THE
FUNDAMENTALS
OF
PUBLIC
RELATIONS

THE FUNDAMENTALS OF PUBLIC RELATIONS

WHAT IT IS AND HOW TO DO IT WELL

BY DR. JOSEPH HARASTA, APR

KUTZTOWN UNIVERSITY

SECOND EDITION

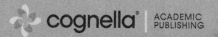
cognella® | ACADEMIC PUBLISHING

Bassim Hamadeh, CEO and Publisher
Carrie Montoya, Manager, Revisions and Author Care
Kaela Martin, Project Editor, Revisions
Jeanine Rees, Production Editor
Jess Estrella, Senior Graphic Designer
Alexa Lucido, Licensing Supervisor
Sean Adams and Allie Kiekhofer, Interior Designers
Natalie Piccotti, Director of Marketing
Kassie Graves, Vice President of Editorial
Jamie Giganti, Director of Academic Publishing

First published in the United States of America in 2016 by Cognella, Inc.

Trademark Notice: Product or corporate names may be trademarks or registered trademarks, and are used only for identification and explanation without intent to infringe.

Cover image copyright © 2012 by Depositphotos / i3alda.

Printed in the United States of America

ISBN: 978-1-5165-3650-4 (pbk) / 978-1-5165-3651-1 (br) / 978-1-5165-7108-6 (al)

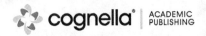

BRIEF CONTENTS

DETAILED CONTENTS

CHAPTER THREE
Legal Implications of Public Relations Practice   49

CHAPTER FOUR
Public Relations Research   67

CHAPTER FIVE
Employee Relations   75

CHAPTER SIX
Media Relations   **97**

CHAPTER SEVEN
Community Relations   **121**

CHAPTER EIGHT
Consumer Relations   **137**

CHAPTER NINE
Social Media   **159**

CHAPTER FOURTEEN
The Future of Public Relations and Tomorrow's Practitioner   **263**

THE ESSENTIALS TO UNDERSTANDING PUBLIC RELATIONS

Chapter Learning Objectives

1. Understand the correlation between interpersonal relations and public relations
2. Apply principles of the Public Opinion Formation Model
3. Recognize the influence of the Two-Step Flow Theory on public knowledge
4. Identify the different Innovation Diffusion Adopters

A FAMILIAR INTRODUCTION TO PUBLIC RELATIONS FUNCTIONS

Often, beginning public relations (PR) students come to the first day of class with either of two perspectives: One, "I know what PR is because I have seen *Sex and The City* or a wedding-planning 'reality' TV show." The other popular response is, "I don't know what PR is but I hear it is about getting people to believe you and like you—usually with some underhanded connotations attached." First off, this book is designed to clarify what PR is—in real reality, not TV reality, and to dispel the notion that the profession is somehow still consumed with hucksterism and spin doctoring. Second, this text will detail the unique nature and responsibilities of public relations and how its success or failure directly impacts the success of organizations and individuals alike. The field of public relations is vast and can be quite complicated; however, this text is intended to explain the practice in simple, familiar, and clear terms so that you can appreciate its purpose while seeing its impact on our everyday lives. In addition, this text will provide you with the essentials in terms of how to develop, implement, and evaluate public relations efforts among the many different groups of people on whom public relations focuses its efforts.

The field of public relations is so diverse and so complex that it often intimidates students because classes often make it seem as though a public relations practitioner must learn some new and complicated means of communication. In truth, public relations is really something that all new students, no matter their level, have had tremendous experience with their whole lives. Public relations is really about learning how to apply this experience in a strategic manner and on a larger scale. But, at its heart, public relations is not that different than interpersonal relations, something in which everyone has experience and knowledge.

YOU ALREADY HAVE EXPERIENCE WITH PUBLIC RELATIONS

When students simply look at the term "public relations," the first indication of their familiarity with it is that they have already had a lifetime of relationship experience—"relations" is simply short for "relationships." From birth, relationships change as we do. The relationship you have with your family is different than that of your best friend's, which is different than you have with your professors. There may be some similarities, but there are certainly many differences as well.

You know, almost instinctively, how to manage and separate them in your life—knowing what you will say when you ask your best friend for a loan is going to be different than if you were to ask your toughest professor for an extension on a paper. You know that you cannot say the same things in the same ways, even though you are asking both a favor. You plan what you will say, how you will say it, and when you will say it to accomplish your goal as well as appeal to your audience. Also, you know that tricking or manipulating them to get what you want may be successful in the short term, but those means can, and usually do, have serious long-term negative effects. Therefore, spin doctoring and hucksterism have no part in successful relationships.

For example, you may feel that your request for a loan from a friend would be more successful if you reminded her of all the times you gave her a ride and say it in an authoritative tone—after all, she owes you, right? However, you know that is probably not going to be the best technique on the professor you want the time extension from. You know from experience in his class that he is unlikely to be swayed to give you that extension unless you can provide some compelling reason. For instance, a family member was hospitalized and you needed to go back home for a few days, which interrupted your ability to finish the paper on time. It may not be a documented excuse according to your professor's book, but you know you can persuade him to give you that extension if you present your case professionally and persuasively—talking about how you never missed a deadline before, your strong performance in the class, and then some mention of your love and loyalty to your family. In doing so, you know you have a stronger chance of receiving that deadline extension when presenting your case this way rather than simply saying, "Can I have until this weekend to get you that paper?" With no evidence and no tailoring of the message in the way you ask him, you know that your request is less likely to be granted. This is obvious to most of us, and it is something we have done for a lifetime—remember when you wanted to stay up past your bedtime when you were seven, or when you wanted to borrow the car when you got your license? You knew then and know now that these types of goal-oriented communications must be personalized to your audience and must be persuasive in their appeal to be successful—being allowed to stay up, using the car, getting the loan, and receiving the deadline extension all depend on presenting your case correctly and persuading your audience to help you.

This is what it means when we say public relations is audience centered. No one-size-fits-all message is going to be as successful as shaping and tailoring them to each audience's needs, experiences, and expectations. You have done it your entire life, and it is really no different for the practice of public relations. To get an audience that is important to your organization, known as a stakeholder group, to accept, like, and patronize your organization, you must do the same things that made you successful in your personal relationships. Of course, with organizations, it is much more complex and even more difficult than in your private life. But at its foundation, the practice of public relations is really not that much different. You can think of your interpersonal relations as micro and public relations as macro in terms of size, but essentially, they are very similar.

Another example of the similarities between your personal relationships and public relations is the changing dynamics of relationships. As you have gotten older, both you and your relationships change—some get stronger, others stay the same, and some just end for any number of reasons. Moreover, to strengthen those relationships you deem most important to you, you know you must manage, maintain, and maneuver them through good as well as bad times. To clarify this aspect of public relations further, think about a relationship that is currently important to you. What are the things you do to ensure it stays positive? Now, think about a relationship, one you deemed important at one time, but now is nonexistent. What happened there? The answers to these questions are all aspects of relationship maintenance—keeping the important ones going and letting the less important evolve into something else, sometimes ending entirely.

Now, think back to your best friend in third grade. Think about the things you two used to do, the ways you used to interact, what you used to talk about, and what you two aspired to. Is that person, who, back then, was so important to your life still as important? Probably not because you evolved and changed just as that best friend did, and maintaining that level of relationship became less important—overshadowed by new people in your life, changes in your personalities, and so on. No isolated incident may have caused you two to separate; it was simply a natural evolution. Now think again about the current relationship that is very important to you. You understand what to do to keep this relationship strong even in the face of adversity. The give and take of the relationship, the sacrifices, and the compromises you and the other person in the relationship make, all contribute to its success—and when not managed well, the lack of such behaviors can damage and even destroy the relationship[1]. If this person needs you to be supportive, you are, and conversely if you need support, you seek it from him or her. Relationships are built on mutual trust and respect. When these two fundamentals of all strong relationships are lost or damaged, the relationship suffers and can eventually end.

These two pillars of personal relations—communicative behavior and maintenance behavior—are the same two as with public relations. The scale and complexity may be different, but at their heart, both are identical. Therefore, you can see that public relations is not as new and intimidating as you may have thought, and it is certainly not what you see on scripted or even "reality" TV—no more than your real lives are the same as those actors' roles. Furthermore, deceit, manipulation, and lying can never be an ingredient to maintaining and growing mutually beneficial relationships.

■ APPLY THE PRINCIPLES TO ORGANIZATIONS

Just as you have important relationships, so too do organizations, and they also must be maintained and strengthened just as with interpersonal relationships. The responsibility of maintaining and strengthening these relationships falls to the public relations practitioner[2]. He or she must therefore understand the dynamics between the organization and the various stakeholder groups just as you understand how to maintain your interpersonal relationships with friends, coworkers, family, and others. For organizations, the equivalent to friends, coworkers, and family are stakeholder groups like community, media, and employees. This is what I call the "**Personal Approach to Public Relations.**"

Undoubtedly, you know from experience that maintaining the relationships in your personal life is often difficult; therefore, you can now start to appreciate the difficulties of maintaining possibly millions of these relationships. To make matters even more complex, the public relations practitioner must maintain and further these relationships between people he or she has no control over. The actions of thousands of employees, media, consumers, and others can influence these relationships' strength in tremendous ways—both positively and negatively[3]. Therefore, the public relations practitioner charged with overseeing the relationship between organizations, their employees, as well as the multitude of stakeholder groups can be intimidating, and as you will see in later chapters, these public relations efforts are not always done well. Just as with your personal relations efforts, there are no one-size-fits-all public relations efforts—each must be deliberated upon and the best options chosen; very similar to choosing the best means to ask for that loan or deadline extension.

Another aspect of relationship management common to both public relations and personal relations is image maintenance. The clothes you wear, the music you listen to, and the friends you choose all influence how and why people think of you the way they do, as well as the way you want them to think. Some may call this a personality[4]. Certainly, personalities evolve and change over the years, influenced by education, experiences, and shifting priorities. This helps explain why that relationship you had with your best friend back in third grade is probably not the same today as it was then. You changed and that person changed, and those changes to your personalities influenced the evolution of that relationship. You found new friends who were more in line with your new interests in style, music, politics, and so on. In your personal life, your personality influences relationships tremendously—it is what people think of when they think of you[5]. Think of the phrase, "You have changed" spoken by someone in a relationship that is probably not at its best. It may not always be accurate, but the personality image is critically important to your interactions with others as well as others' interactions with you[6]. From these interactions, come relationships. This is also true for organizations and public relations too, which by now you can see is simply short for public relationships—fundamentally, good public relations is like good personal relations.

THE FUNDAMENTALS OF PUBLIC OPINION AND PUBLIC RELATIONS

BRANDING AND BRAND MANAGEMENT

While individuals' personalities make up their image, companies have similar personalities, known as **brands**[7]. Every company and organization, large and small, has a brand. Some are of course better known than others. Just as someone's image provides connotations of how and what we think about them, so too do brands. Positive images can be difficult to build and maintain for individuals, and this is equally true for organizations. Strong, well-respected brands are hard-fought and can take years to develop. The responsibility of safeguarding these precious positive brands comes down to the public relations practitioner[8].

As an example, certain companies connote feelings, meanings, and attitudes just as people's personalities do[9]. A company like Apple arouses thoughts of modernity, being cutting-edge, and sleek in most people's minds. Apple did not always elicit these feelings. For some time during the 1990s, the company aroused thoughts of old, antiquated, and low quality as it teetered on the brink of bankruptcy. Through the development of innovative products coupled with a rebranding of the company, Apple was able to change its image completely by the mid-2000s. Other companies rely on long-standing brands, which provide feelings of trust and dependability in their patrons' minds.

Harley-Davidson motorcycles began in a garage over 100 years ago, and while the company has grown tremendously since, it has remained loyal to its brand. Developed during the 20th century, the company's brand today is as valuable as its annual revenues[10]. Few companies have ever been able to develop and grow a brand like Harley-Davidson. To its incredibly loyal patrons the company's brand means freedom, excitement, and individuality. Few companies in the world have had their logo, and with it, its brand, literally tattooed on so many people. That kind of brand loyalty is difficult to achieve and cherished by companies lucky enough to possess it—usually.

Probably the most infamous example of brand management gone awry occurred in 1985 by beverage mega-company Coca-Cola[11]. For nearly a century the company enjoyed unprecedented growth and expansion, going from a pharmacist's counter to the tables of billions of people worldwide. However, that did not stop the world's best-selling soft drink from changing its recipe for success and reinventing its brand. Heralded as New Coke, the company tweaked its formula and launched a multi-million-dollar marketing campaign to sell it to a public that did not want it. Within three months of New Coke's arrival, Coca-Cola re-launched its original formula, dubbed Classic Coke and soon New Coke was relegated to the history books, but not after costing the company millions of dollars and angering millions of loyal customers[12].

As you can see, brand management is a critically important responsibility of the public relations practitioner. The success of an entire corporation can depend on the growth, expansion, and, when necessary and appropriate, the redevelopment of it. To understand how brands and image are managed, it is critical to understand how and why people think and behave the way they do. Much of public relations goes on behind the scenes through research and evaluation, which will be discussed in later chapters; however, the initial understanding of human nature needed by all public relations practitioners is a thorough grasp of **public opinion**.

Essentially, public opinion is the collective opinions of potentially millions or even billions of people[13]. As each individual you have a personal relationship with holds opinions about you and vice versa, so too do large masses of people. From a logistical standpoint, a public relations practitioner could not possibly know the opinions of everyone. Coca-Cola could never know the opinions of all its billions of drinkers, even though more thorough research could have given the company a better indication of the collective opinions of most of its consumers—which might have enabled the company to avoid the costly New Coke mistake. Therefore, it is the amassed collection of prominent opinions that public relations focuses on, which is the definition of public opinion.

A SPORTS ANALOGY

A simple illustration of public opinion in action can be found at any sporting event. The home team's fans dress in the colors and jerseys of their team to illustrate their loyalty and support for it, which is their collective public opinion of the team. However, that opinion can change, sometimes quite quickly. When the team performs well, the opinion is supportive and positive, illustrated through cheers and chants. But, as the team's performance suffers, so too does the fans' opinion of it, usually illustrated by boos, yelling, and leaving[14]. For the team, the public opinion it cares most about is that of its fans. When this public's opinion of the team turns negative, the team can obviously see and hear it. Another example is when a beloved player joins another team.

Because every company and organization is different, a system of analyzing and predicting public opinion exists so that public relations practitioners can make better decisions about how to build on positive opinion as well as reverse negative opinion. Take, for example, when LeBron James left the Cleveland Cavaliers for Miami; the public in Cleveland, who had so supported him, quickly changed their opinions of him, and LeBron went from hero to zero in that city. Conversely, when LeBron returned to Cleveland, most Cavaliers fans welcomed him back with open arms; thus illustrating the fickle nature of public opinion. The following stages of public opinion development illustrate how actions and beliefs influence opinion using the New Coke example to clarify.

THE PUBLIC OPINION FORMATION MODEL

Step One: Uninformed Mass Sentiment. At this stage the public has no knowledge of the situation or of an event that would influence their collective opinions. At this point, everything was business as usual for Coca-Cola's consumers. They had no idea that the company would ever change its recipe, and therefore, remained completely loyal to and supportive of the company and its product. Coca-Cola thought its 200,000 taste tests would deliver a new, more contemporary, and better-selling product. However, nothing will predict step six more than strong, accurate, and sensible research during the Uninformed Mass Sentiment step.

Step Two: The Action or Situation. This stage introduces the public to whatever it is that will influence their opinion, be it an action, event, or situation. Coca-Cola's development of New Coke and its marketing platforms have been developed and are now introduced to the world. People are seeing and tasting New Coke for the first time, as well as realizing that their favorite soft drink does not look or taste like they remember.

Step Three: Public Favor or Dissatisfaction. Following the introduction to the action or situation that will affect public opinion, step three entails the phase when mass opinion starts to be seen—either for or against. Over 1,500 calls flooded Coca-Cola's hotlines, nearly five times the number of daily calls. In a famous story, someone wrote the CEO of the company, believing the autograph of "one of the dumbest executives in American business history" would be worth something someday[15].

Step Four: Debate. Now, the supporters and the detractors debate the issue to arrive at a greater consensus of opinion; essentially, they argue their perspectives in hopes of winning over more supporters to their point of view. By this point, the media was reporting on New Coke's unfavorable arrival onto the soft drink market as illustrated by protest groups against it like the Society for the Preservation of the Real Thing and Old Cola Drinkers of America, as well as petitions and protest songs to return the old Coke formula. While some people may have liked New Coke, the greater percentage of them, or at least the vocal majority, held negative views toward it and the company that introduced it.

Step Five: Time. Public opinion does not happen overnight. It takes time for large masses of people to develop collective opinions about something. Sometimes this stage can take years, as with a presidential election, other times only a few weeks. For Coca-Cola it did not take long for the public to make their minds up that New Coke was not for them.

Step Six: Public Opinion Set. Finally the public's collective opinion becomes set—not necessarily set in stone; it can change, but it is as close to being permanent as it will get during this step. By this point, the writing on the wall made it clear to Coca-Cola that it had made a huge mistake. People wanted the old version of the soft drink back, and they did not want New Coke. Many felt antagonized by the company they had supported for so long—some of them for a lifetime. Here, you can see the damage to the hard-fought and successful brand that Coca-Cola had developed for decades, and now the company needed to restore and rehabilitate it.

Step Seven: Action. Opinions are generally passive, but actions, as the saying goes, speak louder than words. At this step, people are motivated to do something based on their opinions. A clear example is the election of a candidate by the public—public opinion does not elect a person but it does motivate enough people to vote for one candidate over another. Coca-Cola's action to sway public opinion back in its favor was to phase out New Coke and reintroduce the old formula under the name Classic Coke, complete with the traditional red and white swirled logo.

Step Eight: Mass Sentiment. This is the long-term belief held by the public. Public opinion in and of itself can be changed; however, mass sentiment is more permanent and less likely to change as quickly or as dramatically as public opinion. Most people under the age of 35 have never heard of New Coke, which illustrates the long-term mass sentiment held by the public about New Coke—we did not want it, and do not mess with our soda. Coca-Cola learned its lesson as well. Brand loyalty is the second most important commodity any organization can possess, and when it is threatened, the organization is in great danger of angering and losing its most important commodity—its loyal supporters.

PUTTING THE MODEL INTO ACTION

Understanding these steps, and more importantly, how and when to implement public relations plans and strategies within them, can significantly improve public relations success. The Uninformed Mass Sentiment Phase can be thought of as the strategy phase for public relations initiatives. It is at this time that research is conducted and analyzed in an attempt to make the best decisions later—it can best be visualized as the proactive phase. These proactive measures lead up to the Action or Situation Phase when the public is introduced to your ideas. With the help of sound research, the introduction can more assuredly be done well and correctly—this is why research is so important to public relations. For the Public Favor or Dissatisfaction as well as the Debate Phases, public relations work is in high gear. The media is reporting on the developments you introduced and the public is making its mind up about it. If favor is faltering, public relations efforts must be quick and influential to reverse this trend. If public favor is strong, then maintenance and encouragement of those feelings is the duty of public relations. By the sixth phase when public opinion becomes set, the public relations efforts' success, failure, or a mix of both is evident. At this step, public relations practitioners are more passive because people's minds are already set—either they like you or not based on the work already completed. The final two steps, Actions and Mass Sentiment, are reactionary steps for public relations. If things are going well, then maintain the course; if not, then it is necessary to see where and why things went wrong, and then find methods to minimize the damage to your reputation and your organization's brand.

It is important to keep in mind that people who are either strongly in favor of or strongly against something are the most difficult to persuade[16]. Most of the time, it is those who are on the fence who are the target demographic of strategic campaigns. If someone is fervently supportive of your organization, then great, but they are already on your side. The best strategy for them is to maintain these feelings and keep them supportive of you. Conversely, if someone has a strong hatred of your organization, then all of the persuasive messages and million-dollar campaigns will probably not change their mind. It is those people on the fence, who could either become loyal to your organization and its brand or develop a dislike of it, who are the best targets of public relations campaigns. Because they have not decided one way or the other, they are more likely to be influenced by public relations tactics—these people are also called malleable because their opinions can be shaped. The more individual opinions that are shaped in your favor, the more likely overall public opinion will also follow in your favor.

Now that you know about the steps that public opinion goes through from a complete ignorance of something to a near-universal sentiment on it, it is now important to think about the individuals who influence opinions most.

TWO-STEP FLOW THEORY

The **Two-Step Flow Theory** illustrates how information or news travels from its source, is influenced, and then interpreted by the public[17]. It is critically important to understand because even more so in today's world, what the public thinks it understands may be completely different than reality. The Two-Step Flow Theory shows that news or information is changed and manipulated, either purposefully or not, and that this manipulation influences how and why people believe what they do[18].

A SIMPLE EQUATION OF THE TWO-STEP FLOW THEORY

Event or Story + Media Reports + Opinion Leaders Comments on Them = Public Understanding of the Event or the Story

A TALE OF TWO STORMS

To illustrate, let's look at how the event of Hurricane Sandy, or Superstorm Sandy, which occurred in 2012, was not necessarily what people thought they knew about the storm because of this theory's influence.

Hurricane Sandy was the worst storm on record to hit the Northeastern United States. It caused billions in damage and threatened further billions in revenue—specifically for the state of New Jersey, which was hardest hit. Tourism in New Jersey accounts for nearly $40 billion in revenue each year—the most valuable asset for the state. As Sandy struck the New Jersey coastline, the national and international media, of course, covered it at great length. However, some of that coverage would come back to haunt New Jersey leaders when they tried to persuade tourists to come back to their shores the following summer[19].

Erroneous reports of damage being worse than it was, faked stories and Photoshopped images of sharks swimming in flooded highways, and stories of bodies being stored in grocery stores all provided fodder for both traditional and social media. While these outlandish stories may seem silly and ridiculous, they had long lasting and serious repercussions. Rental and tourist polls following Sandy showed that most Americans thought the New Jersey coastline was irreparably damaged—so much so that they were taking their vacations and their money elsewhere. New Jersey needed to embark on a public relations campaign to persuade them otherwise.

Using opinion leaders like Barack Obama and Bruce Springsteen, New Jersey's leadership developed messages, slogans, and images all aimed at dispelling the inaccuracies of the media's reports, and encouraging people to come back to the Jersey Shore. The campaign paid off, and the 2013 tourist season brought in the highest revenues in state history.

As you can see, understanding the power and influence of both the media and opinion leaders is crucial for public relations practitioners. When public relations initiatives are designed to convince and persuade, which they always are, knowing how the public is convinced and persuaded enables practitioners to intelligently plan and implement strategies to affect public opinion in a positive way. Conversely, when public opinion is against an organization, this process can help direct public relations efforts to address and ideally reverse the negativity.

Media influence on public opinion is tremendous. The effect of well-known opinion leaders such as politicians and celebrities also influences how and what people think. However, a third classification of influence can be just as important as the two steps, but often includes those individuals we trust most—our friends, family, coworkers, neighbors, and others.

Through word-of-mouth stories, complaints, and anecdotes, we hear about how other people, whom we respect and trust, feel about products, people, companies, and so forth. Word-of-mouth publicity such as this is often more impactful on shaping people's opinions because of the source. Most of us know that the media is not always as neutral as we would like, and certainly opinion leaders have their agendas, but when the people closest to us say something, it often has more credibility and believability. Because of this, word-of-mouth publicity influences our opinions greatly[20]. For example, imagine you are in the market for a new tablet. You do your research between the brands, and their features and prices. You think you have finally settled on one, but just as you are about to go out and buy one, a close friend of yours tells you about how much trouble she's had with it, how it always crashes, gets viruses, and does not work with her other devices. Even though your research never indicated these problems, which may be isolated, her negative review of the tablet will more than likely influence you to at least reevaluate your decision. Because of this type of influence, the people responsible for shaping and winning public opinion—the public relations practitioner—must understand and appreciate the power of word-of-mouth publicity just as much as the Two-Step Flow Theory.

Several classification systems describe various segments of the population according to their likelihood of accepting and trusting news or new ideas[21]. Because public relations practitioners often introduce new ideas or at least try to influence the ideas that people have about companies, people, and products, understanding this segmentation is necessary when developing persuasive campaigns. In 1962, Rogers and Shoemaker developed a four-part process that describes these influences—it is known as the **Innovation Diffusion Process**[22].

INNOVATION DIFFUSION ADOPTER CATEGORIES

INNOVATORS

The first segmentation is known as the **Innovators**, which encompasses about 2.5 percent of the population. These individuals are known for their willingness to accept new ideas and want the newest and latest in technology. Imagine the people who camp out in front of an Apple Store for a week before the latest iPhone is released for sale—these are the type of people known as Innovators. As long as the product or idea is new and exciting, this segmentation of individuals will be ready and willing to accept[23].

EARLY ADOPTERS

These individuals, who compose about 13.5 percent, admire and are interested in new ideas and new products like the Innovators, but are not as eager for them. Generally, **Early Adopters** are not too cautious with their money and are generally seen as opinion leaders; this segment is the most important for public relations efforts. If public relations practitioners can influence Early Adopters, then it is likely that the Early Adopters can influence the other segments of people.

EARLY MAJORITY

Individuals in this class are known for being deliberate and practical, as well as cautious with their money. At about 34 percent of the population, the **Early Majority** is an important group to public relations practitioners. It is not as easy to influence this group as it is with Innovators or Early Adopters, but the Early Majority is open to ideas as long as they are presented in a way that showcases their practicality and how the ideas or products can help people in the Early Majority.

LATE MAJORITY

Equally as large as the Early Majority (34 percent), the **Late Majority** is much more skeptical of new products and ideas. Seeing new ideas as being risky, this group of people is much more difficult to influence than the preceding groups. Accordingly, public relations practitioners have a challenge before them when trying to persuade these individuals.

LAGGARDS

As the name suggests, this group of people, about 16 percent of the population, are quite set in their ways and very traditional in their thought processes. However, once they are on your side, it is likely this group will remain loyal to a brand or company for the long term. Those individuals who buy the same brand of car over and over again are likely to be **laggards**—they are brand loyal because of the trust and respect they have for a company, its products, and especially the way it treats its customers.

As you can see, individuals must be treated differently depending on how they think and behave. Understanding this classification system enables the public relations practitioner to target and meet the needs of different people in the best ways possible. It is important to remember the fundamental that one size fits all never works well in public relations.

So now that you know the different types of people and why they differ, it is important to understand what most influences their opinions.

THE BUILDING BLOCKS OF OPINION

In many ways this process is similar to the steps that develop general public opinion; however, unlike those steps, the Innovation Diffusion Process looks at individuals' opinion development. This process is important because as larger groups of individuals develop opinions, then overall public opinion begins to form. But, even the most widespread and universal public opinion begins with individuals, and it is from these building blocks of public opinion that public relations practitioners must begin.

The first step in using this process for public relations efforts is knowledge. An individual is exposed to an idea or news and then forms an understanding of it. However, as you saw with the Hurricane Sandy case, sometimes this understanding is flawed and incorrect because the person was exposed to false or misleading information. Because the initial stage of understanding a situation is so important, the public relations practitioner must be constantly aware of what types of information are being disseminated and how people are developing their understanding. If the information is confusing, then the public relations practitioner must clarify it so that it is understandable. If the information is false or misleading, then it is the public relations practitioner's responsibility to address and correct it. The understanding that a person develops initially is often what most influences his or her actions later. It is an important distinction to make that convincing and persuading people are two different things. Convincing is internal—it is a thought process gained and developed by someone's understanding of a product, event, or statement. Persuading is external—it is influenced by the thought processes, but shows itself through some physical evidence. For example, someone may be convinced that a candidate for office is the best choice, but until that person votes for the candidate, that person technically has not been persuaded yet. Clearly, public relations is all about both of these functions, and accordingly, it is important to understand that to get someone to do something for you—such as buy your company's product, vote for your candidate, or spread positive word-of-mouth publicity about you—they must first be convinced to do so. Therefore, this first stage in the Innovation Diffusion Process is critically important to the practice of public relations. People must be made to believe in an organization and/or its brand, and then they will more likely patronize and support it.

CONVINCE V. PERSUADE

The second step in the process is the "actionable" step—persuasion. As mentioned before, persuasion is best thought of as an outward, evident display of someone's thoughts and understanding. Protests are a clear example of persuasion—someone has been convinced that a company's actions are unethical, immoral, illegal, or a combination of all three and they then develop slogans, paint signs, attract media attention, and picket at the company's gates. However, in this scenario, the protestor needs support—no picket of one person will go very far. So, additional supporters of the individual's protests are enlisted—by convincing them to the extent that they will also develop slogans, paint signs, or picket. Remember that the media and opinion leaders have a tremendous influence on convincing someone to do something, and public relations practitioners must enlist their help as well as address their criticisms when necessary.

The third step is the decision step—when someone decides whether to engage in actions that show support or rejection of an idea. This step is clearly close to the persuasion step. Buying products, attending one university over another, or even putting a political bumper sticker on your car are examples of the decision step. Remember that throughout this process someone can change their minds and therefore change their actions or their decisions. This is an important element to remember because too often public relations initiatives begin well but then sputter because they are not maintained. Someone's positive thoughts must be constantly maintained, which introduces the fourth and final step.

The confirmation step is when someone seeks reinforcement for his or her decisions and actions. If the person's decisions are not confirmed, they may change, and the process begins again. An example is a president's slipping approval poll numbers. Clearly, this person was elected president and therefore must have had enough support to gain the office. But as actions, decisions, and policies change, so too does the president's support—either positively or negatively. The economy, foreign policy, and domestic welfare during a presidency all can affect the confirmation of that president's ability to perform well or the need to elect someone else to the office. For the public relations practitioner, this stage illustrates one of the two major functions of public relations: advising management to continuously support public relations efforts to maintain a positive image and brand.

CANTRIL'S AND PUBLIC OPINION

In addition, **Hadley Cantril**, a psychologist who studied the influences that affect public opinion, developed several fundamentals of public opinion formation. These principles of public opinion are useful for students of public relations because they enable clearer explanations as to why people's attitudes can be influenced enough that they shape their opinions on important subjects and decisions[24].

---

1. Important events increase the possibility of opinion change. Elections, terrorist attacks, and even sporting events can influence how and why people believe that they do.

---

2. The greater the magnitude of the event, the more extreme the shift in public opinion. Major events can move public opinion much faster than normal because of the immediacy and severity of the event. The September 11 attacks shocked Americans and their opinion of terrorism, their safety, and patriotism. Public opinion is not likely to return to pre-event levels until the event's impact is stabilized.

---

3. Opinion is usually more influenced by events than words, unless those words are an event. Words, such as major speeches, statements, admissions, and verdicts can count as events because they offer the same impact and effect on people and their opinions, if those words are important enough.

---

4. Actions and statements have the greatest impact on public opinion before individuals' opinions are formed. Similar to the malleability factor of how opinion develops, this principle reinforces the idea that those individuals who have not formed an opinion for or against something are most likely to be influenced by public relations efforts.

---

5. Public opinion does not anticipate emergencies; it reacts to them. For the most part, opinion is reactionary to events; therefore, public opinion does not expect major events in advance, but rather deals with them after they have occurred.

---

6. Opinion is determined by self-interests. Ultimately, most people care first about their wellbeing and those most important to them. When decisions are made, they are influenced most by how they will affect someone personally.

7. Peaks in opinion do not last long unless they continue to be affected by events of self-interests. Major shifts in opinion come and go quickly. Such "temperamental" opinion changes will go back to their original opinion unless whatever influenced the spike continues.

8. Once self-interest is involved, opinion does not change easily. The old adage that people look out for themselves first holds true when opinions are involved. Self-interest, most often when money is involved, will set people's opinion more firmly when they are personally involved.

9. Opinion will take hold before official policy. When public opinion becomes widespread and strong enough, it can influence legislation and laws. However, changes to these official policies occur only after public opinion "forces" these changes to meet the demands of the public's opinion.

10. If opinion is held by a small majority, the remaining people's opinions will more likely be swayed by accomplished facts. The people on the fence of an issue will move after a fact or new information moves them in the direction of acceptance or rejection.

11. Opinion of leadership is much more sensitive during critical times. Public opinion of leaders will shift more severely during difficult or great times than during normal situations. War, economic stress, and public morality debates will affect the public's opinions of leaders, such as the president, more than when times are stable.

12. People are less critical of leadership if they feel as though they have a part in the decision-making process. People are more accepting of difficult decisions, even if they are negatively affected, when they feel as though they have a voice in making those decisions.

13. Opinion is determined by the end goal, rather than the means to attain the goal. Most people care about the end product than the process used to get to it. Especially useful for politicians, this fundamental shows that if people feel the result is important enough, then they are likely to accept whatever tactics were used to attain the desired result.

14. When opinion is influenced by desire rather than logic, shifts in opinion are likely to be dramatic. Akin to the idea that when people think with their hearts instead of their heads, opinion changes can take place rapidly and wildly.

15. The psychological formula of opinion = direction + intensity + breadth + level. The importance of an event, its influence on someone's personal life, the timing of it, the person's influence on the event, as well as leadership during the event all play integral roles in shaping public opinion.

Understanding the preceding fundamentals of opinion development enables public relations practitioners to decide when to introduce public relations plans as well as how to respond to events out of their control. Public relations work is a 24-hour, 365-day effort that must influence and respond to ever-changing public opinion. Armed with the knowledge of how opinions are formed, public relations practitioners are more capable of furthering and maintaining their organization's image and brand.

2 PUBLIC RELATIONS DEFINED

Learning Objectives

1. Identify the two main functions of public relations
2. Understand the differences between managers and leaders
3. Apply the lessons learned from the 1982 Tylenol Case
4. Recognize the contributions of leading historical figures in the evolution of public relations
5. Define the four models of public relations
6. Understand the importance of case study research in public relations

Given the tremendous responsibility and persuasive nature of public relations, it is important to understand its two basic functions: **communicating** and **counseling**[25].

The first of these two functions, communicating, is rather straightforward. Every organization needs consistent, correct, and complete communication between itself and its many stakeholders. Because public relations deals primarily with understanding relationships much more than with its two other strategic communication siblings—marketing and advertising—it make sense that the public relations practitioners within an organization should be the ones responsible for developing and sustaining these means of communication. After all, no one within an organization knows the day-to-day relationships between the organization and its stakeholders or publics more than the public relations practitioner. The public relations functions within an organization can and do directly impact the organization's ability to succeed because successful and long-term relationships depend so highly on communication. The second function, which is no less important, equally influences organizational success, but is less well known than communication.

THE CRITICAL FUNCTION OF COUNSELING

Counseling may at first seem unlikely as one of the two major functions of public relations. However, once you realize that as an organization's management acts so too does the public's opinions of it, you can then see this function's importance. Generally, the public relations practitioner within an organization is not going to be the company's leader—such as the president or CEO. However, because the president or CEO's decisions obviously influence the organization's actions, it is important that those actions be in the best interests of its key stakeholders. Often company leaders focus on revenues and the financial stability of their company. However, sometimes the relationships a company maintains can take a back seat to the money it makes. Often, company presidents and CEOs do not see the direct connection between financial success and relationship success—until there is a crisis. But, the day-to-day functions of any successful organization must include not only the financial decisions of the company, but also its relationship decisions. The clearest example is the relationship between a company and its consumers.

Obviously, a commercial enterprise needs customers to buy its products or services, but it is not just the product that influences consumer behavior, but also the company's brand or image. It is the public relations practitioner's job to safeguard the image or brand. For example, in 2010 the BP oilrig disaster in the Gulf of Mexico created a direct counseling-to-financial-success connection—namely, when BP President Tony Hayward made statements in the media, it affected his company's image quite negatively. As if the actual incident weren't bad enough, Hayward's comments that he wanted the incident resolved as quickly as possible, saying, "I just want my life back," struck many people as callous and insensitive—especially to the millions of people who make their living from the waters of the Gulf of Mexico and who were directly affected by his company's actions[26]. Protests, media condemnation, and even boycotts followed. In this example, Hayward would have been well advised to choose his words carefully (communication) and listen to his public relations team's advice (counseling). It is always important to strategize internally as to what an organization should do and say and then spread that information to the outside world. Often, however, organizational leadership will make hasty comments, say too much, or just say the wrong things—usually attributable to poor public relations counseling.

When this happens, the problems and fallout from it become the public relations department's problem to fix. Therefore it is always best to proactively counsel management on its decisions in terms of how they can influence those stakeholder relationships that took so long to develop. Being a voice in the boardroom is critical to not only public relations success, but also overall organizational success. To gain this voice, it is important to understand the distinction between managers and leaders.

MANAGERS VERSUS LEADERS

Managers are generally task oriented. They are concerned with the "how to" and "must do" elements of singular tasks. Heavy on persuasive threats, they get their employees to work, but never really inspire them to succeed. You can think of these people as those who say comments like, "That's the way we have always done it" or "That's not the way things are done here." On the other hand, leaders are much more goal oriented: heavy on inspiration and producing convincing messages that allow their employees to feel empowered and want to succeed for the organization's good. These individuals develop camaraderie and buy-in from their employees. These people ask such questions as, "What do you [employees] think we should do?" and "What can we do to make this work?" Note the use of the word "we." Leaders empower employees to want to work—not because their paychecks depend on it, but because they see value and worth in their work. For the public relations practitioner, developing this sense of leadership versus management feel within an organization is crucial, and it begins at the top through motivated and empowering public relations counseling.

That is not to say this is easy. Tight deadlines, financial pressures, and busy schedules make the process often easier said than done. However, one element will always gain the attention of top organization leadership—money. For public relations, there are two types of bottom lines: the financial and the relational[27]. Getting leadership to understand and appreciate the second as much as they do the first is the best way to move a company's public relations initiatives from the basement to the "C" suite where the CEO, COO, and other executives make important decisions. Once leadership understands the connection between positive relationships and positive revenues, the sooner they will be on board with public relations' suggestions and decisions. Another aspect is explaining the progress of public relations initiatives.

Generally, organizational leaders are interested in outcomes most. Because, by their very nature, public relations efforts are not always clear-cut in their outcomes in terms of figures and dollars, public relations is not always taken as seriously by leadership as it should be. For example, a company spends $1 million on a 6-month advertising campaign. At its end, the success or failure, or outcome of the campaign is clear—did sales increase during the six months to make the investment worthwhile? Known as **return on investment (ROI)**[28], these types of outcomes allow for evidence of success or failure of a campaign. However, public relations does not always work this way.

Getting someone to like your company's brand does not immediately reflect financial success, which is the type of success that many organizational leaders care about most. Strong, long-term relationships take time to develop. While it is obvious to most people that when people start disliking and criticizing a company, usually via word-of-mouth, that the success of an organization will start to decline is not always accepted by management. Convincing company leadership of it is usually difficult, especially when they care mainly about the immediate returns on their investments. However, public relations professionals have developed a means of illustrating their departments' worth to organizational leadership. Known as Benchmarking[29], public relations initiatives can be measured and their outcomes illustrated to leadership.

THE VALUE OF PUBLIC RELATIONS

Benchmarking in a public relations sense entails measuring the organization's reputation at the beginning, throughout, and at the conclusion of a public relations initiative. It is a way to show that a company's reputation improved and how this improvement resulted in tangible benefits such as greater exposure and sales.

A SMALL-SCALE EXAMPLE

For example, consider a small start-up restaurant in your town. It needs exposure to increase notoriety of it—after all, if no one knows about it, no one can patronize it. However, the restaurant does not have a lot of disposable money to create advertisements and air them on local television stations or print them in the local newspapers. This is where public relations efforts can show their worth. By hosting events like a "locals' night out" or sponsoring an area sports team, the restaurant begins the build notoriety and attracts attention. These initiatives are less expensive than traditional advertising, but when implemented well, they can garner just as many benefits. Remember the local television station and newspaper that the restaurant's owners wished they could afford advertising for? Well, informing the area's media of the locals' night out or the sponsorship deal can attract them to air and publish stories on it. The restaurant gains exposure, illustrates its goodwill to the community, and does it in a way that's more credible and trustworthy than through traditional, expensive advertising. Generally, people will believe a message from a journalistic source like the local television news or newspaper more than the same message in a paid advertisement. After all, everyone expects an advertisement to focus on the positives of the restaurant, but the local media does not have a stake in the restaurant, so it is more likely to be believed by the public. These types of third-party endorsements are critically important to showing public relation's values to those who may not understand it. More people find out about the restaurant, more people patronize it, they spread news of it to their friends, coworkers, and family via word-of-mouth, and the restaurant starts making money—all for the investment of a special event and maybe a sponsorship of the town's little league team,

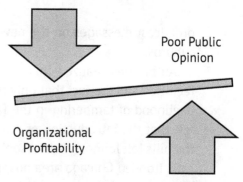

FIGURE 2-1. Organizational Profitability vs Poor Public Opinion

as well as a little public relations work. That is not a bad ROI and shows how the public relations efforts paid off to the restaurant's owners via benchmarking. At the opening of the restaurant, notoriety and revenue was nil, 3 months later, for example, people found out about it through those local stories, and revenue increased. This method illustrates public relation's worthiness to the financial as well as the relational bottom lines.

The preceding illustration presents a hypothetical, yet accurate, picture of public relations affecting opinion and in turn financial success. However, a real-life case illustrates this phenomenon on a much larger scale, and it is the preeminent public relations case study—one that set the standard when it comes to showing that public relations is essential to organizational success—both reputational and financial.

THE TYLENOL CASE[30]

In late September of 1982, a 12-year-old girl, Mary Kellerman, died in a suburb outside of Chicago after ingesting Extra-Strength Tylenol laced with cyanide. Shortly after her death, Adam Janus as well as his brother Stanley Janus and Stanley's wife, Theresa, also died from taking Extra-Strength Tylenol, all from the same bottle, all from cyanide poisonings—10,000 times the amount needed to kill a human. Like Mary's, their deaths also occurred in a suburb of Chicago. Three others would also soon die—all linked by their use of Extra-Strength Tylenol, and all from the Chicago area. Investigators quickly urged Chicago residents to avoid the medicine through

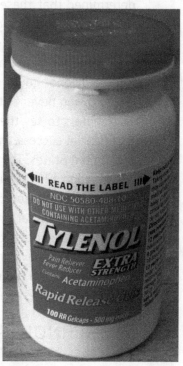

FIGURE 2-2. Tylenol Bottle with Safety Cap
http://commons.wikimedia.org/wiki/ File:Tylenol_bottle_closeup_crop.jpg

broadcast messages on the news as well as police loudspeakers patrolling the Chicago suburbs.

Authorities realized that because the medicine came from different manufacturing facilities, and the fact that only select bottles of Extra-Strength Tylenol were affected, the likelihood of tampering in the factory was unlikely. Both local and federal investigators felt that the introduction of cyanide to Extra-Strength Tylenol must have occurred after the pills left Johnson & Johnson's factory, the maker of the pain medicine. Over 700 phone calls flooded Chicago area hospitals with people reporting symptoms of poisoning after taking Tylenol. Because of the very nature of the incidents, news of it quickly spread across the country. Soon, a few isolated cases from outside Chicago became the most reported news nationwide, even garnering international coverage. Because the incidents included a product that most Americans took and had in their homes coupled with quick deaths of the seven victims, fear quickly took hold over the nation. As with many cases such as these, this fear was exacerbated by numerous, unrelated copycat crimes. Reports of deaths linked to Extra-Strength Tylenol came from states far and wide, which only validated the fears of many. It was no longer a lunatic outside of Chicago who may be responsible, but now it seemed as though Johnson & Johnson may be at fault. It was later determined that these copycat crimes had nothing to do with the Chicago cases—just people taking advantage of the situation to hide their own murders or extort money from Johnson & Johnson. Nonetheless, the reports of these cases did affect Americans' fears about the medicine. The perception that a few people in a region were dying from taking tainted Tylenol could now be a widespread crisis became reality to many people who were vowing never to take the drug again.

Needless to say, the impact this scare had on Johnson & Johnson's image, and in turn, its financial success, was huge. At that time, Tylenol was the number-one pain reliever in the United States. The medicine revolutionized the pharmaceutical industry; up until its introduction, just about the only non-prescription pain drug was aspirin. Tylenol was so important to Johnson & Johnson's bottom lines that it represented 35 percent of the company's billion-dollar revenues. The company had invested so heavily in and depended so greatly on its success, that the permanent removal of the drug from the market and public fear of it might have ended Johnson & Johnson's great success. Billions of dollars, millions of consumers, and thousands of employees all hung in the balance of Johnson & Johnson's public relations response to the crisis—and its lessons would influence the industry forever.

■ TECHNOLOGY OF THE DAY

Because information about the cyanide deaths around Chicago and the copycat murders elsewhere were coming from the mainstream media, Johnson & Johnson's public relations team knew it needed to post company responses and plans where the public got its information—the media itself. Remember the development of public opinion really begins with the organization developing its plans and actions. Even though the event was out of the control of Johnson & Johnson, the response and reaction to it was in its control. In 1982, Americans got their news, or "knowledge" as part of the Innovation Diffusion Process, through the mainstream news media. Long before the Internet, social media sites, and pundit shows on 24-hour cable news channels existed, the local evening and world news and the daily newspapers were the only choices for up-to-date information. Knowing this, Johnson & Johnson embarked on an information campaign in these media to clarify misconceptions, alleviate fears, and encourage trust in its brand and its products. Moreover, because many Americans were fearful of Johnson & Johnson's products and demanding recalls to protect people, the company realized that a voluntary recall in the Chicago area would illustrate the company's commitment to its consumers' safety over its financial bottom line. This action further reinforced the positive image the company needed at this time while also showing its responsibility to safeguarding the public. Recalls cost millions of dollars, but Johnson & Johnson knew that the severity of the situation warranted this drastic measure.

Up until this crisis, Johnson & Johnson was a company known for its health and wellness products and generally a company few people really knew anything about other than its products—if you needed bandages, you bought Band-Aids, Johnson & Johnson's name for them, but you did not need to know much more about the company—just that its products had always been around was enough for most Americans. However, once the crisis took hold, Johnson & Johnson's public relations team counseled company president **James Burke** to appear on television as well as offer interviews to reporters. The company's public relations department knew that fear is the absence of confidence. In this case, people no longer felt confident in Johnson & Johnson's products, and the best way to reverse that was to add a human face to the company. By appearing on national news shows like *60 Minutes*, which had been the bane of many companies, James Burke offered fearful consumers a trusting face to go along with its statements of commitment and reassurance. Part of the success of this campaign was the knowledge that to many people, seeing is believing. This would be a crucial ingredient to Johnson & Johnson's additional public relations efforts.

Because the television media were reporting so greatly on the Tylenol scare, Johnson & Johnson decided to use it as a resource. No broadcast company in the world can send reporters to every story—they rely on public relations professionals to supply some of this information too. If the evening news was going to broadcast interviews and images from pharmacies and customers, then Johnson & Johnson would send its own side of the story. Probably few other responses to the Tylenol poisonings were as successful as Johnson & Johnson's development of video new releases (VNRs) and video news conference (VNCs). These videos were produced by Johnson & Johnson and included statements from key organizational spokespersons like James Burke and images of the company's manufacturing facilities and processes. The video was given to news organizations for their use to edit and include in their nightly broadcasts. Video of consumers stating their fears and anxieties over Tylenol were replaced with images of millions of bottles of Tylenol speeding through Johnson & Johnson's factories, which clearly illustrated the impossibility of someone taking a bottle off the completely mechanized machines, poison it, and then place it back in the assembly line destined for consumers. By seeing the level of mechanization and speed of manufacturing and packaging, Americans began to realize that Johnson & Johnson could not be at fault, and that it really was the work of an outside criminal bent on adding cyanide to bottles of Tylenol after they had already left the factories. Public opinion was starting to shift in Johnson & Johnson's favor. However, even though national poll numbers were showing the public's belief in the company, Johnson & Johnson was not clear of financial ruin.

TURNING THE TIDE OF FEAR

National poll numbers showed that 87 percent of Americans supported Johnson & Johnson and felt that the company was not at fault for the tampering and deaths. However, 61 percent still would not purchase Tylenol. Clearly, Johnson & Johnson's public relations efforts had won the battle over public opinion, but to the company's leadership, the war was far from won. In addition to the media-centered public relations efforts, Johnson & Johnson also embarked on a personal communications campaign whereby consumers could use toll-free hotline to ask questions and received up-to-date information—remember websites were at least ten years away. In addition, the company decided that if fear was the result of a lack of confidence and trust in the product and not in the company as the poll numbers indicated, then the product itself must change.

Up until the poisonings, medication like Tylenol was generally packaged in only a bottle placed in a box. There was no reason to make the packaging tamper resistant because no one had ever really tampered with medicine before. However, after the Tylenol case, Johnson & Johnson introduced the first modern tamper-resistant package. Its triple-seal bottle became the industry standard and reassured consumers of the product's purity. Also, Johnson & Johnson changed the form of Tylenol. First introduced as a capsule, Johnson & Johnson later offered Tylenol as a tablet. The capsule could be taken apart, its contents emptied and replaced with something else, and reshaped to look as though it was not tampered with. A tablet would be nearly impossible to take apart and reform. Moreover, if a tablet gets wet, it turns to mush—something you may have experienced if you have ever taken aspirin without water. By replacing capsules with tablets, introducing the triple-seal package, and reversing public opinion via the media, Johnson & Johnson was able to do what many at the time thought was impossible. By February of 1983, the company had regained 95 percent of its pre-Tylenol-crisis revenues for the product. Such an astounding reversal of such a monumental crisis had never been seen before, and it was the first time that sound public relations efforts were credited for this success[31]. This case clearly showed public relations' worth for a company that was on the brink, and in many ways, introduced public relations as a valuable asset in the corporate boardroom.

An interesting side note to this case is that Johnson & Johnson suffered a very similar repeat incident just four years later. Company officials shook their heads at how this could be happening all over again. However, Johnson & Johnson learned its lesson from the 1982 case so well that the duration and severity of the 1986 incidents did not affect the company as greatly—an example of why case studies are so important and useful for public relations practitioners.

◼ LESSONS LEARNED

In addition to its groundbreaking effect on the field of public relations as far as its now being appreciated by management and needed for crisis recovery, the Tylenol case also provided several case lessons that are as valuable today as they were over 30 years ago. The following have become universal lessons from the Tylenol incident, and they are still used as the principles of effective crisis management.

1. **Social Responsibility Works.** Social responsibility is the idea that an organization or company does what is ethical, moral, and legal not solely for the organization's benefit, for all of society's benefit. Johnson & Johnson was not legally required to spend millions retooling its factories and manufacturing processes when it introduced the triple seal and replaced capsules with tablets. Johnson & Johnson knew that this decision was its responsibility rather than a mandate from a government agency. However, it cannot be underestimated the positives that social responsibility offers organizations using these tactics. No one can deny that they are mutually beneficial for the company and society; however, mutual benefit is also one of the hallmarks of any good relationship and a mainstay of sound public relations.

2. **Good Reputations Can Save.** Johnson & Johnson began nearly 100 years before the Tylenol scare. It was a trusted company whose products became ubiquitous to the American medicine cabinet. The company's products were used by millions of Americans in 1982, but more importantly, their parents and grandparents before them had used Johnson & Johnson products. Americans grew up with Johnson & Johnson's products—everything from its baby shampoo to cutting-edge pain relievers. This trust enabled the company to recover and respond more quickly than a company with no established brand identity, which illustrates why successful brands should be cherished. People trusted the company and its products for generations, and when the

company asked for even more trust during a frightening time, people were willing to give Johnson & Johnson the benefit of the doubt.

3. **Consumers Trust When the Company Commits.** Similar to social responsibility, commitment is something that must be proven. Johnson & Johnson needed to issue an immediate statement; however, all of the statements and promises in the world won't go far without action. Akin to "seeing is believing," "actions speak louder than words" best describes this third lesson. Making promises to protect consumers is great, but if those promises are not kept, whatever trust and goodwill an organization had will quickly go away. Promises are integral to any solid relationship. Johnson & Johnson made good on its promises to protect and safeguard its customers even if it cost the company millions—their safety was more important than the monetary bottom line. However, this measure would of course later affect Johnson & Johnson's economic bottom line as well—a clear illustration of the power of a company's current reputation on its financial future.

4. **Victimized Companies Recover Better.** Johnson & Johnson had their positive reputation and brand quality set in most Americans' minds. The company demonstrated its commitment to its consumers in many ways—from recalls to repackaging. This, combined with official reports from respected agencies like the FBI, helped shape public opinion in favor of Johnson & Johnson. The company, which had been a part of American culture for so long had built a brand of honesty, sincerity, and quality for decades. When a madman in Chicago decided to murder people by tampering with Johnson & Johnson's flagship product, people became disgusted and enraged that such a thing could happen to their trusted company. It was not just the seven innocent people who died from taking poisoned Tylenol who were the victims, but the company that manufactured the product as well. The building and maintenance of Johnson & Johnson's positive image and reputation enabled it to recover its trust more easily than a company without a positive brand. The development and maintenance of positive image is directly the responsibility of the public relations department.

5. **Public Relations Helps the Financial Bottom Line.** This case provides many public relations lessons that have stood and will stand the test of time even in the face of advancing technology. But its greatest impact on the field of public relations was that it finally illustrated that sound, supported, and socially responsible public relations will impact a company's financial bottom line, just as much as advertising and marketing. Before the Tylenol incident, public relations was confused with other strategic communication fields, such as marketing; maligned as inherently deceptive in its practices; and the domain of manipulators and spin doctors. This case, however,

brought the field newfound and enduring respect across multiple industries, and it is one of the main reasons the field has flourished since.

No one has ever been convicted of the 1982 Tylenol murders. Theories and allegations have surrounded the case over the decades. The primary suspect, James Lewis, was arrested for mailing a ransom note to Johnson & Johnson stating that the murders would cease if the company paid him[32]. Johnson & Johnson did offer a $100,000 reward, but all Lewis received was 13 years in federal prison for extortion—not the murders. Investigators have never closed the case, and it is hoped that new DNA analysis technology may shed new light on this case. Ironically, Lewis released a novel entitled, *POISON!*, which he claims is totally fictional and has nothing to do with the 1982 Tylenol poisonings.

A final aspect to the Tylenol case is four major lessons it provided public relations practitioners. As you'll see later, case study lessons are tremendously helpful for public relations professionals—they help guide actions and set up the fundamentals of public relations practice—ones that are seen in case after case.

APPLYING THE TYLENOL CASE LESSONS

1. **Immediate Action Leads to Long-term Results.** Historically, the longer an organization waits to address a situation or crisis, the more severe the damage from it will be to the company's two bottom lines: reputational and financial. More so today because of the 24-hours news cycle than in 1982, the speed of an organization's actions and reactions to issues and problems is paramount to public relations crisis management. The speed of public relations efforts is often as important as the actual effort— timing is everything, but it can sometimes be a balancing act to determine the most appropriate plan. Because news moves so quickly today and nearly anyone can access information anywhere and at any time, organizational responses to issues are also expected to be immediate. However, that can also sometimes be quite problematic to real-world public relations. In 1982, Johnson & Johnson understood the severity of the incidents it faced near Chicago. Because of the life-and-death situation, the company immediately began working with authorities who determined the poisonings, at the early stages, were centered near Chicago. Johnson & Johnson issued a recall of Chicago-area Tylenol, issued statements of concern and remorse to the victims' families, and detailed how the company was working with investigators—all openly and candidly. Most companies up until that time were hesitant to take responsibility for something like a product tampering, but Johnson & Johnson understood that accepting responsibility was not the same as accepting blame. Johnson & Johnson did nothing wrong; however, it was still its product that was linked to the seven deaths. Additionally, issuing recalls are not only expensive, but to some, connote that the

organization knows it is at fault and was ordered to recall their product. Johnson & Johnson willingly recalled their product and made this point known. Moreover, the company continuously updated a worried nation as information became known. When the company did not know the answers to the public's questions, it acknowledged that it did not know, but would keep working to find out and keep people in the loop. However, the risk to making immediate statements and addressing issues is that it might call attention to the problem—more attention and focus than would be if the company did not address it so openly.

On the other hand, the greatest threat to waiting to see if a problem will pass and not making statements is that if the problem does not blow over and becomes a major crisis, to the public, the company looks irresponsible and unconcerned. Generally, the decision to address a situation and the level of concern is dictated by the nature of the incident. For Johnson & Johnson, the seven deaths linked to its product warranted immediate and widespread reaction. A less severe situation may not need such a level of attention—that is the balancing act where case study analyses can help public relations practitioners make these important, yet tricky decisions.

2. **Sound Research is Integral to the Public Relations Decision-Making Process.** As mentioned in lesson one, case studies provide clues and suggestions for public relations practitioners. Johnson & Johnson's 1986 Tylenol scare was not as severe as the 1982 incident because the company learned what worked and what did not and applied it to the second poisonings. These types of lessons come from case study research and analyses. By seeing what organizations and individuals do in certain situations, public relations practitioners can make more informed decisions about how to react to issues or problems. No two cases are ever identical; however, by looking at opinion polls, responses, and actions in different cases, public relations practitioners arm themselves with information to make the best decision for their situation. Throughout the 1982 Tylenol case, Johnson & Johnson continuously monitored national opinion poll numbers to determine which of their responses were resonating best with the public. If poll numbers showed that more people approved of Johnson & Johnson's brand image following airings of video news releases showing the production lines of Tylenol, then more visual evidence like it was developed and disseminated to media outlets. If poll data showed that a corporate response statement was not improving the public's view of the company, a more personal message was written to replace it. Johnson & Johnson learned what worked and what did not as the crisis unfolded. Without sound research, public relations decision making can best be described throwing darts at dartboard while blindfolded. You may hit your target if you are lucky, but chances are you will miss the target and need a lot of darts to even hit the board. Good research

and sound data analyses allow public relations practitioners to home in on the bull's-eye and hit the target with fewer darts—research equals efficient and effective public relations. It is the hallmark of all successful public relations initiatives.

3. **Continuous Communication Furthers Trust and Confidence.** Communication is the foundation on which all good interpersonal relations are built—the same goes for public relations. Johnson & Johnson kept the public involved and informed as the Tylenol scare unfolded. Without this communication, people are likely to believe anything. Rumor mills start turning, misperceptions become reality, and trust and confidence quickly erode. Few elements influence public opinion more than communication from an organization. With it, the public is informed and feels confident about the organization because the information the public is getting is coming from the organization—not a second-hand source. Moreover, today everyone expects this level of communication. In 1982, Johnson & Johnson went out on a limb and decided the open, honest, and thorough communication would be the hallmark of its crisis-management strategy. For the most part, this level of transparency had not been seen from a large corporation before, and once the public got it, it offered a refreshing level of trust and confidence—just the ingredients needed to help replace their fears with trust. Since then, the public has grown to expect communication like this. In addition to this expectation, organizational reticence leaves the public to their own devices to seek and believe what they see and hear. Losing control of a situation is devastating to public relations efforts, and communication is a major part of that control. Sources of information no longer become important to the public as long as they can information and news. The Hurricane Sandy example illustrates this when the public began accepting and believing fabricated stories and manipulated photos. Public relations practitioners must counsel their organizations to remain open and honest, as well as active in their communications—during good times, but especially during bad times.

4. **Evaluate Your Successes and Failures to Learn for Next Time.** Testing the success, failure, and in-betweens from public relations initiatives is key to long-term organizational growth and its lessons. Success and failure in life teaches many lessons for people, and it can do the same for organizations. Johnson & Johnson found convincing people that the company should be trusted worked, but that still did not equate to persuading them to buy Tylenol. The company's public relations team realized that additional steps would be necessary to restore the financial security of the organization. The video news releases, interviews with company leaders, and active communication only went so far. The company also needed to invest heavily in retooling its facilities and revamping its manufacturing process to ultimately persuade Americans to purchase Tylenol. Evaluation inherently goes hand-in-hand with research. Research

provides direction during a campaign or crisis, but evaluation shows what worked and what did not in the long-term, big-picture sense. From these lessons, the public relations practitioner knows what to eliminate in the future, what to emphasize, and what to rework in his or her efforts. Too often, evaluation is not taken as seriously as it should be. Organizations often see results in success or failure—without much regard as to how and why they succeeded or failed. Additionally, real-world public relations results are usually not so cut and dry—generally even the most successful campaign can be improved and the worst failing can provide opportunities. Without evaluation, these two major improvements are usually overlooked, underappreciated, or completely ignored. Successful organizations and strong public relations efforts look back at what they have done to determine their plans for the future.

THE TWO "COURTS" IN PUBLIC RELATIONS

This case also provides the aspiring public relations practitioner the opportunity to understand another key principle to public relations practice: the difference between the **court of law** and the **court of public opinion**. Because public relations is focused on positively influencing public opinion, understanding the challenges, and difference between rather clear-cut rules (court of law) and the fickle nature of public opinion enables practitioners to more fully see the phenomenon of public opinion.

The table below illustrates the two courts that arrive at judgments about people and events—one rationally, the other capriciously[33]. The purpose of this analysis is to show how difficult and unfair public relations work can be. Because public relations deals with the court of public opinion most, the table provides another glimpse into the challenges that practitioners face when trying to influence and maintain a positive image and brand with an often irrational public.

COURT OF LAW	COURT OF PUBLIC OPINION
1. Driven by facts. The defense and prosecution in a courtroom present their cases using evidence to sway the judge or jury to favor their argument. The process is based on logic and the idea that people are generally sensible and rational if given the facts to make a decision.	**1. Driven by a variety of elements.** Anything and everything is admissible as evidence in the court of public opinion. Here, facts can sometimes get in the way of a good story. There is often little in the way of rational decisions because they are driven by emotion and personal beliefs.
2. Based on rules. Courtroom procedures are enforced and must be followed by those presenting their cases. There are also penalties for breaking those rules, which helps to keep the proceedings running smoothly and evenly for everyone involved.	**2. No rules.** Anything goes in the court of public opinion. Because of this, there can be no enforcement of a "right" or "wrong." So-called rules of society are the closest thing, but those change frequently and are generally not officially punishable.

3. Deliberate consideration of evidence. Those making judgments as to the guilt or innocence of someone must think unbiased and clear thoughts to determine an outcome.	**3. Capricious and arbitrary.** Emotions and reactionary thoughts create unpredictable outcomes. Weighing the pros and cons of a case means little.
4. Characters are constant. The judge, prosecution, defense, and jury all have the established responsibilities and duties in the court of law.	**4. Characters change.** Opinion leaders such as politicians and celebrities come and go, and with them go their influence and power. They are replaced with new leaders whose influence could be the exact opposite of the first.
5. Someone is in charge. With set rules come authorities with the capacity to enforce protocols and fairness.	**5. No one is in charge.** No single individual necessarily has influence or dominance over anyone else. Authority is capricious at best, and any power that someone has can quickly go away.
6. Some items are inadmissible. With rules, penalties, and people with authority to enforce them comes guidelines about what can be used to influence others and what cannot.	**6. Everything's admissible.** Nothing is off the table. Anything, no matter if it is true or not, can be used to sway people's opinions.
7. Clear procedures and structure. Everyone has a turn to present their evidence logically and rationally with equality and fairness.	**7. No order or structure.** Anything and everything can happen at any time. There are no rights or guides to make the "proceedings" fair. Often, it is he who talks loudest who gets heard, not he who talks most rationally and correctly.
8. Uniformity. Generally, all homicide cases follow the same process; all burglary, the same. The due process of the law ensures that each person will receive a fair and equal trial.	**8. Unevenness.** No two cases in the court of public opinion are the same procedurally. Times change, people's priorities change, and technology advances—all of these aspects affect how a case is "tried" in the court of public opinion.

As you can see, the court of law is much more straightforward and simpler in terms of persuading others that a "client" is innocent. For Johnson & Johnson, it had to present its case to the world to show its innocence regarding the poisoning case. The company had to contend with rumors, copycat crimes, media sensationalism, and limited access to the public when defending itself. More recent cases provide another example of how these two courts differ. In one of the most infamous cases, the 1993 O. J. Simpson case, when the court of law exonerated him of murder, yet most of the public condemned him as guilty[34]. The 2011 murder trial of Casey Anthony also reflects the difference between the court of public opinion and the court of law. Upon Anthony's not-guilty verdict, thousands of Americans showed their disgust at it through demonstrations and vigils, which clearly showed their belief that Anthony was guilty[35]. The court of law makes determinations based on evidence and predictable procedure. The court of public opinion is influenced by speculation, evidence that may not be true, and the influence of the media and opinion leaders. Accordingly, winning cases in the court of public opinion is much more difficult and can often be more frustrating for the public relations practitioner than for the lawyer.

PUBLIC RELATIONS RESPONSIBILITIES

The responsibilities for the public relations practitioner can be overwhelming; however, by now you can see the primary duties that branch off the two major functions of public relations—counseling and communicating—to win public opinion. The following list includes the sub-duties most common the public relations practice.

1. **Researching.** As you have seen, good research is integral to sound public relations work. There is, however, an important difference between good research and average or just bad research. Good research is focused, appropriate, and well planned to meet specific objectives and gain detailed data. Sound research answers the question, "Where are we, and how can we get where we want to go?"

2. **Advising.** Similar to counseling, public relations professionals must advise their organization's leaders on which steps to take and consider how their decisions might affect the public's opinion of the organization and its brand. Advising also goes to all levels of the organization—remember that one of the most valuable assets any organization can possess is good employees. Public relations is just as much a part of internal operations as it is with the organization's external image. Good advisement answers the question, "Where can we go?"

3. **Strategic Thinking.** Research, analysis, and mindshare, or the use of the collective knowledge of people, all play a role in strategic thinking[36]. Without strategies based on sensible, logical, and realistic knowledge, public relations efforts are on track to fail. Taking into account a situation's past and present through detailed investigation enables public relations practitioners to sensibly plot and plan their organization's future. Strategic thinking answers the question, "What will get us there?"

4. **Strategic Planning.** Branching out from strategic thinking comes strategic planning, writing the map that will be used to guide the organization and further its image and brand in the future. The planning responsibility entails setting goals, objectives, strategies, tactics, as well as the means to evaluate them all. It is the culmination of research that answers the question, "How will we get there?"

5. **Communication Planning.** Communication planning moves public relations work from behind the scenes within the organization to revealing the plan to the public. Action items such as events, news releases, and sponsorship programs are all examples of the public side of communication planning. The tactics from strategic planning, now communicated openly, answer the question, "Are we getting there?"

6. **Evaluation.** The last of the major responsibilities of public relations looks to the past to judge successes and missteps on the way to achieving organizational goals. What worked, what did not, and what we can learn from them for next time encompass evaluation. The major question that evaluation helps answer is, "Did we get there?"

THE PUBLIC RELATIONS PROCESS

These six steps are similar to a long-established public relations formula known as **R-A-C-E**[37].

R—research
A—action
C—communication
E—evaluation

Another well-established formula of public relations also incorporates these functions, **R-P-I-E**.

R—research
P—planning
I—implementation
E—evaluation

Numerous descriptions, models, and formulas describing what public relations is have been put forth over the years; however, they generally all have the same major elements. Research first, developing a plan from research; second, putting that plan into place; third and last, evaluating the plan's outcomes. These components simply and succinctly describe public relations in the big picture. However, within each of these major pieces lie many subsets of jobs, duties, and responsibilities—each focused on specific outcomes, stakeholders, and situations. In reality, the duties of a public relations practitioner are numerous, but all center on making an organization operate as smoothly as possible. And to do so, they maintain and build a solid image and brand for it. Therefore, a basic definition of public relations is:

"Leading an organization to developing and maintaining a positive reputation, image, and brand among all of its stakeholder groups."

HISTORY OF PUBLIC RELATIONS

It is important to look at how and where the industry came from to appreciate its growth, in terms of both size and function. Many survey texts on public relations include histories of PR that go back thousands of years to ancient Egypt and Greece. While interesting, this text focuses on the modern practice of public relations, which really began about 100 years ago. It was during the 20th century that propaganda and publicity evolved into what we now know as public relations.

P.T. BARNUM: HUCKSTERISM AND PR

The changes to public relations practice during the 20th century have their roots in the late 1800s. Much of the negativity aimed toward public relations, such as hucksterism and hacks, those who will say anything as long as it will make money, starts with **P. T. Barnum**. Barnum, whose name lives on today in the Ringling Brothers and Barnum & Bailey Circus, realized in the second half of the 19th century that people would believe his outlandish claims and pay to see ridiculously contrived attractions[38]. With acts such as "The Feejee Mermaid" and General Tom Thumb, a man who stopped growing at age six, became wildly popular attractions for Barnum and his traveling sideshow, named "P. T. Barnum's Grand Traveling Museum, Menagerie, Caravan & Hippodrome." In fact, General Tom Thumb was one of the highest-paid performers of the day. Additional acts included manufactured taxidermy animals composed of several species that Barnum purported to be rare, exotic species. His hucksterism and outlandish personality earned him millions in today's money, and his self-aggrandizing methods also earned him a spot in the history books as one the greatest promoters ever, albeit not one of the most forthright.

FIGURE 2-3. Artist's rendering of Barnum's "Feejee Mermaid"
http://commons.wikimedia.org/wiki/File:Barnum.fidschi.
meerjungfrau.jpg

IVY LEE: COUNSELING AND PR

As the 20th century entered its first decade, the true examples of modern public relations also began. A man named **Ivy Lee** began practicing the principles of modern public

relations that made him famous—social responsibility and counseling. His mandate of "Accuracy,
Authenticity, and Interest" ushered in a new form
of public image management[39]. Much different than
P.T. Barnum's practices of telling the public anything
as long as it makes money, Lee understood that
positive public image equates to positive financial
health—something quite new and controversial
at the time. Additionally, Lee understood that the
media would eventually get the information they
needed to compose their news stories, so there
was no sense in denying, avoiding, or pretending
that a negative event did not happen. In fact, Lee
composed what many believe to be the first news
release following an Atlantic City train wreck in
1906. During the beginning of the 20th century,
mega-wealthy and ultra-powerful industrialists like
J. P. Morgan and John D. Rockefeller had complete
control over America's most important industries:

FIGURE 2-4. Ivy Lee
http://commons.wikimedia.org/wiki/File:Ivy_Lee.jpg

fuel and steel. These men were so powerful that the thought of public opinion never
entered their mind—after all, they were in complete control and could do whatever they
wanted.

MURDER AT THE MINE

Lee would go on to work for John D. Rockefeller, chief owner of the mine in Ludlow,
Colorado, following a rebellion where workers protested their poor working and living
conditions, only to be shot by militia hired to quell the rebellion to get workers back
in line. The rebellion became known as the "**Ludlow Massacre.**" The union movements
in America began during this time as workers started demanding more rights and the
media started reporting the actions of protests, such as the Ludlow Massacre. To illustrate
the state of working conditions, one of the outcomes of the event was an investigation
by the federal government resulting in eight-hour workdays for children. By this point,
the relative naïveté that many Americans had concerning social issues began to erode
as the newspapers started printing stories that detailed true events and editorials that
criticized the once-untouchable magnates of the day like Rockefeller. Because of this
shift in America's consciousness, public image began to take on newfound importance in
corporate boardrooms. Rockefeller hired Lee to clean up his family's name following the
outcry from the Ludlow Massacre. Lee served Rockefeller for many years before starting

his own firm. Lee is credited with the statement, "Tell the truth, because sooner or later the public will find out anyway. And if the public doesn't like what you are doing, change your policies and bring them into line with what people want," which typifies his modern views on public image management, which would be known as public relations. While not without his detractors, author Upton Sinclair dubbed Lee "Poison Ivy" because of is alleged manipulative measures aimed at building his clients' image at the expense of the regular, working man. Nevertheless, his influence on modern public relations is undeniable—so much so that he is named "The Founder of Public Relations."

EDWARD BERNAYS: PSYCHOLOGY AND PR

A contemporary of Ivy Lee, **Edward Bernays** also earned a lofty title as "The Father of Public Relations"[40]. Bernays' fame stems from his work during World War I, in which he came to realize the power of propaganda and the then-fledgling field of psychoanalysis on shaping public opinion. In fact, Bernays was distantly related to Sigmund Freud. Propaganda during Bernays' time did not have the same negative connotations that it does today. Before the world wars, propaganda was akin to advertising. However, following World War I, and its destructive use by Germany, the term took on its negativity. Bernays realized that propaganda needed an image change, so he proposed the term "public relations" instead. However, Bernays' professional career into what would become public relations began before America's involvement in World War I. Working on the Committee on Public Information, also known as the Creel Commission.

SELLING A WAR

Bernays was charged with drumming up support for America's involvement in the war, something that most Americans opposed[41]. President Woodrow Wilson wanted to involve the nation in what many Americans thought of as a European conflict that should not involve the United States. The economic boon the war offered America's industries as well as the sale of war bonds were too tempting. To win public favor of America's involvement in the way, the Creel Commission developed posters, slogans, songs, newsreels, and pamphlets mostly aimed at either scaring Americans into think that Germany would threaten them, or playing on their patriotism to help the downtrodden victims of Germany. The Creel Commission succeeded, and Americans sailed the Atlantic to fight in the war. Bernays used what he learned during his time with the Creel Commission to help establish himself as one of the preeminent experts on shaping public opinion through public relations tactics—known as the "engineering of consent." Using psychology and social sciences as his guide, Bernays was able to influence Americans to do things previously thought of as unacceptable[42]. For example, during the late teen years, cigarettes were the sole domain of men—for women to smoke was seen as immoral and unacceptable. Bernays realized that only half of the potential cigarette customers were buying them. To change society's opinions on women's smoking, he orchestrated events where women would smoke to show their independence, which coincided perfectly with the growing women's rights movement at the time. Sales increased dramatically. Bernays would go on to publicize and sell everything from trucks to hairnets. His legacy is connected most to his introduction of psychology into the practice of public relations—understanding how and why people think as they do, then using that knowledge to influence them. Like Lee, Bernays is not without his detractors. Bernays saw his form of public relations as necessary to democracy because people, left to their own devices, would not be able to make sound choices and decisions[43]. He believed the government needed to influence people to make the best decisions. The destructiveness of this philosophy became apparent during the propaganda campaigns of Nazi Germany. Bernays saw propaganda as a means to reinforce and protect democracy; however, those same techniques could also subvert it.

JAMES E. GRUNIG: ETHICS AND PR

The last of the three individuals who influenced the practice of modern public relations is **James E. Grunig**. Grunig is most well known as a teacher, researcher, and theorist of modern public during the second half of the 20th century. Among many accomplishments, his four models of public relations solidified his place in public relations history. Widely accepted as the standard to explaining the evolution of public relations, his four models illustrate how public relations changed the century in which it advanced most: 1900–2000. The following section describes the four models[44]:

THE FOUR MODELS OF PUBLIC RELATIONS

1. **Press Agentry/Publicity.** This is the most basic and least sophisticated model of public relations. It relies on manipulation and even deceit to persuade people to remember, talk about, and want to know more about an idea. It is most connected with overt self-promoters like P. T. Barnum. Communication in the Press Agentry/Publicity Model goes only from the source to the consumer. For example, P. T. Barnum would create a fake attraction like a mermaid, spin a wild story about it, have a bizarre image of it made, and then disseminate to the public in an effort to stir people's imaginations. Akin to the antiquated notion that "Any publicity is good publicity," users of the Press Agentry/Publicity Model do not care if the public believes the message, as long as they remember it. Barnum used this method quite successfully during a time when

people were a bit more willing to believe and wanted to see the bizarre and fantastic. In today's skeptical society, this model would not work well for very long.

2. **Public Information.** Second only to the Press Agentry/Publicity model in its simplicity, the Public Information Model is designed primarily to disseminate information without much regard for the public's ability to receive and understand it. Essentially, an organization sends out information, and it is up to the consumer of that information to find it and make sense if it. Clearly, this model is rather limited in its usefulness today; however, some organizations still rely on it for their communication methods. Usually associated with government agencies, the Public Information Model enables them to create communication platforms and messages without too much regard for the public's ability to comprehend these messages. For example, imagine someone is using federal student loans to pay for their college expenses. Upon graduation, that student must begin paying back those loans; however, the student may not know all of the repayment options available to him or her. A first-year student entering college using loans may not know that according to recent legislation, the duration and amount that he or she must pay when leaving college could be greatly less than he or she thinks. The law is on the books, and the program was developed to help students, but generally, it is the students' responsibility to find this information and understand it. Additionally, each year the Internal Revenue Service adds, changes, and eliminates many tax laws and allowances, but for the most part, private-citizen taxpayers are expected to know this information before filing their returns. In both cases, the information is available, but it is the individual who must locate and then understand it for his or her own situation. The reason that the government uses such a model is that the government does not have any competition. In other words, where else are you going to file your taxes other than through the IRS? In a commercially competitive industry where several companies are vying for your business, however, each commercial company develops communication methods aimed at making their customer experience better than their competitors'. In this way, the consumers' communication experience improves. For those using the Public Information Model, there are few if any competitors to worry about. Because of this, communication is directed in one way—from the organization to the recipient with no regard for the recipients' ability to ask questions or provide feedback. Generally, it is an ineffective model for true, meaningful communication between an organization and its stakeholders.

3. **Two-Way Asymmetrical Model.** Now the public relations models begin to take shape into what we think of as modern public relations. In the Two-Way Asymmetrical Model, the recipient of information now has the ability to communicate back to the organization. In this model, research also plays a large role because the organization needs to

know which methods of communication are most effective. Generally, this model is associated with competitive, for-profit commercial businesses that must remain one step ahead of the competition who are pursuing the same consumers. This capitalistic approach to communication makes the experience better for the consumer. In doing so, the organization is better able to convince and persuade the public that their organization is better than the others. However, even though the recipient of information has the means to communicate back to the organization, the level of communication is not equal. In other words, an organization will research how certain people respond to certain messages and then use that knowledge to create more persuasive and appealing communications. Generally, the Two-Way Asymmetrical Model is typified by organizations seeking recipient input as a means to make messages more persuasive. Because of this, the Two-Way Asymmetrical Model includes two-way communication, but it is uneven, and therefore, asymmetric, or out of balance. Overall, the organization has more communication "power" and influence on the recipient than the recipient has over the organization. For example, a customer who is not happy with her purchase may feel the company that made the product should refund her money. The company may offer a refund policy, but only if the return includes the receipt. She lost the receipt, but still wants a refund. The store refuses because their policy will not allow a refund without a receipt. In this sense, the store has the power over the consumer even though the store is willing to listen, but they will not pay attention to the customer's reasons for not having the receipt, and therefore, no refund. The Two-Way Asymmetrical Model is the most widely utilized model of public relations because of its effectiveness for organizational goals, as well as it practicality in the real world.

4. **Two-Way Symmetric Model.** The final model of public relations is the method of communication that public relations practitioners are supposed to aspire to—in a perfect world. Here, both the organization and the recipient have equal communication power and influence. It is a lofty goal, but one that is difficult to implement in reality. The mutual power and respect between the organization and the individual is difficult to enact because a large corporation could not possibly be able to listen, respond, and arrive at a mutually beneficial outcome with every consumer. The logistics behind the Two-Way Symmetrical Model make it a goal to aspire to, but one that is difficult to attain at all times. At best, the public relations practitioner can use its fundamentals from time to time, but creating communications that are truly Two-Way Symmetrical Model is impossible. Because of this, organizations try to level the playing field between companies and consumers in an effort to improve communication. Organizations such as the Better Business Bureau act as relationship enforcement liaisons between the two groups. Because a private consumer will never have the same influence as a large company, these groups act as unions of consumers to keep organizations as close to the

Two-Way Symmetrical Model as possible. In addition, groups like the Public Relations Society of America (PRSA) work to enhance and further the ethical and positive practice of public relations on the organizational side, including the Two-Way Symmetrical Model.

Overall, the primary focus of public relations is on building mutually beneficial and successful relationships between organizations and stakeholders. It is important to remember that public relations efforts will never be 100 percent successful 100 percent of the time. But, by understanding the principles, purposes, and procedures associated with public relations, practitioners can become as successful as possible. Additionally, by studying and understanding the backgrounds, concerns, and positions of public relations' most important stakeholder groups, practitioners will find that their success rates rise dramatically. Later, we will look at those groups in detail and see how they influence organizations and how organizations can influence them to build these mutually beneficial relationships. Before that, however, it is important to look at public relations function No. 1—research.

For the remainder of the text, we will look at public relations functions through a hypothetical situation. Imagine that you are responsible for the public relations functions at your college or university. Because you are leading the efforts to build, maintain, and further its reputation, image, and brand, you must control a tremendous amount of information and number of messages and actions on the part of your organization. Now imagine that it is 9 a.m. Monday, and the new workweek greets you with angry phone calls from local residents complaining about a fraternity that threw a loud, late, and destructive party the previous Saturday night. What should you do first?

Very often novice public relations students will answer this question with responses such as, "I'll call the dean of students and get the fraternity members to account for their behavior" or, "I'd put the fraternity on probation" or even, "I would make the fraternity members do community service." At first, these may seem like positive public relations practices, which they are. The problem is that you do not know for sure if the phones calls are legitimate, accurate, or appropriate. Many times, neophyte public relations practitioners will jump into a situation, make decisions, and implement actions without the most important ingredient to their success—research.

RESEARCH

Research is the single most important skill a successful public relations strategist can possess. It is the hallmark of professional, well-trained, and experienced public relations practitioners. As you saw in the previous chapter, research is the first step in all models of public relations processes. So much rides on correct and meaningful research because the information it provides enables public relations practitioners to plan and execute programs as successfully as possible. Public relations, like all communication-centered professions, is really humanistic in nature. That is, public relations is a study in human nature, and human nature can often be quite unpredictable. It is unlike a "hard science" like mathematics, were the same formulas will produce the same results over and over again. Five times ten will always produce 50. People's opinions on a company's handling of an oil spill, however, can shift and change from case to case. The best means to predicting what these opinions will be is through research and analysis. There is no such thing as 100 percent assurance with any public relations decision; however, research is the only assurance that enables these decisions to be most likely the best. It is public relations' best friend because it gives insights, suggestions, and motivations for why a public relations initiative should go this direction and not another. Again, without sound research in place, public relations efforts are like throwing darts at a dartboard while blindfolded—you may hit the bull's-eye once in every 100 tries. Research removes the blindfold and improves your chances of hitting the bull's-eye with much more frequency because it offers the direction to it. Perhaps that fraternity party resulted in only some trash blown from the frat house into the neighborhood; maybe it ended at midnight instead of 4 a.m. as was reported; or maybe it never even happened. Without researching and knowing for sure what did happen, you may wind up making inappropriate and unnecessary actions and end up looking quite foolish, or worse, in the process.

There are numerous means of research available to the public relations practitioner. In this chapter, the most common and useful methodologies are described. Overall, the chapter is intended to introduce you to the fundamental importance of the practice of research in public relations.

PUBLIC RELATIONS CASE STUDY

THE USE OF CASE STUDY IN PR

The landmark Tylenol case provided many lessons on how public relations functions can aid and rebuild a company's reputation when it is experiencing a product-tampering crisis. While the case introduced many best practices for such a scenario, it is not an airtight set of directions on what to do and how to do it. If your product is not a medication, then some of Johnson & Johnson's tactics might not be appropriate for you. If your crisis does not involve fatalities, then some of Johnson & Johnson's tactics might not be for you. The point is that you cannot expect the same actions that an organization made in the past, even if it is in a similar situation as your organization, to always work and produce similar results. The best that **case study research** offers are suggestions and clues as to what is *likely* to happen.

As you saw with the Tylenol case, a great deal of knowledge and insight is gained through case study analysis. Case studies are integral to public relations because they provide as much "evidence" of what worked in the past, which can be used to determine the outcomes of similar future results. Of course, it is never going to be an absolute guarantee; however, in a field with no guarantees, it is the next best option. The following is a rather famous case study, and from it, you'll see several lessons and plausible suggestions for public relations practitioners facing similar situations, but even if it is similar, remember it is never going to be exactly the same.

THE NEEDLE IN THE PEPSI CAN

A bizarre finding in 1990 started a case of panic and deceit, and put one of the world's largest companies directly in line for serious brand and reputation damage. PepsiCo is the second-largest soft drink bottling corporation in the world—narrowly edged out by mega-company Coca-Cola. PepsiCo operates bottling facilities all over the world to satisfy its millions of customers who daily consume billions of gallons of Pepsi and Diet Pepsi. One of them, an Ottawa bottling plant, came under investigation following a store clerk's discovery of a hypodermic needle in a bottle of Pepsi. The clerk notified Canada's Department of Health and Welfare who discovered that a disgruntled employee probably inserted the syringe, but no other needles were found, so the case ended there—for a while[45].

Fast-forward 3 years to another eerily similar discovery, also involving Pepsi. On June 9, 1993, an 82-year-old man from Tacoma, Washington, reported that he heard a clanging sound from his can of Diet Pepsi. Thinking it was a prize, he discovered a syringe in the can after he poured its contents into a glass. The news media reported on this extraordinary story, and soon widespread reports of similar finds in Pepsi cans spread across the nation. In total, 52 official reports of people finding objects in cans of Pepsi were made in 23 states.

FIGURE 2-5. Can of Pepsi
http://commons.wikimedia.org/wiki/File:Pepsi_Cola_2008_(Alter_Fritz).JPG

THE PROBLEM GROWS

However, people began to get creative with their finds. The reported finds ranged from multiple syringes to bullets to crack cocaine vials[46]. As the investigation unfolded, the Food and Drug Administration quickly ruled out the possibility that these objects were inserted in cans and bottles of Pepsi, Diet Pepsi, and Caffeine-Free Pepsi. Clearly, the spread of copycat finds in cans of Pepsi was a result of people hearing about the story from the news, and then creating their own case in hopes of getting monetary settlements or some glimpse of fame from PepsiCo. The fake finds from across the country were perpetrated following the only legitimate find—the first one in Washington State. However, investigators never could determine the source of that needle, and several unusual circumstances surrounded its discovery. The syringe was bent in a fashion that diabetics use when discarding needles, yet no one with diabetes was involved in the case. Also, the Diet Pepsi can in question was found in a case of regular Pepsi. No charges were filed in that initial case. Nonetheless, the firestorm of cases across the nation sparked fear and panic in many people, turning many loyal Pepsi drinkers to Coke drinkers. PepsiCo knew its financial future was at stake, and the best way to ensure that future would be bright was through public relations initiatives.

SEEING IS BELIEVING

Following the investigators' conclusions that the finds were bogus, PepsiCo began its reputation-rebuilding efforts. Note that PepsiCo waited until verification from federal investigators that it was not to blame for the incidents before the company began its campaign. Public relations professionals at PepsiCo realized that the best way to persuade Americans that Pepsi was safe was the allow them to see the evidence for themselves. At the time, PepsiCo operated 150 plants producing about 2,000 cans per minute, which equals 2.7 billion cans an hour. With that much output, PepsiCo relied on complete mechanization of the process—and that mechanization would be the proof Pepsi needed to clear its name. PepsiCo offered to open the doors of its manufacturing facilities to the media so they could film and broadcast the powerful visual evidence into American homes via the nightly news. After all, it was the nightly news that first reported on the bogus finds, and in doing so, created the panic—what better way to reverse the damage than to go to the source? Viewers at home saw the blinding speed of Pepsi's bottling operations; the production lines moved so fast that a can of Pepsi was open for only nine-tenths of a second. No one can insert any object into a can that fast. Americans saw for themselves the impossibility of someone at Pepsi tampering with the product; the only explanation was that the people claiming to make the finds were likely to same people inserting them.

In addition to the "seeing is believing" evidence, PepsiCo also embarked on a nation-wide advertising campaign that reinforced the conclusion that Pepsi was the victim of the hoaxes. Additionally, federal investigators' findings were disseminated, which provided corroboration of Pepsi's statements. Of the 52 cases, authorities made 20 arrests from people who made the claims for the fun of it, to extort money from Pepsi, and even from individuals who wanted to be on the local news that evening—a very short 15 minutes of fame. Ultimately, Pepsi was able to recover its reputation from the previously wary public who believed that anything could be lurking in their can of Pepsi.

ILLUSTRATING THE IMPORTANCE OF INDIVIDUALIZED PUBLIC RELATIONS

As you can see, this case has many similarities to the Tylenol case; however, the differences between the two illustrate how a "standard" response to a crisis, even if similar, can never be achieved in public relations. Each case is different enough to require specific strategies and tactics for that individual case.

For example, the following shows how both PepsiCo and Johnson & Johnson managed their crises. Notice the similarities, as well as the differences to each company's responses:

JOHNSON & JOHNSON	PEPSICO
Joined local and federal investigators to determine the origins of the poisonings. Issued a statement pledging it would do whatever it took to ensure the safety of its customers. Initial reports could not conclusively state that the addition of cyanide came from within the Tylenol factory or not—Johnson & Johnson did not accept blame, but took responsibility for its products' safety regardless of what future investigations may find.	Worked with investigators to determine the plausible source of the alleged syringe find. The company was not as vocal with its statements because the syringe was quickly found to be from an outside source. Because of this, PepsiCo did not want to call too much attention to what might be an isolated hoax, which could have possibly be contained in the Northwestern region of the country—where the first syringe was found.
Issued a recall of Tylenol because of the magnitude of the crisis. At this point, several people had died from direct contact with poisoned Tylenol.	PepsiCo did not issue a recall because no one was ever injured from the so-called finds in their soda and because issuing a recall may have added fuel to the fire. Recalls are tricky—not recalling can be interpreted as callous. Issuing a recall can also be seen as an admission of guilt that your product is unsafe. Because PepsiCo knew that its tampering was coming from outside the Pepsi bottling facilities, it knew that the blame was not on the company.

Continuously monitored the media, and in turn, public opinion on the status of Johnson & Johnson's brand and reputation. Because of this, the company was able to tweak and change its response strategies to align with what the public wanted and expected the company to do.	Monitored media reports and sales of its product. PepsiCo's central office took control of the crisis, which in retrospect may have caused the panic and reports of additional tampering to spread. Had the company relied on its Northwestern United States' offices to handle to crisis where it began, it might not have taken off throughout the country as quickly as it did. Consequently, more copycat tampering took place, more media coverage about it was aired, and the crisis took longer to resolve and created more damage than necessary.
Developed video news releases, media conferences, and appearances on major network new programs. Johnson & Johnson took control of the crisis immediately and never let go. The visual evidence seen by millions of Americans that showed the implausibility of tampering happening on the assembly lines left the public believing the company was not to blame.	PepsiCo released footage of its bottling plants illustrating the impossibility of someone within the plants inserting an object like a syringe into a can of soda. This visual "proof" showed that the people finding objects in their sodas were also the people who likely put them there in the first place.
Created an advertising campaign in the months following the start of the crisis to lure customers back to buying Tylenol. Coupons, safety pledges, and new packaging gave Americans a sense of trust and re-belief in the company they had supported for so many years.	The company started running a series of advertisements under the slogan "Nothing" to illustrate the safety and purity of the product.

THE POWER OF PERCEPTION

As you can see, while there were many similarities between the Tylenol poisonings of the early 1980s and the Pepsi tampering of the early 1990s, the differences between the two warranted strategies specific to each case. Whereas Tylenol was pulled from shelves, Pepsi remained available to consumers because of the difference in the gravity of the cases, and the differing outcomes of investigations into the causes of the incidents. Both companies relied on the visual evidence of "seeing is believing" in convincing the public that the organization was not at fault, and both launched advertising campaigns to bring customers back to their products. Overall, both cases provide lessons and clues as to what strategies are appropriate for different situations. Here, case study research demonstrates the fine line between accuracy and immediacy: perception = reality. People believed that all Tylenol was potentially deadly early on in the crisis. Similarly, multiple reports of unusual items in Pepsi cans added credibility that it was not just an isolated hoax. Whereas Johnson & Johnson acted quickly to quell fears via the news media, PepsiCo's slower response meant that more damage occurred to its reputation because it left the public to its own devices to believe what it wanted. Clearly, however, PepsiCo's strategy was pre-determined in the post-Tylenol era. Having studied and researched the tactics Johnson & Johnson used ten years earlier enabled the public relations practitioners at PepsiCo to develop and disseminate video news releases showing the speed and mechanization of the company's bottling lines. As you can see, this research into the Tylenol case enabled PepsiCo to learn from Johnson & Johnson's tactics. However, because the Pepsi case was different enough from the Tylenol case, not every tactic Johnson & Johnson used would be appropriate. Unlike the Tylenol case, the Pepsi incident shows when pulling the product is not best. PepsiCo proved why a recall was not necessary. While seeing-is-believing strategies worked for both companies, PepsiCo's crisis did not involve deaths or even injuries. Also, investigators realized that the tampering must have been taking place outside of the bottling facilities, whereas the addition of cyanide to Tylenol was less sure. Lastly, both cases illustrate the power of the media in shaping public opinion and the fact that the resolution of the incidents is often buried in the media.

UNDERSTANDING THE MEDIA

The media did not create the story—that was done by someone outside Chicago and in Washington State and by the copycats across the country. However, the media certainly spreads the news of the story, which may or may not be entirely factual or unbiased in its reporting. Clearly, public opinion depends heavily on what the media reports, as well as how the media shapes its reports. Tylenol's quick reaction to the crisis enabled Johnson & Johnson to quickly influence the media, which in turn, influenced the public toward Johnson & Johnson's side. PepsiCo's late response enabled the media to report on the cases of tampering springing up across the nation, which left the public to hear only the allegations and not the resolution that the syringe came from the consumer, not the company. Researching these cases shows that organizations facing crises of trust in its product must influence the media through news releases or statements. because the media will report the story anyway, and without the organization's side of the story communicated, the reporting becomes much more one sided. It is like being on trial and never having the opportunity to tell your side of the story. The jury, in this case the public, will believe whatever it is told regardless of the facts or your defense, which usually will not result in outcomes favorable to you. In this sense, public relations practitioners are like lawyers in a court of law—only here it is about public opinion, which is why it is called the court of public opinion. Unfortunately, the resolution to a crisis often will never get the same amount coverage, so the court of public opinion is far from fair. A case of a syringe in a can of Pepsi is front-page news; the outcome that it was planted there is buried in page four. That is just the nature of public relations.

As you can see, case study research provides public relations practitioners with tremendously important clues and suggested practices to implement in similar situations.

However, it is never a case of "If it worked for them, it will work for us." Each case is unique, but case study research provides trends and best practices to consider when making strategic decisions.

Another important aspect of public relations research is that of the law—the court of law. Because public relations practitioners constantly work with building and maintaining public trust, understanding the importance of the legal consequences connected to strategic decisions and tactics is crucial. Much of the legal research that public relations encompasses is very similar to one of its most important stakeholder groups: the media.

IMAGE CREDITS

3

LEGAL IMPLICATIONS OF PUBLIC RELATIONS PRACTICE

Learning Objectives

1. Define the major government agencies that regulate communication
2. Identify the different forms of privacy invasion
3. Identify the defenses against privacy invasion lawsuits
4. Define defamation
5. Identify the defenses against defamation lawsuits
6. Apply the lessons from the *Times v. Sullivan* case

Much of public relations law is very similar to media and journalism law. Issues dealing with First Amendment rights, defamation, and privacy affect public relations practice as well. The following will look at public relations law and illustrate the common ground with journalism as well as analyze a benchmark legal case that influenced media law more than any other.

◼ THE GOVERNMENT AGENCIES ASSOCIATED WITH PR LAW

First, it is important to understand the agencies charged with enforcing the laws that often affect public relations practice. These agencies are often the sources of the law, so researching and understanding them helps to better understand the laws they enact and enforce. More importantly, when a public relations crisis occurs, these agencies are the sources of corroboration and substantiation of the company's statements. The Tylenol and Pepsi cases illustrate this function. Because these agencies have no stake in any company's future, they are seen as trustworthy and credible third-party sources of information, which can add a great deal of believability to a company's statement—think of them as witnesses in the court of public opinion.

The Security Exchange Commission (SEC) oversees matters concerning finances. Often when you hear of embezzlement or insider trading, it is the SEC that investigates and resolves such issues. The role of the financial public relations practitioner, which is one of the highest in terms of responsibility, must understand the reporting mandates set forth from the SEC. Items such as news that might affect stock reports or a company's annual report need to follow strict guidelines because of the sensitivity and importance of this information. For instance, if a company decided to issue a recall, it could undoubtedly affect the company's stock value. Imagine someone within the company selling all their company stock before the news of the recall is released. That person will benefit from this information because the sale price of his or her stock is higher than it will be after the recall news is released. This type of activity is known as insider trading and is illegal according to the laws put in place by the SEC.

The Federal Communications Commission (FCC) enforces codes that all broadcast communication must conform with. Clearly, the public relations practitioner must understand these rules to ensure that his or her company's communication is compliant with FCC regulations. Developing video news releases, taped speeches, and advocacy advertising must be done with the FCC in mind. Failure to conform to its rules can result in fines and regulatory action such as suspensions. The most common example of the FCC's work is the ratings system for television. Programs must indicate their ratings using the FCC's guidelines, such as TVMA for mature content.

The Food and Drug Administration (FDA) regulates all food, pharmaceutical, and beverage ingredients, as well as how companies can market these types of products. Clearly, the FDA played a large role in the Tylenol case because it substantiated Johnson & Johnson's assertion that the company was not to blame for the poisonings. Developing campaigns, communication platforms, and marketing materials for food and drug items all must conform to the FDA's regulations. For example, an advertisement for a new drug for Alzheimer's disease must include all known side effects. Until recently, pharmaceutical companies did little in the way of overt advertising their prescription drugs, but over the past decade, all drug companies began marketing their products directly to consumers, which was quite unusual in years past. With this new push to market directly to the public came added responsibilities for the people developing the advertising campaigns. For example, when a drug is recalled from the market, part of the response is certainly public-relations focused. Therefore, public relations practitioners must research and be up to date with FDA regulations.

The Federal Bureau of Investigation (FBI) is well known for its role in investigating major crimes. However, the agency also plays a larger role in more mundane, day-to-day crimes as well. In any case that involves product tampering, deceit, deception, theft, or physical harm, the FBI will likely be involved in some way. Both the Tylenol and Pepsi cases illustrate the role of the FBI when it comes to determining the source of the crimes. Also, because the FBI exonerated both Johnson & Johnson and PepsiCo of blame, the bureau aided in the public relations recovery efforts as well.

The final major regulatory agency important to public relations is the Federal Trade Commission (FTC). The FTC's main function is consumer protection. Clearly, because much of the public relations' focus is on customer relations, the FTC plays what is arguably the largest role for the public relations practitioner. Essentially, any practice deemed as deceptive in nature to a consumer would fall under the jurisdiction of the FTC. Unsubstantiated claims of a product's effectiveness, for example, would be cause for the FTC to investigate. Therefore, any communication such as an advertisement or news release must be truthful and candid. Because public relations practitioners are often the ones responsible for the content of these items, they must understand the rules as well as the penalties for infringing them. As important as these rules are, it is equally important to understand the agency's definition of what constitutes deception. **Deception**, according to the FTC, includes three major elements[47]:

1. The representation must be highly probable that it will deceive. Essentially, representation entails anything that a company uses to communicate its products' worth and appeal. The most obvious example is advertisements. If a television commercial for a new detergent shows that it will instantly remove any stain, then the product must remove any stain instantly. Using production techniques such as cutaway photography or time-lapse fast-forward to show the detergent's effectiveness must be made clear to consumers that what they are seeing is not what they might believe they are seeing. Such a practice could be determined as deceptive because consumers may think that when they try to remove stains, the product will work just as quickly and perfectly as it does in the advertisement. Clearly, if this were the case, the detergent company's consumer relations would suffer, and it would be the job of the company's public relations department to resolve the issue.

2. Part of the problem with researching and understanding public relations law is that it is ambiguous in its terminology. The previous element illustrates this point in the fact that representation must be highly probable that it will deceive. The problem with such a statement is what is highly probable to one person may not be to another. Therefore, a universal definition of what highly probable means must be provided. This is the second element. The courts use what is known as a "reasonable person" to determine what judgment calls like "highly probable" means. Accordingly, a reasonable person is one who has the ability to understand, analyze, and come to a decision using the faculties available to a normal functioning adult. As you can see, even this definition is a bit vague—after all a normal functioning adult may constitute different things to different people. However, this is the means that courts of law use to judge and determine what terms such as "deceptive" mean. There is no one, universal definition. What is deceptive today may not be deemed as deceptive 50 years from now. The terminology must be able to be flexible to change with society and technology.

3. The last element used to help in understanding what deception for a public relations practitioner means in a court of law is the outcome of the alleged deception. What was the result? The courts have an outcome that results in material injury to help define deception. For example, if someone feels as though the detergent advertisement deceived him or her, then what was the result? For deception to exist, it must have led to some form of material injury. It is not enough for someone to claim deceptive practices injured them if they say it hurt their feelings. That is not necessarily a material injury. The loss of the $5 they spent on the detergent, however, could be material injury. The element is most clearly seen with pharmaceuticals. A new drug's television commercial that claims to aid in weight loss, but doesn't, would be deceptive only if: (a) the commercial was designed to be deceptive, (b) a normal functioning person agrees that the commercial was deceptive, and (c) the deception resulted in some form of physical or material loss.

As you can see, the complexity of public relations law forces up-and-coming practitioners to research and understand it because the consequences of not complying with them can be devastating to the company or even send the practitioner to jail. The last components of public relations law that will be discussed deal with the two most common areas that practitioners may find themselves in—issues dealing with **privacy** and **defamation**. Like deception, the determination of what constitutes either privacy infringement or defamation can be complex, but like deception, the judgment is by a normal functioning person.

PRIVACY

The right to privacy is more implicit than explicit. The Constitution does not directly guarantee it as a right like it does for freedom of expression. For the most part, privacy law evolved over time; as new cases and precedents were established, the laws regarding privacy were developed. For our purposes, the four major components as to what constitutes privacy infringement will be described, as well as their roles in the practice of public relations.

For someone to legally claim that their privacy was infringed upon, they must prove one of three elements: **appropriation**, **intrusion**, or the dissemination of **private facts**.

APPROPRIATION

Appropriation entails using the image or likeness of an individual without his or her consent. The easiest way to understand appropriation is for endorsement purposes. Celebrities and sports stars get millions of dollars to support a product or company because they can bring the company tens of millions of dollars in sales. Imagine Nike without Michael Jordan. Now imagine Nike using Michael Jordan's name or likeness in an advertisement without Jordan's permission. Clearly, Michael Jordan's image and likeness are far too valuable to be used without some compensation, and therefore, Michael Jordan would have a clear-cut case for appropriation. A clearer public relations example of appropriation is with promotional materials such as employee publications. Often employee newsletters or even news releases include names, photos, and descriptions of the people who work at a company. Imagine a news release from a pharmaceutical company that included the names of the scientists and chemists who developed a groundbreaking drug. Theoretically, if one of those scientists or chemists did not consent to their names being in the news release, they could have a case against the company—specifically, its public relations department. It is for this reason, that employees often must sign consent forms for their name and likenesses to be used for future promotional materials at the time of their hire.

INTRUSION

A second form of privacy invasion is intrusion, which entails invading or disturbing someone's solitude. At its heart, privacy is a matter of trust—trust that certain areas, conversations, and actions will not be broadcast to the world. A private discussion at the water cooler between you and a coworker is implicitly private. Someone in the conversation may not have the nicest words about a coworker or even the boss—that person should feel as though he or she may speak his or her mind (as long as no one else is around).

Someone eavesdropping on a private conversation and then telling others what was said would feel like an intrusion of privacy. However, for the public relations practitioner, it is a bit more complicated than that. Imagine you are the public relations director for a university. As part of an effort to increase enrollment, your department along with the office of communications is developing an online advertisement to be posted on the university's website. An element of that advertisement includes snippets of video from around campus—some practice sessions at the athletic fields, a band rehearsal, or class lectures. All seemingly innocuous and innocent enough; however, after your videos have been airing for a week, your office gets several calls from unhappy students who say they never thought their participation in practice, rehearsal, or class would ever show up on the Internet. Technically, they could claim intrusion because it is assumed that the football field, the music hall, and the classroom are private and the actions that take place at those places are private. For the university's public relations professional, it means he or she needed their approval or consent before the videos were uploaded to the Internet for promotional purposes. As you can see, the legal implications can be subtle, but the effects can often be immense.

PRIVATE FACTS

The third of the four major categories of privacy infringement likely to affect the public relations practitioner is private facts, or more specifically, the dissemination of private facts. Everyone likely has things in their past that they would rather not be broadcast to the world. They may be embarrassing, humiliating, or just plain ridiculous, but for whatever reason, they are private to us and should not be made known. The problem is what may be considered embarrassing, humiliating, or just plain ridiculous to someone may not be embarrassing, humiliating, or just plain ridiculous to someone else. So, like deception, a definition of what constitutes a private fact needs to be determined—in this case, the courts use a "reasonable person" to define what is private and what is not. It is important to note that private facts are just that—facts. Rumors, speculations, and falsehoods connected to someone do not apply. Private facts must be able to be substantiated as true or not and previously unavailable to the public. For instance, someone may want to hide the fact that he was arrested for DUI ten years ago, but because that is public record, it is not protected as a private fact. In addition to being private, the dissemination of the fact must also have no legitimate purpose behind its release. As an example, suppose that person with the DUI was never charged, but someone knows that the police only gave him a warning. That same individual who was not charged now is applying for a job as a school bus driver. The person who knows about the uncharged DUI contacts the school district where the person is applying as a driver and explains what happened. While the uncharged DUI is not public, the fact that his driving under the influence was reported could be excused in court if an infringement of privacy was claimed. The reason—disseminating that information, which for all intents and purposes, seems private, could be judged as being in the public's best interest. After all, bussing children needs a responsible person with a clear driving history, which in this instance, may not be the case. For public relations professionals, private facts can be difficult to determine. Remember the pharmaceutical company's news release with the scientists' and chemists' names in it? Undoubtedly, the news release would include some background information on them. You find out that one of the scientists is a single mother, and thinking that it would be an inspirational angle, you mention it in the news release—after all, to accomplish so much and be a single parent shows the person's determination and character, right? Well, the single mother scientist is less than pleased with your decision and regards the fact that she is a single mother as a private fact. If she is able to demonstrate some level of physical harm associated with the publication of her marital status, she may have a privacy infringement lawsuit against you. Moral of the story: always check what you assume about people with those people first—it is always better to err on the side of caution.

FALSE LIGHT

The last category of privacy violation is **false light**. As the name suggests, this category includes making people seem as though they were in a situation or did something that they did not—in other words, putting them in a false light. The connotations of words, edited photographs, and misplaced modifiers can all lead to inadvertently putting someone in a false light. However, the good news is that for someone to claim a legal violation of privacy under false light, they must also prove that whoever put them in the false light did so with a "reckless disregard for the truth." The defendant did not conduct due diligence in his or her research or published information about someone maliciously—not accidentally. However, proving that something was done maliciously and not accidentally is not always easy. A famous case of false light came from a newspaper story about an investigation into the backdoor dealings of a particular "gentleman's club." Apparently the owners of the establishment were arrested for narcotics and prostitution, and the local media was obviously reporting on such a scandalous story. To add interest to the story, a newspaper sent out one of their photographers to take some snapshots of the front of the building for the next edition of the story. The photographer took several pictures of the building and the police tape around, but also captured something else—a man walking to work. In the photo, the man's clothes and face are clearly visible against the closed business's façade. The picture was published the next day, and the newspaper's editor received a call from the man who just happened to be walking by at the very moment the photographer captured the image. The man claimed that the newspaper put him in a false light. Given the context of the story, he stated that several friends had called him and asked about his involvement with the story and its salacious overtones. The man, of course, had nothing to do with the story, but because the photo implicated him in it, he felt his reputation and image were damaged. He successfully sued the newspaper for false light invasion of privacy. A more public relations-focused example occurred when a bridal shop decided to do its own PR work. The owners of the bridal shop obviously wanted to highlight their designs in their brochures, which would be handed out to brides-to-be at open houses and bridal shows. The owners realized they did not have the permission of previous clients to use their image in their promotional materials, so they thought they were wisely altering an image of a bride by editing the photograph to depict on her silhouette. A few months go by, and the owners receive a letter from a lawyer stating that a past client is suing them for using her image without her consent. How could this be? The client in the silhouetted photo recognized herself because of the one-of-a-kind veil she wore. Her false light lawsuit was settled out of court, but she did have a case. For the professional, as well as the amateur public relations practitioner, even the most innocent use of someone's identity and well-thought-out plan can backfire. Researching and knowing the legal implications of privacy is critical to successful public relations practice.

As you have seen, getting into legal hot water can be easy, but there are defenses to get yourself out of it. There are three defenses available to the sued public relations professional when it comes to privacy: newsworthiness, consent, and fault.

DEFENSES AGAINST PRIVACY LAWSUITS

NEWSWORTHINESS

The first defense of newsworthiness entails disseminating private facts, but it is done so for the good of others. The school bus driver scenario from earlier would fall under this defense. Someone who knew about it, while not on public record, disseminated the news of the "unofficial" DUI, to the school district's officials. The person implicated here would seemingly have an open-and-shut case of privacy infringement from the release of private facts. However, because this information would be for the benefit of society, specifically the students who would be riding the bus every day, it is defendable because of the newsworthiness of the information in question. Even using the names of photos of the scientists and chemists in the pharmaceutical company examples could be defended by the newsworthiness defense because the drug's breakthroughs are of enough importance to society that they should be published. Measuring the extent of newsworthiness can be difficult. Again, it is a matter of what a reasonable person would determine as newsworthy enough to warrant the information's dissemination.

The second defense for allegation of privacy invasion is consent. This is arguably the best and easiest defense for privacy cases. As you can probably gather, consent is just that—the individual in the story or communication in question provides consent and authorization to use his or her image, likeness, name, or another form of identity in your public relations productions. Usually included in any employment contract is a clause that stipulates the hiring organization has the right to use the hiree's name, image, etc., for future promotional materials when the circumstances warrant. Chances are that when you signed your acceptance paperwork from your college or university, somewhere tucked within it was a legal disclaimer stating that you may be included in the school's promotional materials in the

FIGURE 3-1. The Newseum in Washington D.C.
https://commons.wikimedia.org/wiki/File:Newseum-tablet.jpg

future. Here you can see how the university in the previous example of using video of day-to-day campus activities on the school's website can easily be done by the public relations staff. Senior students may see themselves in the video, and even if they don't like it, it is still legal because they signed the paperwork before their freshman year. Consent forms and waivers are the best and simplest way to avoid and defend oneself from privacy infringement lawsuits.

FAULT

The last defense against these lawsuits is fault—specifically who was to blame for the violation of privacy and under what circumstances. Any individual must prove that the dissemination of their private facts was done because of either carelessness or maliciousness, and that it was not done to aid the public's interest. In other words, if a public relations practitioner does not do his homework when it comes to getting the facts straight in a news release, and not as a result of negligence or an accident, then he may be liable for privacy invasion. For example, a newspaper story about an individual's misappropriation of funds may not include "Jr." after his name. His father, the senior, may try to claim false light because of the omission of the junior, claiming he was damaged because he is now implicated as an embezzler; however, if the reporter can demonstrate that it was an honest mistake, then the lawsuit may have no merit.

Privacy law for public relations practitioners can be quite tricky and complicated at times. But, the public relations practitioner who researches, understands, and takes the necessary precautions against privacy lawsuits can easily avoid the courtroom.

DEFAMATION

The second of the two major areas of law that often affects public relations practice is defamation. Like privacy, several major elements must be proven to validate a defamation lawsuit, as well as multiple means of defense. However, the public relations practitioner fortunately does not have to demonstrate the burden of proof—that responsibility falls on the plaintiff arguing that he or she was defamed. The court system allows as much freedom of speech and of the press as possible to facilitate open, honest, and critical media. Because public relations is so intertwined with media, specifically the news media, much of the protections afforded journalists also apply to public relations professionals. As you will see, proving defamation is quite difficult for a plaintiff to do, and often the time and expense of court proceedings make the decision to sue moot. There is little sense in suing a media outlet for $1 million when court and attorney fees may reach $2 million. Additionally, because of First Amendment rights, demonstrating innocence against defamation lawsuits is much easier than proving defamation occurred. The scales of justice are definitely tipped in the favor of the communicators (public relations, journalists, marketers, and others).

First, it is important to understand what defamation is in a communication sense. Defamation is any form of a statement that injures someone's reputation, image, or character so much that it diminishes others' opinions of him or her. There are two basic categories of defamation that affect public relations. The first, **libel**, is any written form of defamation. Clearly, published articles in newspapers, magazines, and journals or newsletters fall under this category. The second type is **slander**. Slander is the same as libel, but in a broadcast form. Television coverage, movie, video, and in-person statements would include libelous material. Essentially, there is little difference between libel and slander other than the format or medium that carries a libelous or slanderous statement. The same criteria to prove defamation apply to both libel and slander, as well as do the defenses against them. The terms "libel" and "slander" have developed over the past decades; however, today the line between print and broadcast is blurry at best. Online content contains both. However, the principles of defamation—either in a written or broadcast form—remains the same even for new media like Internet content.

There are a few aspects of defamation that are important to understand before looking at the specific criteria to prove defamation as well as to defend against it. The first is someone cannot sue for defamation on someone else's behalf unless the individual in question is a minor. For example, you feel that a news story defamed your best friend because the report called her a "party girl." Your allegation of slander may have merit, but your friend, whom you believe was defamed, just wants to forget it and not pursue legal action against the network that aired the statement. As angry as you may be, you cannot sue the station for her defamation. Only the person who is allegedly defamed can pursue legal action. If your friend is 17, then it may be a different story. Being a minor enables her guardian to pursue legal recourse. Generally, corporations and government agencies cannot sue for defamation because they are organizations and not people. There may be other legal steps the management of these organizations can take, but companies do not hold the same rights as individuals—people have the right to sue for defamation, not corporations. The last fundamental to know regarding defamation is the concept of "libel proof." Some individuals, because of their position or circumstances in life, lose the ability to sue for defamation—that is why they are considered libel-proof, or unable to be libeled or slandered according to the law. Examples of these types of individuals are those with so high a status in society or so low a reputation that no matter what someone says about them, they can no longer seek legal recourse. Barack Obama, because of his position as president of the United States, cannot sue a newspaper for libel regardless of what it prints about him. On the other hand, someone like Charles Manson, who over the past half century has gained infamy as a crazed psychopathic murderer, cannot sue a television news magazine for slander regardless of what it airs about him. The individuals on the extreme ends of the spectrum of public opinion are generally considered libel-proof.

Now that you understand the fundamentals of defamation, the steps needed to prove defamation will be analyzed. A defamatory statement can take many different forms—body content, headlines, photo captions, advertisements, and even cartoons. It is important to remember that anyone suing for defamation must prove all of the following, which corresponds to the fact that the burden of proof rests squarely on the shoulders of the plaintiff. This also illustrates the great difficulty in winning defamation lawsuits.

CRITERION NUMBER ONE: IDENTIFICATION

As the name suggests, identification is just that—clearly proving the plaintiff is included in the defamatory statement in question. However, identification is not as clear-cut as it may seem. Obviously, certain criteria clearly identify people such as names, photographs, and job titles. But identification can take additional forms. A plaintiff could prove she was identified in a defamatory statement through a description of her, her nickname, her signature, a caricature of her, or even circumstances. For example, imagine that a news magazine publishes a story about an up-and-coming company CEO who made racial jokes at a recent convention. The magazine does not publish a name, picture, or even a description of the CEO. However, the story in the magazine does state, "He was seen at the bar looking drunken and disheveled. His tie was half off and he clearly was intoxicated as he rambled off a tirade of racial jokes. Afterward, he needed a cab to return to his hotel and his black Maserati was towed the following morning." Within these few lines lies enough information to clearly identify the CEO who is now trying to sue the magazine for libel. How? If he can prove he was the only person wearing a particular tie that night and that he is was the only conference attendee with a black Maserati, then he may have enough evidence to prove identification. As you can see, proving that someone was identified is not a simple as it may seem—an important lesson for any communication professional to remember when writing and editing stories about people.

CRITERION NUMBER TWO: PUBLICATION

The second proof a plaintiff must demonstrate is publication. Like identification, this step seems rather straightforward at first. On the face of it, publication should entail the printing or airing of defamatory statements. However, in addition to dissemination of information, publication must also include two other elements. It must include the defamed, as proven in the first step of identification, and it must include the defamer, or the person who is making the defamatory statements. It is important to note that publication, or the printing or broadcasting of defamatory statements with the defamed and defamer identified, does not have to be widespread. Neither thousands of newspaper nor millions of viewers are necessary to prove publication. One, single issue or one uploaded YouTube video with no views can count as publication. It is a record that somewhere someone was defamed by someone else. In many ways, the publication criterion acts as a witness to prove the defamation happened.

CRITERION NUMBER THREE: FAULT

In addition to the two previous proofs needed by the plaintiff to move a defamation lawsuit forward is the third criterion, fault. Fault in defamation law is quite similar to fault in privacy law—the question is whether someone was negligent or malicious when he or she made a defamatory statement against someone else. An important distinction must be made here between public figures and private citizens. Private citizens have a much easier time proving that fault or negligence is a result of the defamer's actions. Public figures, such as celebrities, politicians, and sports figures, have a much more difficult time proving fault. The reason is that the courts have acknowledged that if people want to be a movie star, a senator, or even a great first baseman, then they have to expect that some of the benefits of being a private citizen must be lost. In other words, if you want to have all the benefits of stardom (money, fame, privileges not afforded ordinary people), then you will lose some of the benefits of anonymity, one of which is the ability to sue for defamation as easily as a private citizen. Public figures cannot have their cake and eat it too, or you cannot have it both ways—public life when it benefits you and private life when it benefits you. One of the principles of fault, and defamation in general, is the notion that public figures must prove "a reckless disregard for the truth." This means that celebrities must prove beyond a shadow of a doubt that a publication or a television show defamed them because of negligence or viciousness. Because of this heavy burden, few celebrities ever sue for defamation, which is why publications like the *National Enquirer* and *TMZ* can get away with making seemingly very libelous and slanderous statements and allegations against celebrities. The lawyers for public figures know that the battle to win defamation lawsuits in court is an uphill one at best. Successful celebrity defamation lawsuits are few and far between because of the need to prove fault.

CRITERION NUMBER FOUR: FALSITY

In addition to identification, publication, and fault, plaintiffs filing a defamation lawsuit must also prove falsity. Essentially, falsity is the probability that a statement is untrue. You will see later that the best defense against a defamation lawsuit is the truth—if something is true, no matter how negative it may be, then that is always going to favor the defendant. You will notice that falsity entails that a statement is probably untrue—until the statement in question can be validated as false, then it is likely inadmissible as evidence of defamation. Famous cases such as lawsuits filed against the *Washington Post* during the Watergate scandal illustrate the importance of falsity. The *Washington Post* published stories implicating the Nixon Administration to the break-ins at the Democratic office at the Watergate Hotel. However, much of the newspaper's evidence came via a confidential informant. Because the material published could not be validated completely or dismissed completely as false, those statements are inadmissible in a defamation lawsuit against the individuals implicated in the break-in. As you can see, the courts continuously leave a good deal of interpretive "wiggle room" so different cases can be tried based on their individual situations, yet still under the umbrella of established law.

CRITERION NUMBER FIVE: PROOF

The fifth and last proof necessary to successfully establish a defamation lawsuit is personal harm. Like privacy, the affected individual must demonstrate that the defamatory statement against him or her resulted in some form of damage. Unlike privacy though, proving personal harm can take on non-physical injuries such as mental anguish or psychological distress caused by a libelous or slanderous statement. Additional evidence of personal harm includes damage to one's reputation. Often both of these evidences of personal harm will result in some monetary loss. For example, a news story alleges that a school principal had improper relations with a student. If the principal can prove identification, publication, fault, falsity, and personal harm, then this individual may have a chance of winning the lawsuit. In this scenario, the principal may state that the allegations caused his reputation to falter at his school; he endured comments made by students as he walked the halls; he needed to take a leave of absence because of it. The leave of absence affected his salary, and therefore, personal physical harm can be demonstrated from emotional stress. As you can imagine, evidence of such a situation would warrant documented medical and psychological proof from doctors.

Looking at these five "proofs" that a plaintiff alleging defamation must clearly demonstrate shows the difficulty in successfully filing and winning such as lawsuit. Remember that all five must be proven, and that famous people have a much harder time to sue for defamation than a private citizen has. To further illustrate the burden of proof set on the plaintiff, the following defenses against defamation are much simpler to prove. In addition, unlike the plaintiff, a defendant needs to demonstrate only one of the defenses to be exonerated of a defamation lawsuit.

There are four major types of defense available to someone facing a defamation lawsuit: truth, opinion, **absolute privilege**, and **qualified privilege**. Often defamation cases do not get much further than opinion because an opinion is just that, someone's personal feelings about something that do not need proof or reasoning.

DEFENSES AGAINST DEFAMATION LAWSUITS

DEFENSE NUMBER ONE: TRUTH

The truth defense relies on a statement, no matter how damaging, be accurate and factual. After all, people cannot sue for defamation against something that is true, even if they wished it were not. Someone arrested for burglary cannot sue a news station for airing a story about the arrest even if the person is found not guilty later. The fact is that person was arrested for burglary—the news station may air a follow-up story later that focuses on his innocence in the court of law—but the news station is not required to do so. Granted, that person's reputation may be damaged severely to the point of long-term personal harm. But because the police did arrest him, and it is public record, it therefore did happen and can be reported. This person's innocence may be validated in the court of law, but the court of public opinion is of course a very different place.

DEFENSE NUMBER TWO: OPINION

As you can imagine, plaintiffs trying to claim that their reputation was damaged because of someone's opinion could not go very far in a court of law. Everyone is entitled to their opinion, and the courts have agreed that opinions are protected forms of speech, and therefore cannot be used as evidence of defamation. Satirical programs like *Saturday Night Live* or *The Daily Show* could not exist if people could claim that opinions defamed them. People defending themselves against a defamation lawsuit can simply say that the evidence a plaintiff is using for the lawsuit was just an opinion. You can see now why it is so difficult to win a defamation lawsuit.

DEFENSE NUMBER THREE: ABSOLUTE PRIVILEGE

Because the courts must uphold the right to free speech, additional defenses were established to allow certain individuals, acting in their official roles, to speak freely without fear of a defamation lawsuit. At its most basic level, privilege rights afford certain individuals the ability to protect their speech against threat of legal action. Politicians, legislators, and those running for office have been granted this right through absolute privilege, which is the right to make statements during hearings, speeches, and debates. As you have probably seen during elections, the statements made by challengers and incumbents to office often seem to attack their opponent to the point of defamation. Often statements concerning one's ability to handle the job based on their past become fodder for debates, slogans, and political advertisements; critics define these statements as mudslinging or smear campaigns. How can they get away with making such outrageous and damaging statements? Absolute privilege protects their speech against the threat of defamation lawsuits. Absolute privilege also protects statements made during hearings and other official business activities, even if the comments are intentionally made to harm someone's reputation, also known as malicious intent.

DEFENSE NUMBER FOUR: QUALIFIED PRIVILEGE

Whereas absolute privilege protects political speech, qualified privilege protects anyone's speech as long as it is done in the course of officially recognized business. It allows people to give comments and opinions about people without the fear of retribution, even if those statements can and do cause personal harm. There are several criteria needed to employ a qualified privilege defense. The first is that the statement must be made in good faith. In other words, the statement was true and accurate as far as the person who said it could know. The second is that the statement must be made for the purpose of some official business relating to the situation. For example, if someone you worked with asked you to give him a reference for a new job, but you do not believe he or she would be good for that job, you should give him a negative reference. Naturally, the negative reference can cause personal harm to the person you providing the reference because he might not get the job because of it. But, your statement was made during official business because you were asked to do so based on your capacity to provide an accurate reference. The same would apply to a teacher talking about a student who is a minor to her parents or if the police asked you for a character reference for someone you know. What you say may not be too positive and could harm them greatly, but because it is your duty to do so, your statements are protected. However, unlike absolute privilege, qualified privilege does not protect statements made maliciously. For example, imagine you did not like the person who asked you for a job reference—not because of his job performance, but because of personal reasons. And based on the personal reasons, you decide to give him a negative reference out of spite; then those statements are not protected. The source of many of these protections began in the early 1960s with what is arguably the most important court case in journalism and public relations communication history—the *Times v. Sullivan* **case**[48].

The Times v. Sullivan Case

Before you can appreciate the precedent-setting importance of this case, it is necessary to understand what was happening in this country during the time. The 1960s in America was the most socially turbulent time during the 20th century. The decade began with large-scale civil rights demonstrations and protests in the South spurred by individuals like Dr. Martin Luther King, Jr. Opposition to civil rights was strong, not only among private citizens, but local and state leaders as well. The *Times v. Sullivan* case focuses on one of those leaders.

Montgomery Alabama Public Safety Commissioner L. B. Sullivan, who acted as the city's police chief, sued *The New York Times* for libel. The case hinged on a 1960 advertisement in the newspaper called "Heed Their Voices," which was developed to solicit donations for Martin Luther King's legal defense as he fought an Alabama perjury charge. In its attempt to persuade people to send money, the advertisement made claims against the Montgomery police force, which were not all completely accurate. For example, the ad stated that Reverend King was arrested more times than he was by the city's police, which made the city's police look more severe than it was. Even though L. B. Sullivan was never identified in the advertisement, he sued *The New York Times* for defamation because he claimed the ad implicated him as a corrupt official who furthered a racially biased police force. However, even at that time, defamation lawsuits needed to go through a difficult task of proving their merit. For instance, the state court in Alabama required that *The New York Times* be given the opportunity to retract the statement, but its editors and publishers chose not to comply. Instead, they published a letter questioning L. B. Sullivan's reasons for the lawsuit, saying they did not understand why he was suing them since he was never mentioned in the ad. Sullivan continued his legal fight, and eventually the Alabama court awarded him $500,000—a very large sum of money in 1960. *The New York Times* appealed the ruling to the United States Supreme Court. The highest court in the nation reversed the Alabama court's decision citing the fact that the Alabama ruling did not provide enough evidence to warrant the possibility of stifling freedom of speech as stipulation in the Constitution. Essentially, the court's ruling stated that even if a statement is untrue about an elected official, it is still protected as long as the statement was not made with actual malice. The addition of the term "actual malice" is the primary reason this case is so important.

Up until that time, malice meant that any false statement could be interpreted as malicious because if the person made a damaging false statement about somebody, then it was automatically assumed that it must have been made with the intent to harm. However, this definition did not take into account the fact that many false statements could be made because of poor research or investigation, editing errors, etc., and not out of a desire to intentionally harm someone's character. The court found that *The New York Times* did not maliciously go after L. B. Sullivan's character to ruin it. *The New York Times* did not recklessly publish the advertisement that offended Sullivan. In other words, it did not publish the statements knowing that they were incorrect. Even if a statement is false, it may still be protected under what the Supreme Court would later find as a safeguard against a chilling effect on free speech rights when it tested the *Times v. Sullivan* precedent in later cases. The new standard for actual malice set forth from the *Times v. Sullivan* case extended speech protection beyond what it had been and, in turn, established stronger freedom of speech protections for both the media and those who work with it, such as public relations practitioners. The ability for public figures to sue for defamation would forever be toughened by these findings. However, because the ambiguity of malice still exists, it is not impossible for public figures to sue successfully for defamation. But, clear evidence of actual malice and a reckless disregard for the truth would be needed for all such cases after the *Times v. Sullivan* case.

IMAGE CREDIT

Fig. 3-1: Copyright © 2010 by David Monack, (CC BY-SA 3.0 US) at https://commons.wikimedia.org/wiki/File:Newseum-tablet.jpg.

4

PUBLIC RELATIONS RESEARCH

Learning Objectives

1. Understand the differences between primary and secondary research
2. Identify the most common research methods used in PR
3. Recognize the steps to developing a successful survey

The preceding research strategies into case studies and the legal fundamentals and precedent-setting case *Times v. Sullivan* illustrate the importance and usefulness of studying history. That is, public relations practitioners using these research and data sources did not have to find the information themselves. The actions from the case studies were, of course, already done by the organizations that implemented their plans and strategies. The communication and public relations law principles came from years of trials, decisions, and precedents set in place by the legal community. This type of research is not only rich in useful data, but the work in getting the data is already done for you. This type of research is known as **secondary research**, so named because it comes from secondary sources—in the previous examples from Johnson & Johnson, PepsiCo, and the Supreme Court. The next category of research important to the practice of public relations is **primary research**, so named because practitioners complete the research and compile the data themselves. For example, when Johnson & Johnson continuously gauged the public's trust in Tylenol, the company needed to complete this research for itself. Primary research is generally much more tailored to a specific circumstance or the individualized needs of an organization than is secondary research.

PRIMARY RESEARCH

Primary research is critical to making sensible and appropriate decisions when strategizing and selecting the best tactical options among all available possibilities.

Using the example of the hypothetical role as a public relations professional working for a university or college, imagine the university's board of trustees deciding that their recruitment efforts were not getting the results they wanted in terms of both quality of students and quantity of applicants. They come to you with the job of improving these efforts. Where do you begin? The answer is research. You can use secondary research such as investigating what other universities like yours have been doing and what is working for them. There is nothing wrong with using these data as a starting point; however, because those universities are not yours, you cannot be totally sure that their efforts will work for you. You use the secondary research as a starting point to help direct you to asking the right questions about your own university's needs, which is primary research. So, in your secondary research you find that tailoring messages to each student's interest attracts them best, at least at those other universities. In addition, you find that those students who visit the campus while making their decision about which university to attend are 60 percent more likely to select that university than its competitors. With this knowledge you now have a direction to move forward with in developing your primary research strategies.

Armed with this knowledge, you can begin researching and asking questions about your situation. You know that personalizing the materials for prospective students seems to work for other universities like yours. Therefore, you can begin selecting the methods you will need to use to find out if these tactics will work for your university too. You now need to decide whom you will ask to see if these methods would work. Where better than your own university? Asking the students who already attend your university and who fit the profile of students your board of trustees wants to attract is a good starting point. But now the question is, how best to ask them?

After arriving at whom you will ask, then comes the question of what to ask them. Selecting your participants is critical because they must match the type of people whose opinions you need most. After all, there is no sense in asking the entire student body questions about successful recruitment efforts if they do not match the profile of prospective students you want. You know you need the opinions of the top ten percent of students at your university because they match the profile of students you want to attract. These top ten students are known as the sample from the population, which is the entire student body. In addition to skewing your data, asking the entire population will probably be costly, in terms of money and time. After selecting the most appropriate sample of students, you now need to decide on what method you will use to find out what they think about effective recruitment strategies specifically for other students like them—top students.

RESEARCH METHODOLOGIES

After selecting the sample you will research, deciding on which method or research methodology you will use is next in the process of primary research. There are many different methodologies available to researchers, but the most common ones used by public relations practitioners will be discussed here. There are two major categories of research methodologies: **qualitative** and **quantitative**. As the names suggest, one type is numerical based, quantitative, and the other is more interested in delving deep into thoughts and opinions, qualitative. Below is a list of some common public relations-focused methodologies from both categories.

QUALITATIVE	QUANTITATIVE
Focus Groups. This method entails gathering a group of people and asking their opinions about a specific topic. The aspect unique to focus groups is the dynamic that occurs when people listen and contribute to the group's discussion. Often, topics and ideas that would not be possible with one-on-one interviews materialize in focus groups, providing a richness of data.	**General Survey.** Often the most widely used of all quantitative research methodologies, surveys enable researchers to find out the collective thoughts of large groups of people and arrive at statistically significant results. Interviewing a million people is impossible, but by selecting an appropriate sample size, researchers can arrive at statistically proportionate number and data that best reflects the opinions of the population of a million people.
Interview. Asking probing questions and follow-up questions enables researchers using this methodology to find very specific data from one person's perspective on a topic or issue.	**Intercept Study.** This type of methodology is quite similar to survey research, but where survey research is generally anonymous, intercept studies include asking survey-type questions to individuals on the spot. An example is when participants are stopped in locations like shopping malls to provide answers about their spending habits right there and then.
Case Study. As you have already seen, case study analyses provide a wealth of information about what has and has not worked in the real world. It provides clues, not rules, about how and why different public relations tactics succeeded or not.	**Feedback Survey.** These surveys ask respondents their opinions following the use of a product or survey. Often found as customer service surveys in places like restaurants, they specifically target people who have used a particular product or service and ask questions about how to improve them.

THE IMPORTANCE OF THE MIXED-METHODOLOGY

In your hypothetical position as university public relations director, you decide that researching the top ten students on campus is most feasible by selecting a sample of them and conducting a focus group. You set up various times and places to have your focus groups administered so you will get a good cross-section of your sample. Using your data from case studies on recruitment, you devise a list of open-ended questions that will elicit straightforward answers as well as those that will generate conversations and discussion among the group, which is why you chose a focus group methodology. You find that the first few focus groups enable you to devise and perfect later focus group questions because you learn new perspectives and insights into the phenomenon than you had at the beginning of your research agenda. Following several rounds of focus group sessions, you are ready to analyze your data.

Because focus group data are generally qualitative in nature, you decide that analyzing and coding the respondents' discussions and answers will provide you the specific information you need to strategize and build your public relations plan to increase and improve recruitment at your university. From your analyses, you find several trends that will help you make the best plan possible. For example, you find that this specific group of students does not care as much about on-campus visits as they do about knowing the specifics of the programs a university offers and how they will help students achieve their professional goals. This finding is the most common and universal among all the focus group sessions. Armed with this knowledge, you can then begin your campaign strategy. Remember that your case study research revealed that visits to campus influence the choice to attend a university greatly. If you had only relied on this datum, you would have missed the most important aspect that influences your targeted group of students: academic programs that lead to professional success. You would have invested great amounts of time and money and your results would have achieved success in recruitment, but not of the group of students you wanted. Needless to say, your bosses on the board of trustees would not be happy. As you can see, it is crucial not to underestimate the value of primary research. There is no other way to find critical information necessary to making educated decisions about your specific situation than through primary research.

What often happens is a combination of efforts is more successful than just one methodology. In this example, a mix of case study and focus group research provided you the direction and data you needed to complete your task. However, often a combination of both quantitative and qualitative can provide even more information. Using your knowledge gained from the focus groups, you decide to further your efforts to the top 20 percent of students. Because there are too many students in this group, focus groups would be impractical. However, a survey of them would enable you to find statistically significant data. Imagine there are 1,000 top 20 students on campus; you would then need to receive completed surveys from a specific number of them to make your findings statistically relevant. Generally, the more surveys received, the better your chances are of knowing what most of the 1,000 students think. Below is a chart of the number of surveys needed and the **margin of error** you would have in your data.

MARGIN OF ERROR (+/-) %	SAMPLE SIZE REQUIRED FOR 95% CONFIDENCE
10	96
9	119
8	150
7	196
6	267
5	384
4	600
3	1,064
2	2,400

THE IMPORTANCE OF STATISTICAL SIGNIFICANCE

The lower the margin of error, the more likely your survey responses are to be like those of the whole population of 1,000 students. For example, if you received 384 surveys back, your data will have a margin of error of ±5, meaning that 95 times of out 100, your 384 responses would match those of the 1,000 students. If, for example, a response rate to a question about the importance of extracurricular activities on students' decision to attend a university came back at 68 percent saying it was very important, then you know that between 63 and 73 percent of the 1,000 believe the same on extracurricular activities. Why? Because the original finding of 68 percent with a ±5 margin of error equates to 68 − 5 = 63, and 68 + 5 = 73. If your margin of error was ±10 then you would subtract 10 from the original finding (58) and add ten to it (78) to determine the accuracy of the responses about extracurricular activities on the population of 1,000. As you can see, if you were strategizing your recruitment plan, you would be much more assured and likely much more successful in your efforts with a lower margin of error. Therefore, this consideration is critical when using surveys, which again are the most utilized method of quantitative research in public relations.

DEVELOPING THE SURVEY

They are, however, not the only key considerations when developing surveys. Others include:

1. Is survey research really the best means to get the information you are after? Using surveys should not be a knee-jerk reaction whenever public relations data are needed. You did not need a survey for the top ten students because focus group research provided the information you wanted.
2. What will you do with the results? Often questions are posed that offer little or no real data that will help your planning later. If asking the age of the top 20 students may offer no real significant data, then do not ask.
3. Are you asking the right people? Surveying all prospective students would offer few useable data; only the top 20 should be included.
4. How much time is needed? Surveys generally take a long time to develop, implement, and analyze to make them worthwhile. If your trustees want your plan in a few weeks, then a survey may be out of the question.
5. How will you analyze your data? There is a plethora of statistical analyses available, but do you know them? Receiving a high response rate from your survey on students is great, but if you cannot process them correctly, then they are worthless.
6. How much will your survey cost? Even today's online surveys take a great amount of time to develop and analyze. If there is a less costly means of asking those top 20 students and achieving the same results, then go with the latter.
7. Are you asking the right number of people? Remember that survey data are quantitative and therefore must adhere to the law of numbers. Receiving 100 surveys from students will offer little in the way of meaningful, useful data.
8. Would qualitative data provide more information? Surveys show the opinions of large groups of people, but if you are looking for perspectives deeper than just opinions, like with the top 10 students, then surveys may not help you.
9. Is this the time to survey? Surveys, like all research, are snapshots in time. In other words, what people think today may be very different tomorrow. Surveying the top 20 students in September of their junior year in high school may provide data that are significantly different than their opinions in June of their senior year. Time can have a

tremendous impact on how people think and how their opinions on the same subjects change over time.

10. Can mixing surveys with other methods provide greater insights? Often, public relations practitioners use what is called mixed-methods to achieve greater insights into people's thoughts. A survey shows the big picture of how those top 20 students think, but including several in-depth interviews with a few of the top 20 students adds insights into what the numbers mean. Combining quantitative methods with qualitative enables you to know what people think, but also why they think that way.

11. How can you ensure you are asking the right questions? In addition to preliminary and secondary research, there exists a means of perfecting a survey as much as possible—pretesting. Pretesting requires sending out your first draft of your survey to a few top 20 students and asking their opinions not on recruitment per se, but rather their thoughts on the layout, the questions, and the clarity of the survey itself. This extra step enables you to ask the right questions the right way before you invest all the time, money, and energy in the full-blown survey later.

In every public relations process, the first step is always research. Quality research sets the professional, respected public relations practitioner apart from the hacks and untrained. Research is all about the acquisition of knowledge and then the application of that knowledge into action. Whenever you see successful public relations efforts at work, you can be sure a great amount of quality research went into the efforts long before they were ever implemented.

5 employee relations

Now that you have a foundation in the fundamentals of public relations as well as its essential function of research, the next few chapters will detail the specific principles and applications associated with various **stakeholder** groups. As chapter one outlined, each group must be dealt with individually for your public relations efforts to be successful in the long run. A one-size-fits-all approach to stakeholder relations will never work for very long, just as treating all of your personal relationships the same will result in confusion, mistrust, and eventual destruction.

Everyone expects to be treated as individuals with his or her own specific concerns, questions, and cares. Of course, public relations is different than interpersonal relationships because of one fact: public relations works on a macro level whereas interpersonal relations is much more of a micro level. No matter how many friends, coworkers, family members, and others someone may have, it will never be to the level of thousands, millions, and more relationships that an organization will need to manage. Because of this, stakeholder relations is the best means to approach large-scale relationships on a manageable, logical, and doable level. While it is of course impossible to speak to each person's wants and needs, by categorizing and individualizing public relations efforts to specific groups, practitioners can effectively and efficiently speak to many people's wants and needs. These people are grouped according to their relationship to the organization, as well as their related characteristics, similarities, and psychographics, or the ways people think.

The following chapters focusing on each stakeholder group will analyze each one according to their acceptance, reliance, and maintenance behaviors needed from a public relations perspective. As you can imagine, the more stakeholder group relationships you can manage positively, the better your public relations efforts will be, and therefore, the likelihood of organizational success rises exponentially. First, the importance and necessity of positive employee relations will be discussed.

EMPLOYEES: THE ORGANIZATION'S MOST VALUABLE RESOURCE

While at first, employee relations may seem like an odd choice for public relations work, it is arguably the most important stakeholder group of them all. It is helpful to think of employees' current feelings and actions as the backbone of all future public relations work. After all, if your employees are not happy, they are not productive. All public relations efforts begin at home; in other words, within the organization. If things are not going well at home, you may be able to put on a façade that all is well. However, this act will last only so long. The damaged relationships eventually make themselves apparent in public. The biggest destructive force of negative employee relations is that fact that all of your other stakeholder relationships will suffer if your employee relations is poor. Those other groups will see your negative relationships within the organization as a failure on your part to treat your own members with respect and admiration. They would say, "If they cannot even make their own employees happy, how can they expect us to like them too?" or "Look at the way they treat their own people. Imagine what they really think of us." The power of strong employee relations must not be underestimated when it comes to how the outside world views your organization. Clearly, if they have a negative view of it because of negative employee relations, then all of your relationships with the outside stakeholder groups will suffer. Remember that your organization's image, reputation, and brand all depend on what the world thinks of your organization—internal problems will always create external ones.

If your employees feel unimportant, they are unempowered. If your employees become discontented enough, they can start becoming your worst public relations nightmare. It is helpful at this point to think of employees as the foundation on which any organization is built—the better the foundation, the stronger the structure. As the foundation begins to deteriorate because of rumors, mistrust, and general anger toward management, the faster and worse problems will affect the organizational structure. Contented, empowered, and generally happy employees make the job of the public relations practitioner much easier. As employee relations go, so too does the organization, and it is the public relations practitioner's job to ensure this relationship is a positive one.

No doubt you or someone you know has had jobs where employee relations can be described as less than positive. Think about those jobs as we move forward. Why were they so bad? What made your boss difficult or frustrating to deal with? Why was there nothing done to improve employee relations? What was the effect of this negativity on the organization? How could the atmosphere have been improved?

Often, employee relations hinge on developing an atmosphere of trust—trust in the employee and the employee's trust in the organization. This is the focus of employee relations efforts, sometimes referred to as internal relations because it takes place within the organization. Now, some common scenarios will be analyzed to determine the source and results of poor employee relations—some of which may be quite familiar to you.

THREE EXAMPLES OF POOR EMPLOYEE RELATIONS

Imagine that has been snowing all night; there are about six inches of snow on the ground, and you have to be at work by 7 A.M. Clearly, the roads are not completely passable, and your rear-wheel-powered, manual-transmission car is far from its best in these conditions. You finally make it in at 7:30 A.M., and see your boss is not happy and wants to talk to you in his office. He berates you for your inability to get in on time because, as he repeatedly puts it, "You should have left earlier!" Your white-knuckle drive into work means nothing to him, and your frazzled appearance goes unnoticed. Of course the fact that you live 30 miles away and have never been late means nothing. You compose yourself, apologize, and make your way to your cubicle and begin the day's work. What do think the quality of your work and the productivity of your day will be?

Another scenario: You have started working for a large university as an administrative assistant in the office of university relations, also known as public relations. After 5 years of hard work, you have made it to director of university relations. To move up the ladder so quickly you must have done some great things, such as increasing enrollments of the top 10 and top 20 students in the country by 30 percent in two years—much to the delight of your board of trustees (that research really paid off). Based on your success, you want to implement a campaign to retain existing students—after all, attracting students to your university is one thing; keeping them is another. You start your research by looking at other successful programs in the country and put together a proposal for the university president, who will give the final approval for your plan and its budget. After weeks of preparation, number crunching, and intense presentation practice, not to mention the best PowerPoint design ever, you are ready to pitch your ideas. You begin, and 5 minutes into your 45-minute presentation, the president stops you and says, "We don't have the money to do this. Don't you know that?" You begin to explain that your research shows that losing students who transfer to other schools does more financial harm to your university than any other factor, which you would have gotten to in a few minutes had you not been interrupted. The president refuses to believe your statistics, and simply states, "Our students love it here! We're not going to mess with something that's already perfect! Thank you, good day." So ends your weeks of work and preparation and your attempts to provide meaningful and important innovations for your employer. Dejected, you walk back to your office to begin your day-to-day tasks. What do you think you will do with your future ideas and initiatives?

Scenario number three: You are working your way through college at a pizza place down the road from your school. This is your first job where your income will go to paying real bills like rent, food, and transportation. Because you know so much is riding on this job, you are enthusiastic, willing, and excited to impress your employer with your drive and ambition—getting a raise sooner than later would not hurt either. The first couple of weeks go by rather uneventfully. The mundane tasks of cleaning the fryer, mopping the floors, and your favorite, scrubbing the bathroom, go on without much recognition, or even notice by your boss. After about a month, the enthusiasm you had at day one is a long-distant memory, and you realize that there is no sense in working harder than anyone else there, so why bother? As your work slips in quality, no one really cares. Your boss comes in late, sometimes not at all, your fellow employees are much more interested in checking their Facebook page than the food preparation, and then you are witness to your boss's customer service skills. After waiting 15 minutes for a cheesesteak, an angry customer asks, "What's the holdup?" to your boss's monotone response, "Comin' up next." Another five minutes pass, and eventually the customer gets up and leaves, but not before a few choice words for your boss and your pizza shop. Your boss's response: "Whatever." He returns to watching the game on the TV up in the corner of the shop. What do you think the pizza shop's future will be?

EMPLOYEE RESPECT

All three of these scenarios illustrate common sources of poor employee relations. While fictional, they all are grounded in the realities of the work-a-day life of employees. However, it is the organization's influence on the work-a-day life that ultimately determines the success or failure of employee relations. In the first scenario with the late employee, you were treated with disrespect and disregard for your efforts to come to work despite adverse conditions. Your boss's response was belligerent, unconcerned, and selfish in that he wanted things his way all of the time. Clearly, you are left in this situation feeling dejected, unappreciated, and despondent. It is not difficult to imagine that your performance that day will suffer, and that your feelings may linger for some time. So distressed, you seek support from fellow employees. Hearing of the events of the morning at lunch that day, your fellow employees feel your outrage and they become angered and unmotivated as well. The virus of discontent is now affecting the whole organization, and its result is unmotivated and unproductive employees.

APPRECIATION

The second scenario points to the practice of appreciation—arguably the most important ingredient to long-term employee success. After years of hard work and clear evidence of past successes, your work as the university's public relations specialist seems perilous. You had always thought that you found your career home at this university, but after today's meeting with the president, your confidence in that decision is shaken. Hours of work and preparation fell on deaf ears, despite the fact that your efforts entailed working nights and weekends. In just five minutes, hundreds of hours of work were disregarded and ignored as if they had no value whatsoever. You believed in your work. You felt that you were going above and beyond on your job description and your employer's expectations, which was what enabled you to rise through the ranks so quickly before. No doubt, you feel as though there is no point in reaching beyond your basic job duties anymore. Your assurance in your job security also runs through your mind—after all, the university president is your boss. If he is not happy with your efforts, what does that mean for your future at the university?

THE EFFECTS?

So, you decide to keep your head down and go on with your day-to-day work, which becomes boring and tedious. Your drive to motivate and innovate at work is gone. Student retention slips, as you predicted, and now the university is cutting budgets to make up for the lost revenues. Guess whose job is next? Fortunately, you have record of success, and it is not too long before you get a new job at a local community college as director of communications. Your enthusiasm returns, and you bring your ideas to your new employer, who accepts and welcomes them happily. In a few years, the once small community college is bustling and expanding to accommodate all of the new students, and much of the success attributed to your efforts. And what about your previous employer? After years of dropping enrollment (you are not there anymore to keep your programs running) and increasing transfers to other universities, it is forced the cut spending everywhere—programs are eliminated, student services cut, and extracurricular activities are all but extinct. Needless to say, the university's ranking continues to drop, endowments dry up, and the university becomes a pale version of what it once was.

MOTIVATION

The last scenario illustrates the destructive force of motivation, or lack thereof. The pizza shop had a great asset ready and willing to help make it a success. You were on time, stayed late, and worked on your days off when they asked (usually because the other employees didn't show up for their shift). However, your efforts were increasingly ignored and irritated the other employees because who were you to come in and ruin their good thing of getting paid for doing little to nothing? Eventually, you agreed. Their bad habits, lazy work ethic, and general malaise to anything close to effort infected your formerly energetic and enthusiastic employee persona. As business slipped, so too did the already bad work environment, and the competitors down the road began picking up all of your organization's potential patrons. The reputation of your pizza shop quickly deteriorated in the community as the owner feverishly made last-ditch efforts to save his failing business by cutting corners wherever possible—store hours, product quality, and eventually staff numbers. (Coincidentally, this is the first time in two months that you have seen the owner since you were hired. It seems he had more important things to do than run his business.) The writing was already on the wall, and the pizza shop closes just four months later.

These examples clearly show the importance of employee relations and employee morale on organizational success. No company in the world can operate successfully for very long with unhappy, unmotivated, and unappreciated employees. They truly are the lifeblood of any organization. Now, the factors that influence employee trust and motivation most will be discussed along with the public relations tactics that can encourage strong employee relations.

MASLOW'S HIERARCHY OF NEEDS

One of the longstanding, fundamental theories that explain what motivates people most is **Maslow's Hierarchy of Needs**. This psychological principle describes where motivation comes from and what people care most about as they and their relationships evolve[49]. Remember that much of public relations comes from understanding the psychology and why people think the way they do and in turn, why they behave the way they do. Essentially, if public relations practitioners know what makes people tick, they can then develop programs to encourage positive behaviors—such as motivating employees and improving employee relations.

The model works on the premise that everyone must satisfy their most basic needs before they can advance to wanting to satisfy more advanced needs. Achieving the highest of the five levels in the model results in a content, whole person who is willing and able to do their best in life.

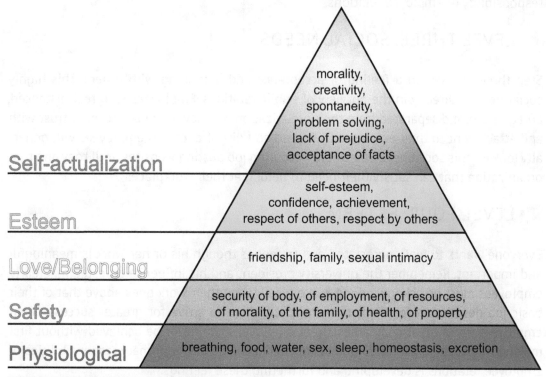

FIGURE 5-1. Maslow's Hierarchy of Needs
http://commons.wikimedia.org/wiki/File:Maslow%27s_hierarchy_of_needs.svg

LEVEL ONE: PHYSIOLOGICAL

The first step is satisfying the most basic needs of life. After all, you cannot expect someone to develop great initiatives if they are worrying where their next meal is coming from. You may think that this step is out of the scope of public relations functions. However, focusing on employee relations, you can imagine that financial stability would play a large role in satisfying these basic needs—food, shelter, warmth, etc. So, at its heart, employees do look to their employers for these basic needs, and if they feel as though these requirements are in jeopardy, their work will undoubtedly be negatively affected.

LEVEL TWO: SAFETY

The second step entails providing stability, absence of fear, orderliness, and protection from harm. While public relations may not offer the same protections as the police do, it does offer the means for employees to feel safe. Job security plays a tremendous role in determining employees' trust levels in their organization. When an employee feels as though their company may go out of business, downsize, or outsource, their anxiety levels increase exponentially. Providing a feeling security or at least honesty is a major responsibility of employee relations.

LEVEL THREE: SOCIAL NEEDS

Step three focuses on a feeling of acceptance and belonging with others. This highly social need is directly in the purview of public relations. Employees who feel distanced, antagonized, and separated from their organization will never feel any level of trust with and attachment to their employer. Distanced and disenfranchised employees will generally look for this social need elsewhere—scouring job posting websites until they find that organization that can satisfy their need to belong at their workplace.

LEVEL FOUR: ESTEEM

Everyone wants to feel appreciated and to feel as though his or her work is meaningful and important. Remember the university president and his influence on esteem? Clearly, employees must be acknowledged and praised when their work goes above that of their basic job description for them to want to continue to strive for greater success. Great employees make great companies. Great employees can never be achieved without first making them feel appreciated and acknowledged. One of the primary responsibilities of employee relations is developing and furthering these feelings.

LEVEL FIVE: SELF-ACTUALIZATION

The final step to a fully developed and completely evolved person is the realization that their full potential has been achieved. Self-actualized employees are worth their weight in gold. They continuously seek to find ways to achieve and become even better tomorrow than they are today. This last component of the hierarchy of needs is always dependent on the strength and success of the previous four building blocks. In other words, self-actualized employees can and will falter if their feelings of physiological, safety, social, or esteem needs are no longer being met. Therefore, it is critical to continuously monitor and maintain employee relations efforts toward the goal of a workforce of all self-actualized employees.

Now that you understand the factors that affect employee relations, the public relations tactics and efforts that can help improve them will be analyzed.

METHODS TO IMPROVE EMPLOYEE RELATIONS

There are five essential components to positive employee relations: respect, honesty, recognition, listening, and encouragement. As you will undoubtedly notice, these five essentials correspond to many of the building blocks of the self-actualized employee and are the opposites of many of the problems you saw in the three scenarios earlier.

RESPECT

The first, respect, is a basic right that all people expect. Employees expect respect from their organization, but the question is, how can employee relations efforts encourage an atmosphere of respect? For it to be meaningful and long lasting, respect must be mutual—the employee must respect the organization and vice versa. Respect is also dependent on trust—just as with your personal relations, if trust is damaged or lost in a relationship with a friend, loss of respect for him or her is not too far behind. The same is true in employee relations. The primary ingredient of trust, of course, is honesty. The more honest and forthright an organization is with its employees, the more likely the employee will respect the organization. In doing so, employees will become more honest in their relationships with their employer. However, as you know, honesty is not always pleasant. Being truthful can sometimes be hurtful as well. When there are difficult decisions to be made and uncomfortable conversations to be had, these honestly cannot take a backseat, even if it seems like the easy way out. Outsourcing, downsizing, and layoffs are all realities of professional life, even more so in today's economy. When these difficult-yet-necessary steps are taken, then the responsibility of communicating them falls to the public relations practitioner. Sugarcoating, obfuscating, or avoidance of difficult topics like these will never build an organizational culture of trust, and without this trust, respect is impossible. An organizational culture of trust and respect will exist only by being forthright, open, and honest about such difficult information. Granted, those employees directly affected by outsourcing, downsizing, and layoffs will never be happy about the news; however, they will respect the organization if it gives the news straightforwardly and with sound reasoning for the decision—for example: "If we did not downsize our workforce by 10 percent, the company would go under, and everyone would be laid off. We hope this cut will be a temporary one, and we can then rebuild." Moreover, the remaining employees will also respect the organization for handling the situation truthfully and professionally.

HONESTY

The second element, honesty, is clearly a major part of all of the components to successful employee relations—just as it is a major component of all successful personal relationships. Remember in chapter one, the principles that the honesty, sincerity, and authenticity of someone's character dictate a person's reputation and image, and the same applies to an organization's image and its brand. Never forget that as the internal workings of an organization go, so too does its reputation to its external stakeholders. Honesty builds trust, which builds respect. In addition, an organization's reputation of honesty also helps fight the number-one most destructive force on positive employee relations: rumors. Rumors are the scourge of employee relations and can quickly infect an entire organization if they are not kept in check. The best way keep them in check is the stop them before they start. What is the best proactive measure? Honesty. Being upfront about news like layoffs keeps the realities of the layoffs out in the open and discourages the backroom and water cooler fear mongering that can devastate employee morale. Imagine that a company must cut 500 jobs from its workforce of 15,000 employees because of dropping sales and falling stock prices. Employees are extraordinarily on guard when their organization is doing poorly, so these types of atmospheres are ripe for the rumor virus to grow and spread. Without direct, honest communication from the company, the employees are left to their own devices to decide what the "reality" of the company's health really is—and it is never a good idea to let a stakeholder group be left to their own devices. The company's public relations office must develop clear, concise, and correct communication of the reality versus the employees' perceived reality—remember the correlation between perception and reality from chapter one? Accordingly, every attempt must be made to inform employees of the company's actions and keep them in the loop as new developments arise. The company can remain healthy and free of the employee relations disease that is rumors only by being open, honest, and accurate in its communication with its most valuable asset—its workers.

RECOGNITION

When you think about what motivates employees to perform well and produce valuable, meaningful work, often incentives like salary, benefits, and a prestigious title come to mind. However, many studies over the years point to one element that repeatedly has been shown to encourage, empower, and excite employees to come to work every day and contribute their skills to the success of their organizations: recognition[50-52]. Even the best salary with the fullest benefits package and a great title and office will keep employees happy for only so long. After a while, discontent, discouragement, and disdain for the job invariably develop.

People need to feel appreciated beyond what their paychecks say. There are countless stories of high-paid executives packing in their high-powered jobs to pursue simpler, more rewarding professions. Unlike high salaries and corner offices, simple employee recognition is free. Telling people they did a great job and encouraging them to continue to excel does not require great investments of money, or even time. Passing words of praise in the hallways about a specific project that was done well provides just as much recognition as a monetary bonus to most employees. Those who care more about the money probably are not working toward the betterment of the organization anyway—it is much more likely they excel to make money for themselves. As long as the bonus gets to them, they really do not care about the long-term success of their organizations. Those types of employees are obviously not the ones who are invested in the organization and who offer the greatest benefits to it. Usually, the employees with the most to offer are the ones who also respond best to recognition in the form of verbal praise. Additionally, they are also the ones who provide the most benefits to the organization.

Remember your hypothetical public relations position at the university where you worked above and beyond to develop and promote your university for its benefit? Remember the reaction from your university's president? And the result? Even if the president did not understand or even like your plans, a simple acknowledgment of your hard work would certainly have lessened the blow you received. As a result, you felt dejected and any future plans to improve your organization for its own sake, and not because it is in your job description, were lost. Eventually, you felt so unappreciated, you took your talents where they would be acknowledged and valued.

Recognition can come in many forms, from simple acknowledgment in the halls to employee of the month awards. All these steps are simple and affordable for any organization regardless of its size. Even the pizza place example illustrates how lack of encouragement ultimately results in lack of motivation and poor performance—not because the employee cannot excel, but because he or she sees no point in it. Malaise, boredom, and stagnation are all signs of an organization in serious need of employee recognition efforts. It is impossible for people to move up the ladder of the motivation without at least some acknowledgment that their work is recognized, appreciated, and valued—regardless of the job or the industry.

INSTILLING POSITIVE EMPLOYEE RELATIONS EFFORTS

THE TWO-WAY MODEL OF COMMUNICATION

In organizations with poor employee relations, communication between employees and employer often takes a one-way form. Remember the two weakest models of public relations also take a one-way direction of communication. Essentially, one-way communication is all about talking and not listening. Often, organizational leaders and managers assert their authority over their employees through communication. A fundamental of employee communications is that the immediate supervisor holds the greatest influence for employees. The person they know and interact with on a daily basis is also the person who can influence their opinions and knowledge most. Therefore, it is critical that public relations initiatives for employees include training all levels of supervisors on not only what to say but also how to communicate effectively. Being spoken at, not spoken to, and being heard, not listened to, are all hallmarks of poor employee communication. Being listened to means being acknowledged and appreciated as well. It means that your input is valued and understood. It also means that you are included in a conversation. Too often, however, managers are good at tasks like meeting deadlines, but poor at understanding the big picture of employee relations. The manager in the previous scenario heard the situation and trials of the employee doing everything in her power to get to work through a snowstorm, but her boss never listened to her side of the story. Listening connotes a sense of interest, understanding, and sometimes empathy. Hearing is simply the physiological process of picking up sounds with your ears—it is like having a TV on in the background—you hear it, but you are not paying attention to it. No employee wants to be like a TV in the background. Conversations are mutual two-way exchanges of thoughts and ideas. The university president never included you as the university public relations manager in on your own conversation about recruitment possibilities. His quick dismissal of your plans and your hard work equated to a dismissal of your abilities, creativity, and drive.

THE IMPORTANCE OF INCLUSION

Productivity is inherently linked to a feeling that an employee's input is valued and utilized by the organization. Additionally, it includes a feeling of inclusion in decision-making processes. An additional benefit of inclusion and encouraging employees to feel as though they are being heard is when difficult decisions must be made, the outcomes are much easier on those affected if they were in on the difficult decisions in the first place. For example, if layoffs are needed to help ensure the life of a business, those facing layoffs will take the news much better if they felt as though they were in on the decision to cut jobs. That does not mean that every employee sits in on the board of directors meetings. Rather, it means that all employees are kept in the loop that such discussions are taking place, as well as seeking their opinions about how to improve the economic status of the business. Where can we make cuts other than in our workforce? Enabling them to understand that unless 100 jobs are cut, all 1,000 employees face termination because of imminent bankruptcy helps to lessen the blow and create an atmosphere of understanding as to why the cuts are needed for the overall health of the company, and that those 100 employees were not singled out for personal or performance-based reasons. One fundamental of public relations is the fact that people will be more likely to accept news that negatively impacts them if they are involved in some way in the decision-making process than if they are not[53]. Simply keeping everyone abreast of the situation as it materializes increases honesty, trust, and communication—all requirements to sound employee relations.

ENCOURAGEMENT

Like recognition, encouragement draws out the best in employees. Recognition can best be thought of as the product of positive employee relations. Encouragement is the first element needed to get to that product. The two go hand in hand. For employees to perform well and illustrate their intelligence, insights, and interest in seeing their company succeed, they must be encouraged to believe in their work. Having a boss who never encourages, let alone one who does not acknowledge employee performance, results in a depressed and ineffectual workforce. The university president who never appreciated the extra efforts will likely not see future extra efforts from his employees if he treats them as he did in the previous scenario. The manager at the pizza shop will never understand the correlation between employee encouragement and organizational success. As a result, the enthusiasm and determination of his employees will quickly vanish, only to be replaced with indifference and disregard for their work and their employer. Like recognition, encouragement costs the organization nothing other than learning new employee approaches and forgetting bad habits. Simple phrases like, "Great job," "Nice work," or "We're lucky to have you" impact the positivity of any organization tremendously. Employees who feel encouraged keep moving forward to excel higher and higher. Like many of the steps needed to instill a positive working environment for employees, the primary ingredient is solid communication. Communication from the organizational leaders can directly affect the productivity of employees. When it is negative or nonexistent, employee efforts slip and the organization's overall performance slips with it. Positive communication focused on respect, honesty, recognition, listening, and encouragement create an atmosphere where employees want to try harder and achieve greater success, which translates into better organizational performance. The responsibility of explaining this to the leaders of an organization falls to the public relations practitioner. Remember that the two primary functions of public relations are communication and counseling. Here, counseling plays a huge role in changing and improving the communication between leadership and employees. Practitioners who clearly illustrate the connection between positive employees and positive company results understand the power of counseling. Developing programs, training sessions, and communication opportunities like company picnics, minimizes the separation between the heads of a company and their employees and bring the two closer. The days of CEOs sitting in their office atop skyscrapers, avoiding their employees at all costs are long over. Only those organizations that nurture and improve the relationships between all levels of an organization's hierarchy can expect to maintain and build positive outcomes in the future.

DEVELOPING LOGICAL EMPLOYEE RELATIONS INITIATIVES

Of course, it is one thing to think about all the possible ways to encourage and improve employee relations, but it is another to sensibly and logically decide which ones are the best for any given organization. Remember that public relations efforts are never a one-size-fits-all proposition. Any effective and efficient efforts must first be understood—it is not as though picking an idea such as a company picnic will end in favorable results for all organizations. First, you must decide what is needed in your situation and then decide how to implement it. Therefore, the first step to developing sound, personalized employee relations initiatives is also the first step to all public relations initiatives: research.

Research is required before any public relations program designed for any stakeholder group can begin. When it comes to understanding employee relations, the obvious starting point is within the organization. Often, public relations practitioners make the mistake of assuming too much when internal relations is concerned. Because you are in the organization every day, and may have been for several years, you might start to assume you know everything about the company. However, this is just as dangerous an assumption for employees as it is for any stakeholder. Only by stepping back and looking at the organization from a fresh, third-party perspective can you hope to really see what is going on inside your organization. Generally, initiatives aimed at gaining this accurate, but not always pretty, picture of your organization are collectively known as **internal audits**.

INTERNAL AUDIT

The internal audit is a full investigation into your organization aimed at finding what the reality of the day-to-day functions, perceptions, relationships, opinions, etc., of your workforce is in reality. Often, upper management as well as the public relations department will not realize what is going on in their organization—akin to the idea of "not seeing the forest for the trees." Sometimes, being immersed in a culture every day makes people not notice the same aspects of that culture as someone seeing it for the first time—organizational cultures are no different. An internal audit allows public relations practitioners to see all perspectives. For internal audits to be as accurate as possible, they must be conducted regularly.

CONSTANT RESEARCH

Times change, people come and go, and economic and personnel pressures constantly change an organization over time. No company stands still and remains the same for very long. Because of this, internal audits need to be a continuous project for the public relations department. Remember that research in general shows what is happening only in small chunks of time—what and how people think and behave today may be very different tomorrow. This is why constant internal research is necessary. You always want to have your finger on the pulse of the organization and understand what is really going on, and not what you think is going on if you hope to create sound, informed, and meaningful public relations programs.

CONSISTENCY

In addition to the constancy of research, internal audits should also be characterized by consistency. Comparing apples to oranges will always yield inaccurate and inappropriate information when it comes to research. Because internal audits need to be an ongoing effort, they must also seek the same information because it is the only way to ensure that you will be able to see trends, compare data, and more accurately predict future behavior. Seeking opinions about upper management's leadership qualities needs to be sought over several years and several administrations to clearly see what affects employee opinions about their bosses. Asking completely different questions during each round of an internal audit will produce data piecemeal and will not offer information that can be used to understand and predict employee opinion trends.

PERSONALIZATION

The third component of internal audits is the personalization of the process. Because the people being researched are part of a team of individuals the organization relies on, the methods of research need to incorporate connotations of trust and mutual understanding. If employees feel as though they are guinea pigs in an experiment of some kind, they may become hostile to the research process, which is designed to provide information to develop programs for their wellbeing. Personalizing the process for the employee and making it a part of the institutional culture will provide faster, more accurate data than springing surveys on them sporadically with no clear explanation as to why they are being surveyed.

HONESTY

The fourth element to sound internal audits is honesty. Being clear and up front with your research agenda and what will become of the data enables employees to more fully appreciate that the process is for their benefit. With this, employees are more likely to provide accurate and meaningful responses rather than simply "toeing the company line" and providing what they believe are the answers that you are after, or ones that will not get them in trouble. With honesty in research comes trust and believability of the data. Inaccurate data from dishonest research will provide nothing for the public relations practitioner to use when developing employee relations-centered programs.

COMMITMENT

The last aspect of internal audits is the opportunity for management and leadership to illustrate their commitments to their employees. This aspect is more in line with what the research is supposed to be designed for: the workers. If, for example, your internal audit illustrates that three quarters of employees fear for their jobs, then you know you need to push management to increase the accuracy and immediacy of communication dealing with company finances. Armed with these data, the organization's leadership can show its employees that it will do something with the data, and that the internal audit process is not being done for the sake of doing it. Any research is worthless if it does not have a purpose—internal audits are no different. Now that you have a better understanding of the process of employee research, it is important to understand what questions must be asked for you to understand your organization and what it needs to succeed from within. Those questions encompass **issues management**.

ISSUES MANAGEMENT

When it comes to sensibly and accurately responding to public relations issues of any kind, research will always be the first step in creating the best programs possible. As with all areas of public relations, employee relations is no exception. There are many ways to research employee sentiment toward an organization, as well as means to build and maintain positive relations. One of those methods is issues management analysis. Issues management is by no means restricted to just employee relations initiatives. This system works for a multitude of stakeholder groups and public relations goals. However, it can be clearly understood by looking at its application to employee relations programs. For this illustration, your hypothetical position as community college director of communications (remember that meeting with your former employer, the university president) will be used. While you may not think of students as employees, for any college or university, they are the most important internal audience, so to illustrate the diversity of internal audiences, this underutilized population will be used in this scenario.

Step One: Identify the Problem

The first step entails finding an issue or opportunity that can improve the internal relations of your staff, faculty, administrators, and others. It is important to note that even though the step calls for identifying a problem, it is equally important to seek opportunities, which may not necessarily be linked to problems. For this example, you find both. You realize that many students attending your college are nontraditional—that is, they are past the average age of 18 to 21, and most have careers and families. With this knowledge, you start thinking about how you can attract traditional-aged college students to improve your college's attendance rates. After all, the more students who attend the college, the more revenue and funds are available to expand and improve its offerings. With this idea, you have determined the problem is a lack of students attending your college directly from high school. In addition, you have identified an opportunity to improve your college and its ability to teach and service students. Now, you must understand this phenomenon a bit more.

Step Two: Analyze the Causes and Effects

Here, you begin the hands-on research process. Without this knowledge and plans or recommendations to attract more traditional-aged students would be guesswork and not likely to succeed. Therefore, you need to know why 18- to 21-year-old students do not attend your college in the same numbers as non-traditional students. So, you begin questioning where the traditional students are going and why. You look at area universities that are attracting the students you are after and realize that their numbers of 18- to 21-year-old students are down as well. Now, you see you are not alone. The next question to answer is why these students are not choosing your college or the larger universities. You decide it is time for some secondary research. Looking at enrollment data nationwide, economic trends, and news stories on soaring student loan debts, you start realizing that much of the restrictions keeping traditional-aged students from your college come down to money. You start to see a trend that as tuition costs rise, enrollments decrease. Armed with that knowledge, you begin exploring primary research options that will provide data specifically for your situation—no amount of secondary research can give you tailored information for your individual case. Even though your college does not have a large population of traditional-aged students, you have enough to embark on some quantitative research. You develop and pretest a survey for these students, asking them what motivated them to attend your community college compared to the universities and why they chose your college rather than the other county college options in the state. Your data show that most students opted for your college because of two major factors: (a) it was more affordable and (b) its credits transferred more easily to four-year institutions than the state's other community colleges. Now, you have a starting point to develop programs to attract more traditional-aged students. However, the surveys you sent out provided good statistics, but lacked the meanings behind them. You want to delve a bit deeper before spending time and money implementing your ideas. You decide to interview a few of your target students. You solicit their opinions on which programs attracted them, the resources available to them, and the outcomes they expected to accomplish at your college. Now, your mixed-methods research provided you with the overall reasons students do or do not attend your college, as well as some insights into the specific reasons. You have the information you need to start the planning process.

Step Three: Strategize

Your research provided you with valuable information that now enables you to develop sensible and productive ideas aimed at attracting more traditional-aged college students to your campus. The data revealed that cost is the number-one factor keeping them from attending. Furthermore, fear of staggering student loan debts deter them from funding their education via loans. Additionally, students who knew about the transfer options and the ease of matriculating from your college to a university were more likely to attend community colleges. You now have the basis to develop plans to increase your traditional-aged student population. If students fear the rising costs of post-secondary education, then they need to be informed of the many payment options available at your college, as well as the affordability factor that your college has that the large universities do not. You realize that most students this age do not actively seek information like this, so you plan to visit all area high schools and present the real costs and options to them to actively clarify the misconception that all college is expensive. Furthermore, you want to reinforce the ability of your college's credits to matriculate to other four-year institutions, furthering the value of your college's two-year degree. You decide that all marketing materials from the college must highlight this factor. Lastly, based on your interviews, you want focus on the programs at your college that most attract the student population you are most interested. You decide testimonial evidence can clearly and persuasively communicate this attribute. The next stage is to organize and direct your ideas.

Step Four: Develop Plan

Any public relations plan can best be thought of as a map. Just as a roadmap provides you with your overall direction and turn-by-turn route, a public relations plan enables everyone working with it to see his or her duties as well as the overall, big-picture direction the plan is moving. Based on your strategizing efforts to illustrate the affordability of your college, the different payment options, its transferability of credits, and its job-focused programs, you develop a plan. You create new slogans, keyword statements, high school visit materials, and marketing platforms to get 18- to 21-year-old students accurate and personalized information that will motivate them to attend your college. Your plan has an overarching goal, measurable objectives, strategies, and specific tactics and evaluative methods to measure its success. It is clearly laid out so anyone working with it can understand his or her part and how it fits into the big picture. The plan is written, and now it is time to put it in motion.

Step Five: Implementation

This is the action step. Everything preceding this step was all in preparation for it, and now the researching, strategizing, and planning efforts begin to materialize. This is also both the most exciting as well as scary part of the process because you can never be 100 percent sure that your plan will work—it is the real world, and anything is possible. Your new brochures and information packages sent to prospective students highlight the affordability factor in clear charts and graphs at the beginning of the pamphlets. You include testimonials from current students reinforcing the applicability of their current majors to real-world jobs later. You add statistics on the income of college graduates versus high school graduates and the median incomes for the types of careers your college prepares students. You partner with local universities to implement an advertising campaign that features their programs and how students can begin their college careers at your college for less, and then easily transfer to the four-year institutions. You begin your high school presentations, bringing your new marketing materials and a persuasive appeal that provides aspiring college students with incentives and excitement that a college degree is within their reach without the need for heavy loan burdens later. You even recruit some current students to speak with potential ones—you find they listen to and believe them more than they do you. The months pass by, and your efforts continue, but at some point, you must stop and see if all of your efforts were successful.

Step Six: Evaluation

The last stage requires you to step back and measure your effectiveness. Part of this last process focuses on what you did, but more importantly, on how well you did it. Your goal was to increase the number of traditional-aged college students on your campus. Did you do it? The first indicator of your success is of course the enrollments of 18- to 21-year-old students the following fall. You must have a benchmark to measure. The previous fall's numbers will do this fine. You know that last year's enrollment of traditional college students was just 15 percent of the incoming class. A year has passed, a lot of researching, strategizing, planning, and implementing took place, and now you see that this year's class is 30 percent 18- to 21-year-olds—by all accounts, a great success. You wanted to increase enrollment of this demographic and you did.

RETURN ON INVESTMENT

However, before you celebrate too much, it is important to look at your investment versus your outcome. For example, if your efforts cost the college $100,000 and the increase in enrollment brought in $75,000, then the success of the program was somewhat mixed. Granted, you accomplished your goal, but remember that the purpose of the program was to improve the funding and resources on campus. If the initiative cost the college $25,000, then it was not successful in accomplishing what it was planned for, which was increasing enrollments to improve the financial outlook of the college. This is known as your return on investment—but not to despair. Remember that public relations efforts are not just about the first bottom line of dollars and cents; they also focus on the second bottom line, which is all about image and reputation. Even though your efforts may not have paid off this year, all indications show that keeping the plan going can result in substantial improvements each year (going from 15 percent to 30 percent in one year is quite impressive). As the plan moves forward and evolves, it gets better and more successful, eventually to the point where you are accomplishing your goal of increasing traditional-aged students to improve the financial picture of the college. To do so, you must constantly evaluate and test each component of the plan to determine which aspects of it work best, which can be improved, and which can be eliminated. Through this process, your plan becomes not only more effective, but also more efficient in its use of resources. The fewer the resources expended, the better your return on investment in future years. Your evaluation of the plan's progress shows that the high school visits were the most influential in persuading students to attend your college. The material on affordability was the number-one influencer from these presentations. With this knowledge, you plan to develop a complete marketing plan centered on the affordability of your college, which becomes a huge success. By the plan's third year, your enrollment of 18- to 21-year-olds rises to 50 percent. As you succeed, your plan changes and adapts to ensure its long-term success. You begin placing advertisements about the low costs of college on YouTube videos and even develop a free app that allows students to calculate their true college costs at your institution versus their perceived, fearful costs of college in general. The plan is constantly updated and improved because of your constant evaluation and reevaluation of it. Remember that every aspect of public relations is constantly moving and transitioning, and the successful public relations practitioner not only acknowledges this aspect, but also embraces it.

Overall, effective proactive measures lead to positive results in public relations. This is especially true of internal relations. Remember that any organization is only as good as its internal stakeholders—from each level of employee to the executive suite, as well as those internal publics that you may not think of at first, such as students at a college. The positives of good internal relations must not be discounted. The most valuable asset any organization can possess is a positive internal operation.

THE PAYOFF FROM GOOD EMPLOYEE RELATIONS

The advantages to organizations that come with good employee relations are numerous, but in summary, they include:

1. **A Common Culture.** Everyone is on the same page and informed and educated about the realities of the organization—a no-rumor zone.

2. **Access to Information.** Research enables the organization to see itself as it really is. Only when an organization is honest with itself can it realistically and tangibly improve its inner workings.

3. **Effective Communication Channels.** Too often, communication flows from the top of an organization down. True, effective communication, however, must move up and down. Two-way communication requires listeners and speakers from both sides—the entry-level workers should feel that their voice is just as loud as those of the board of directors.

4. **Reduced Fear.** Because people's jobs provide so many means of motivation and support for them—both physiologically and psychologically—their workplace environments must also be positive and supportive. Positive environments lead to positive employees, and positive employees work for successful organizations.

5. **Backing Up Words with Actions.** Lip service will go only so far for so long. Internal publics must see their organizations accomplishing something instead of constantly promising with no action. Some actions may not be successful, but inaction will always result in failure.

6. **Replacement of Managers with Leaders.** Often such comments as, "We don't do it that way" or "We've never done that before" are hallmarks of ineffectual and ineffective organizational leadership. The people running an organization must accept the realities of their workplace and see the need to do something about it. The person responsible for making them see it?—the public relations practitioner.

As you have seen, internal relations with employees, special groups such as students, and even vendors connected with your organization, all need specialized treatment and acknowledgment for them to help the organization succeed. They are by no means the only stakeholder group important to all organizations, but they are arguably the most important. Internal audiences are the foundations of organizations—when they suffer, the organization suffers—when they collapse, so too does the organization.

IMAGE CREDIT

Fig. 5-1: Copyright © 2006 by J. Finkelstein, (CC BY-SA 3.0) at http://commons.wikimedia.org/wiki/File:Maslow%27s_hierarchy_of_needs.svg.

6 MEDIA RELATIONS

At some point, every organization will need to deal with media in some way. It might be a positive, proactive measure that helps the organization establish itself in the public's mind. Or, it could be a reactive crisis response where the life of the organization is at stake. In either of these two extremes, the strength of the relationship between an organization and the media will often determine the outcomes. Of course, between these two extremes of media relations are the day-to-day operations and tasks associated with public relations work. Second only to your internal operations, your relations and dealings with the media are likely to be the most integral to public relations success. The strength of this mutually beneficial relationship is often determined by the actions of an organization's public relations department. The public relations practitioner is the link between the internal operations of an organization and the outside world. Access to the outside world is very much controlled by the media. Therefore, it is imperative that a strong, beneficial relationship be established and improved constantly through sound media relations work.

However, before you can begin developing and expanding a relationship, you must first understand the dynamics of it.

The media, which includes the news media as well as the media critics and pundits who are so popular and influential today, operates on several principles. The better you know these principles, the more likely you are to maintain positive relations with it. Most of these demands fall to the public relations practitioner. Historically, the relationship between the media and public relations is great when it is good and terrible when it is bad. Remember that the media are one of the two main influencers of public opinion—part of the Two-Step Flow Theory. Additionally, because the media controls the means of public opinion leaders like celebrities' and politicians' access to the public, they are the most important influencers. The media's power lies in their ability to control access to the public. An important fundamental to understanding, and then ultimately using the media's power, is appreciating their means to direct public opinion.

You will recall that the formation of public opinion goes through many steps and can take a long time to establish itself. From the initial stage of Latent Mass Sentiment, the process evolves through several steps. The most important of these steps in determining what public opinion will become is the knowledge of the issue and then the debate of it. Remember that perception to many people is just as accurate as reality. Many people believe what they hear first, and even when that information is countered later, the initial news is usually the longest lasting when it comes to affecting people's opinions. Because public relations is interested primarily in favorably affecting these opinions toward an organization, influencing the initial reports of an issue is hugely important to influencing opinion. If you can influence the influencers, in this case the media, and what as well as how it reports about issues important to your organization, the better your chances of affecting public opinion to like and support your organization. To illustrate this, a major public issue will be analyzed through the lens of media influence to help show the fact that what the media reports directly influences public opinion.

Debates and opinions concerning climate change and the environment are one of the most important issues facing people today. But, what influences people's opinion about this important subject, and how will knowing this help public relations practitioners? The following will answer these questions. The topics of global warming, climate change, and environmentalism have been around for some time. Beginning in the 1960s, more and more Americans became aware of the correlation between pollution and poor ecosystems. Movements such as Earth Day and even recycling laws arose from this newly mainstreamed understanding and helped move the issue from the privy of scientists' and ecologists' discussions to the general public's consciousness. In the 1990s and 2000s, questions over increasingly erratic and destructive weather took these concerns to a new level. Now, it was no longer the clear and logical conclusion that pollution leads to damaged environments and ozone depletion, but rather why weather conditions all over the world seem to be changing as well. By this time, evidence of the polar caps melting as well as rising global temperatures pointed to one thing: pollution leads to poor environmental conditions, and poor environmental conditions lead to global warming. A new issue found its way into the public opinion process, and the media would directly influence the outcome of that opinion.

New reports introduced the topic of global warming to the general public. How these reports were presented impacted people's ability to comprehend and then believe or discredit global warming as real or not. Videos of polar bears stranded on ice floes caused by melting glaciers affected people's belief and then their emotions about the topic. Remember that emotions can have a tremendous effect on opinion. On the other hand, unconditionally proving global warming was not easy. In news magazines and investigative programs to morning radio call-in shows, the "evidence" was presented and the public debate began. On one side, the proponents in the global warming camp reinforced the evidence of changing meteorological conditions punctuated with images of monsoons, tsunamis, and tornadoes. On the other side were the disbelievers, highlighting their view that either climate change was natural and not influenced by pollution or that it did not even exist. The sides were set, and now the media and the opinion leaders would take the reins.

In the early 2000s public interest in global warming debates was relatively low. However, that would change by the middle of the decade. Toward the end of 2013, opinion polls showed a dramatic increase in public debate over global warming[54]. Whereas the early 2000s showed little change in this debate, by September 2013, it had become a major public debate. Why?

When Hurricane Katrina slammed into Louisiana in September 2005 it brought catastrophic flooding to many areas, most notably to New Orleans. The most destructive hurricane in U.S. history naturally brought with it unmatched media attention. Nothing could compete with the compelling and staggering statistics and footage associated with the storm. Every night, Americans' televisions were inundated with the most recent fatality, homeless, and missing persons numbers. The coverage would eventually move from content over the storm to that of the mismanagement and misuse of authority and resources from those charged with dealing with the disaster. Emotion-heavy visual evidence of people stranded on rooftops for days, bloated bodies floating in canals, and the throngs of people pushed into The Super Dome led to Americans' outrage and disgust over the crisis. However, at the end of the day, the question of why this storm was so bad lingered in many peoples' minds. Naturally, as Americans began to question to ability of its leaders to manage the response to Katrina, political maneuvering quickly took hold.

Finger pointing and excuse pandering soon took the debate over global warming to a new level. Spurred on by the events of Hurricane Katrina, the issue now rested solidly in Americans' consciousness. Debate over the inadequacies of Katrina's response still lingers, but debate over climate change hit new levels in the months and years just following the event. The presidential elections of 2008 offered the perfect opportunity to really amp up this debate. Public opinion over global warming was influenced most by both the democrats' statements made in support of researching and alleviating it from and anti environmental votes by republicans. The arguments, criticisms, and name calling on each side played out in the media. The democratic side supported by networks like CNN and the republican side by Fox News turned the public debate about climate change from that focused on weather to a debate between the differences of the parties. Following Barack Obama's election to the presidency, focus on global warming began to subside again. It no longer had the spotlight like it did before. However, it was not long before it crept into the forefront of the public's consciousness yet again.

FIGURE 6-1. Former vice president Al Gore
http://commons.wikimedia.org/wiki/File:AlGoreGlobalWarmingTalk.jpg

In December 2008, the film *An Inconvenient Truth* was released, spawning new focus on the issue. However, by this point the believers versus the naysayers debate was well established and both sides were set. The film only reinforced this. After all, it was former democratic vice president Al Gore's film about climate change and it reignited the democrat-versus-republican perspectives on the issue. The media once again focused on the differences between the two parties and less on the issue itself[55]. Global warming had moved from a general public's issue to one between political ideologies. The outcome of general public opinion on climate change still fluctuates between weather events like Hurricane Sandy in 2012 and elections.

FIGURE 6-2. New Orleans residents stranded on rooftops after Hurricane Katrina
http://commons.wikimedia.org/wiki/File:Katrina-14512.jpg

However, the media's spotlight on the debate ebbs and flows in direct relation with public interest in it. As you can see, an event like Hurricane Katrina set public debate over climate change in motion, but it was the media that influenced what people knew about it. It went from facts and science to arguments and philosophy. The media possesses tremendous power concerning public opinion. A long-established theory explains this critically important fundamental of media relations.

Agenda-Setting Theory explains how the media tells people what to think about when it comes to acknowledging and understanding important issues like climate change. Most of society first heard of climate change, global warming, or any combination of terms from the media. It is the media that sets the ball of public opinion rolling. It is where news like climate change comes from, and what it includes or omits in its coverage as well as what the connotations of this coverage directly impact public opinion. The media does not necessarily tell you what to think, but it tells you what to think about. It sets the agenda of what the public will debate. Of course, the media did not create Hurricane Katrina. However, the media's focus on certain aspects of Katrina like the bodies in canals and Federal Emergency Management Agency (FEMA) conference bungles, as well as more coverage of a republican point of view than a democratic one, certainly affected people's perceptions of Katrina. The perceptions would later directly influence public debate over climate change. But what does this mean for the public relations practitioner who wants to harness this power of the media?

AGENDA-SETTING THEORY

Understanding Agenda-Setting Theory helps practitioners get media attention to focus on their organization's agendas[56]. It helps explain how the media can be used as a means of "popularizing" your company's position. What do you want people to think about your organization and its agenda? Remember that an agenda is just a set of issues important to your organization that must be communicated. You must influence the media and the way you want them to report about you. If you can do this, then your stakeholders will be well on their way to thinking the way you want them to about you. In other words, you have set your organization's agenda in their minds through the media. There exists what's known as a "dynamic interplay" between the media, stakeholders, and policy makers ... all of which are interdependent for their own success. It's not a linear model as in the past where the media sets the agenda, and then influenced public opinion, and that set policy. Now, it's multidirectional. For example, texting-while-driving laws are not a direct result of traditional media agenda setting, but rather organizations using the media to spread the word on the dangers of texting while driving, which then creates enough interest to develop laws prohibiting it. The media cannot be everywhere. The media depends on public relations for its agenda too.

A simple list for you to remember on understanding and harnessing the media's power for public relations initiatives is:

1. Media coverage influences what the public thinks about.
2. Public relations can affect media coverage.

3. When media coverage includes an organization's public relations efforts, the public knows about them.
4. As the public knows about these efforts, they will develop positive opinions about the organization.
5. Positive public opinion via the media improves the organization's ability to succeed.

For example, a hospital opens a new research facility. The hospital's public relations department wants to spread the word about it to boost the hospital's image. They invite the media for a ribbon-cutting ceremony, which gets good exposure ... for the day. But, for the hospital to remain part of the public's agenda, the hospital's public relations team needs to keep the story "fresh" with follow ups about how the new research facility is saving lives and by setting up interviews with doctors, patients, and others. That keeps the story, or the agenda, in the public's eye, and in turn, long-lasting positive public relations is built. The hospital's public relations team used the media to set the public's agenda about the hospital being modern, cutting-edge, etc. This, in turn, boosts revenue for the hospital.

However, creating enough interest in your agenda to then influence the media to cover your news, events, etc., is not easy. After all, every organization in the world with a decent public relations practitioner is competing with each other for the same coverage. The question then is how you can create enough media interest in your organization and what it takes to garner their attention. To answer this question, it is necessary to fully understand the media's needs and what it wants from public relations practitioners when they present "news" to the media.

There are several classic descriptions of what makes something worthwhile, or news-worthy, to the media. The time-tested five W's and H are a good place to start. You can imagine your roles as public relations director for your community college to understand these aspects more.

THE FIVE W'S AND H OF THE NEWS MEDIA

Who. The media loves people-centered stories. After all, if people cannot hear about themselves, then the second-best option is to hear about other people. Of course, the importance of the person plays a huge role in making his or her actions interesting enough to warrant media coverage. As public relations director for your college, you understand the importance of developing positive media relations and creating meaningful news for them to cover. Just like the hospital's new research facility did, you know that getting your organization's positive aspects into the media often equates to more revenue, better image, and improved relations with all of your stakeholder groups. Using the newsworthy factor of people, you decide that the best way to attract media attention is to use a high-profile individual. Because of your success in recruiting more students, your college decided to open a new department of student success, which helps incoming students acclimate to college, as well as returning students get back in the groove of college life. While the new department is interesting, it probably would not attract a lot of media coverage. Therefore, if you use a person to publicize the new department, the likelihood of increased media coverage improves. So, you decide to invite the governor to come to your campus and cut the ribbon on the new department. The governor's appearance enhances the newsworthy element of your story.

What. This is the "so what" factor what all good media-targeted stories must possess. Without it, your story will be quickly dismissed, and one of your competitors' stories will take its place. You must identify and emphasize the importance of your story on your media targets' audiences. These people are the end consumers of media coverage, and because the media outlets like newspapers and television stations rely on their patronage, the media cares about their interests most. How is your story important to them? Always remember that at the end of the day media outlets are businesses that depend on revenues. Their revenues come mostly from advertising. The more viewers and readers a media outlet has, the more they can charge for advertising, and the more money they make. This is the number-one reason to always tailor your stories not just to the media outlet but more importantly to the people who read or watch that media outlet's coverage. With this knowledge, you realize that your story on the new department must be meaningful and interesting to the people who read the newspapers you are pitching the story to and the people who watch the news programs you are pitching the story to. What makes the department important to them? You decide that the ever-present stories about skyrocketing tuition costs and the sluggish economy would make a great segue to your media pitches. By emphasizing the costs of college education and the concerns of parents and students about it, you now emphasize the magnitude of your story about the new department. The new department, after all, is all about making the transition into college as easy as possible, and therefore as successful as possible, meaning fewer dropouts and fewer people paying for an education without a degree. Also, you emphasize the affordability factor of your college and how the new department will help students understand their financial options—all important aspects of the story that the media consumers care about, and if they care about it, then the media will care about it.

When. Timing is everything with newsworthiness. By its very definition, news is new information about something important or interesting. The time when you pitch a story to the media goes a long way in affecting the interest level in the story. Certain events like fires and scandals receive media recognition first. Your story, however, does not have the immediacy factor of these types of events, and you may therefore think that the time your pitch you story will be unimportant to its chances of finding itself in the news. However, even the story on the new department includes a timing element. Think about what your story's focus is on—the new department, yes, but the new department's usefulness and meaning for potential students. The time you should pitch the story on the new department should also coincide with the time that potential students would be most interested. You decide that late April would be best because potential students are winding down their high school careers and now realize that college will start in a few months. Pitching this story in October, for instance, would not capture as much attention from the people consuming the news, and therefore, it is less likely the news media would cover your story. You can increase the likelihood of media coverage of your stories by having them coincide with annual events, holidays, and seasons that match your focus. The immediate news like disasters or major crimes will also receive media coverage. The difficult job for the public relations practitioner is to make the not-so-impactful news like new departments, hires, promotions, and products just as interesting to the media. Timing can help accomplish that.

Where. Clearly if something happens in your town it is much more interesting to you than a similar event halfway across the country. People care about what is happening near them—the closer, the more interesting. This phenomenon explains why local news stations and newspapers exist. If people did not care most about what was near them, then all the public would need is one news channel and one newspaper. Localizing your stories to the areas where you want them to air or be published is critical to getting them placed in the media. Your story focusing on the new department certainly lends itself to local coverage. It is a community college after all. Therefore, getting coverage in the local daily newspaper should not be too difficult. However, the story would be much more impactful for your college if it were also carried in the city newspaper. However, as the importance of readership of a newspaper goes up, so too does the difficulty in getting a story in it. Fortunately for you the governor agreed to open the new department, which should garner bigger news outlets' attention. But for argument's sake let us say that the governor's plan to visit your campus fell through—now what? Because you know your community so well, you know that the city's sports teams garner tremendous media attention. Therefore, you decide to reach out and partner with the city's football team to encourage their support of student success in college. Because the team also wants good publicity, they agree and will send out two of their star players for the ribbon-cutting ceremony. This certainly gets the city media's attention.

Why. The media must know the reasons for the stories you are pitching. Where do the ideas behind stories involving new products, services, advancements, and even new departments come from? What is the use of them, and why were they created? What will your new department do, and what was the reason for its development? You understand that your college's new department will aid students in many facets of their college experience—most importantly with their financial and academic success. However, just because you know this, or think it is obvious, does not mean the media will understand this element. Remember, the editors and reporters who receive pitches like yours also get hundreds of similar ones every week. They cannot possibly pore over each one to extrapo-late their newsworthiness. It should be clear and obvious to anyone. Therefore, you must highlight the reasons behind a story—why did you college develop this new department? It sprang from the fears from potential students about the rising costs of college and the uncertainty of today's economy. Emphasizing these aspects not only reinforces the "why" factor, but also increases the attention-getting elements of your story, which will only help its chances of being published or aired.

How. The last of the six elements of newsworthiness focuses on the benefits or services and general effects your story's focus will have on people. Major news events, or hard news stories, on fires, shootings, layoffs, etc., clearly answer the "how" question. But, stories such as that of the new department are less obvious. Therefore, they need to be spelled out so that the people who make the decisions whether your story will be published or aired will be persuaded to run it. Often, these individuals are editors or producers, and are collectively known as **gatekeepers**. The term "gatekeeper" comes from the idea that these people control access to their newspapers, television stations, and radio airwaves. They either open or close the "gate" on your story to access their media channels: newspapers, television stations, magazines, etc.[57] In fact, the entire process of making your stories as newsworthy as possible is done in an attempt to persuade these gatekeepers to open the doors to their media channels and allow your story in them. Therefore, you must present a compelling story as to how your new department will benefit the gatekeepers' readers, listeners, and viewers. It is not enough to say your new department offers services and programs aimed at increasing and bettering the college experience for all students; you must explain why it will as well. Your pitches include evidence that supports these claims. In doing so, your story becomes more credible as news and not simply an advertisement disguised as news. Nothing turns off the media faster than self-promotion made to look like something meaningful and useful to the public. The media developed these six ele-ments a long time ago, and if public relations practitioners hope to include themselves in the media's system, then they must play by their rules.

Because the media controls itself and its channels, radio and television stations and newspapers and magazines for example, it also possesses a rather egocentric relationship with those trying to use these channels—especially public relations practitioners. There is an old saying that you do not pick fights with people who buy ink by the barrel. This decades-old adage means that the media is in control, and they know it. Media outlets can run your stories if they want, or may not—there is no one saying they have to, and no one saying they need to be fair either. You could develop the best story and greatest pitch and news release, but the media can do with it as they wish. It could make the front page or the recycle bin. It is totally up to them. Furthermore, trying to argue with the media over its coverage, or lack thereof, often will result in them criticizing or ignoring you as much as they want. Remember, the gatekeepers have total access to their channels every day and do not need your help to fill their broadcasts or their newspapers, or so they think. The grudging relationship between public relations and the media is nothing new. They think they do not need public relations and sometimes public relations thinks it does not need the media. However, nothing could be further from the truth. Today's 24-hour news cycle needs content. It is impossible for any media outlet to have reporters everywhere all the time. That is where public relations comes in by supplying the stories the media cannot cover. Conversely, public relations needs the media because the public gets its information primarily from the media. This coverage clearly influences public opinion, and because public relations is focused on managing public opinion, it cannot function without partnering with the media. As you will see later, the media can be a public relations practitioner's best friend or worst enemy. Even though the media can act erratically at times, managing media relations is really about understanding how the media functions and want it wants, such as truly newsworthy stories versus self-aggrandizing promotion. The media does not want to be used, and by following their rules, they are less likely to feel that way and more inclined to work with you. Treating the media as just a means to an end will inevitably result in poor media relations and can end in devastating results, especially when a crisis develops. In addition to understanding the basic nature of what makes an item newsworthy to the media, it is also necessary to understand the unwritten rules of positive media engagement. Public relations practitioners who know and abide by these fundamentals maintain stronger and more beneficial relationships between themselves and the media than those who dismiss or ignore them. It is impossible for any public relations practitioner to develop and maintain a strong organizational reputation and brand without positive media relations. Below are seven fundamentals to creating and improving media relations.

Developing Positive Media Relations

1. **Know the Media Markets.** Every geographic area is different in its population composition. Miami is different than Los Angeles, which is different than Philadelphia. The lifestyles, backgrounds, and public opinions of these areas all affect the media outlets there. Miami, for instance, with its larger retiree population, certainly cares about major issues differently than Philadelphia with its working-class, blue-collar makeup. The media outlets in these cities also must reflect the lifestyles of those who live there. If they did not, the citizens in these areas would not consume these media outlets, and they would be forced out of business. Remember that media is a business that relies on customers just as much as any manufacturer that sells tangible products like automobiles. Therefore, if public relations practitioners have any hope of getting their organizations' news into these media outlets, they must tailor their stories to reflect the mentalities of the populations residing there. The same story would, theoretically,

need to be written five different ways for five separate markets. Each version would appeal to the unique characteristics and concerns of these five different markets. Remember, one size fits all never works with public relations efforts, especially its communication efforts. Even the same market can have different media channels that each appeal to a different segment of that market's population. In Philadelphia, for example, the two major newspapers are *The Philadelphia Daily News* and *The Philadelphia Inquirer*. Each of these newspapers appeals to different subsections of the Philadelphia population. *The Daily News* is more sports-, entertainment-, and pop-culture-oriented, while the *Inquirer* is more global and in-depth in its coverage. That is not to say that one is necessarily better than the other; they are just different. It means that public relations practitioners who want their stories published in Philadelphia not only need to know the city's market overall, but also the subsections of that market and different media outlets that cater to them. For example, your story about the new department at your college would probably not find its way into the *Inquirer*; however, if one of the two football players who are cutting the ribbon have a Philadelphia connection, then you might have a chance with the *Daily News*. You would then need to emphasize the fact that there is a Philadelphia connection for the *Daily News*'s editors. Media placements are all about making your message and story appeal to these gatekeepers—knowing who they are by knowing where they are is a good start.

2. **Know the Gatekeepers' Audience.** As you saw in the previous rule, tailoring your messages must be a priority for successful media placements. It is very difficult to make your message appealing to these important people without this knowledge. They are the ones in control of your story's fate, and therefore, they expect you to have done your homework when it comes to giving them something that they can sell to their customers. You must research their customers, that is, the area radio stations' listeners, the television stations' viewers, and the newspaper and magazine readers from each area. With this knowledge, you can write stories that attract each demographic interest, and in doing so, you will appeal to the gatekeepers who control the media content in the areas you want your stories disseminated. It is imperative to remember that you must customize your communications to each region and the population that resides there.

3. **Help the Media Workers Do Their Job.** Journalists' jobs are not easy. They work under tight deadlines and demanding schedules to fulfill their duties. They also must work with uncooperative individuals under difficult circumstances. Because of this, their tolerance for public relations practitioners who do not tailor their work to the needs of their media outlets can be quite limited. The aim of media placement is of course to

get your organization's news and story content into newspapers, television broadcasts, and radio airwaves. You can better accomplish this by following the guidelines and deadlines of the media workers. Understanding their deadlines and job demands better enables you to develop a professional, mutually beneficial relationship. Remember that the media needs public relations work just as much as public relations needs the media's ability to communicate to the public. By understanding their jobs, you have a better chance of creating trust between and building respect. In doing so, you also create lasting relationships that will be very useful when you really need their help, such as with public relations crises. For example, if you know that a newspaper reporter's deadline for the next day's edition is 7:00 P.M., then by all means provide information to him or her well in advance. Additionally, it is important to work on the media professional's schedule, not yours. You might have a nine-to-five job, but you can be sure the media professional's workday is not so standard. It is important to provide them your contact information for the entire 24 hours of a day, not just the eight when you are at the office. Today, every public relations practitioner is expected to be available at all times. The consequences of not being available might be that your story does not get published or aired. In its place will be your competitor's story because that person was available for follow-up questions and confirmations that the reporter needed. The 24-hour news cycle is just that—24 hours a day.

4. **Know the Right People.** Every media outlet is filled with specialists who were hired because they know how to connect their thoughts to the right people. Again, this means that a one-size-fits-all mentality to media relations, or any stakeholder relations for that matter, will never work well for very long. A newspaper's layout illustrates this point. Every newspaper is arranged by differing content—front page news, local, international, business, sports, etc. The lead reporter for the business section certainly does not contribute much to the sports section. Each reporter and more importantly, each editor, does his or her own job within their areas of expertise. This means that every public relations practitioner must know who covers which area within every media outlet that the public relations professional works. For example, your story about the opening of the new college department could appeal to several editors of several sections of the local newspaper. Clearly, the sports section would be a good place to solicit your story because of the football player angle. Also, the local or communities sections might be a wise choice because of the importance of your college to the local community However, you must understand that each of these two sections require customized content. For instance, the sports section needs emphasis on the football players and their connection to the college more than the communities section, which would require more focus on the actual department's programs and how it will benefit the area's residents. Each story would still

include the most important information about the department, but its content layout would be arranged according to each story's focus. Part of understanding the needs of media professionals is understanding their reporting style. Just as you consider and understand their work schedule, you must also know their writing and editing styles. Journalism is quite different than traditional English composition. It follows its own style and rules. Every public relations professional must know the style, which is called Associated Press Style[58]. An Associated Press Stylebook is arguably the most important tool that any public relations professional can own. It lays out the types of content and more importantly, the punctuation and grammatical style unique to journalism and news media. For example, Associated Press Style, or AP Style, requires that all numbers from zero to nine be written out in text, and all numbers above 10 must use numbers. These seemingly small details are extremely important to gaining the respect of media professionals. If you consider that a reporter or editor receives dozens of news releases each day from public relations practitioners, and they only have a limited amount space to publish and air them, who would get this valuable space—the news release written in AP Style or the one that is written as if it is for an English class? The answer is obvious. Understanding and following the media professional's work schedule and style enables you to develop this very important relationship. The better your relationship with the important figures in the media such as the reporters and editors of the outlets you depend on most, the better your organization's publicity efforts.

5. **Do Not Expect Results Overnight.** You know that you must adhere to the media's writing, reporting, and scheduling demands; however, every public relations practitioner who tries to appeal to the media also follows these guidelines. That means that every public relations professional whom you compete with for print space and airtime might already have a great working relationship with the reporters and editors at the media outlets you are interested in. Therefore, you cannot expect to move to the head of the line right away. Media professionals are rather skeptical of public relations to begin with; they might understand the necessity of public relations, but that does not mean they adore practitioners. Often, media professionals see public relations practitioners as necessities or means to an end. Accordingly, gaining their trust and respect is often an uphill climb. To make that climb easier, you must understand the points of view that they have for public relations. At some point, nearly all public relations practitioners have the same view for the media, especially when their organization is negatively reported. Gaining their trust and respect is not impossible, but it can take time. Their pessimism over public relations inherently reins in their likelihood of accepting a new public relations practitioner overnight. This relationship is hard fought and is dependent on your ability to work to their styles, schedules, and systems of how

things are done. Just as with any solid relationship, media relations takes some time to establish itself, and like relationships in general, can be damaged quite badly by one misstep. Because the media is in control of this relationship, both because it controls the media channels and in turn its egocentrism, the public relations practitioner's job is to avoid causing unnecessary angst and aggravation.

6. **Expect to Be Rejected.** As mentioned previously, media space is highly prized and every competing organization is trying its best to gain this space. Because of this competition, someone's story and publicity effort will be dismissed. It is an inevitability that one of your stories will not make into the media. Despite all of the hard work and effort you might put into a news release from the inception of the story to its dissemination to the media, it can go unnoticed. That is a reality of public relations life. The best insurance against it is to develop meaningful, useful stories for the media written for and adhering to their guidelines. Remember, that all rejections and disappointments offer lessons to learn from—accepting these rejections as learning opportunities offers every public relations practitioner the chance to become better. If a story of yours was not published or aired, think about why it did not make it. Was it too long, confusing, the wrong outlet or editor, or was there something else more important happening that day? Armed with this knowledge, you can then adapt and change future stories so they better fit to these circumstances. For instance, the best day to pitch soft news items like your story on the new college department is generally midweek—Tuesday through Thursday. The reason is that Monday is a catch-up day when the media updates the weekend's stories, and by Friday, everyone including the media is looking forward to and reporting on the weekend. If your story somehow relates to the weekend then it is also best to submit stories by Wednesday because reporters and editors need to know them in advance so they can prioritize them. Springing these stories on them on Friday will not likely result in publication or broadcast. The same rule applies for holidays as well. Connecting your story to them can facilitate their acceptance and dissemination by the media. Perhaps your story on the new college department could coincide with your school's Thanksgiving efforts at providing food to those in need in your community. These extra interest-gaining elements increase the likelihood of your story being accepted and published or aired. You always need to remember the newsworthy elements—the more of these elements you can appeal to, the better your story's chances of media acceptance.

7. **Always Be Honest.** Every relationship depends most on trust and truthfulness. Most relationships fail because of a loss of these critical foundations of lasting and strong relations. The same is very true of media relations. Remember that many media professionals and gatekeepers feel that public relations professionals need them more than

they need public relations. Accordingly, these hard-won relationships are very fragile and the smallest misstep can result in long-lasting damage. Therefore, it is imperative to be truthful and forthright in every communication you have with the media. For example, any news release that provides inaccurate or inaccurately presented information will not only miss media publication, but also it can also result in a negative reputation on the part of the public relations practitioner who uses these methods. Positive reputations and good images are descriptions that everyone wants, and as you know in interpersonal relationships, dishonesty will inevitably result in damage to those reputations and images. As an example, if your news release on the new department indicated that it would accomplish goals that you cannot guarantee, then it is dishonest and will likely be dismissed by the media. If, for example, you stated that your college's new department will graduate 90 percent of all students, then it is inaccurate. You cannot guarantee that it can accomplish this because for one, the department does not have a track record yet, and because human nature dictates that nine out of 10 people will not always graduate from your college. It is always best to err on the side of caution and not overstate something that you cannot guarantee.

The preceding are seven of the most important fundamentals to remember when working with media professionals. It is easiest to remember lessons when there are negative effects from them—essentially, learning from mistakes. To further illustrate the principles of media relations, the following top 10 list of negative media relations practices will reinforce the fundamentals of positive media relations.

10. **Poor Preparation.** Media professionals are generally highly trained and experienced individuals who gained their positions because of their ability and success rate. Accordingly, they expect the people they work with to be the same. Lack of research will always result in subpar public relations. The same is true of media relations preparation. As you saw, the importance of tailoring your message to each media market and their consumers is critical to gaining the trust and respect of media gatekeepers. Likewise, all media contact should be well prepared and double-checked for accuracy, style, and content. The extra few minutes spent re-editing a news release may result in its acceptance into a media outlet.

9. **Inability to Connect with the Right Audience.** Media outlets such as television and radio stations depend on their consumers for continued success. Without readers, listeners, and watchers, no media outlet can exist for long. Accordingly, media content is always tailored to specific target demographics. The magazine section in any bookstore illustrates this point—there is a different publication for every interest. Likewise, there are individualized media outlets for each section of the population. To

gain access to them, every public relations practitioner must customize their content to match that of the targeted media outlet. As mentioned earlier, subsections of the public can have subsections, such as the difference between the *Philadelphia Daily News* and *Philadelphia Inquirer's* content—same city, but different focuses. Therefore, even messages like news releases sent to the same areas must still be tailored to individual interests.

8. **Indifference to Acknowledging Responsibility.** The defiance to taking responsibility for your organization's actions can lead to damaged media relations. The media, in general, exists to report the facts of a situation, and sometimes those facts can be rather unpleasant for an organization. Scandals, recalls, and lawsuits all lead to crises that public relations professionals must manage. Remember that even the strongest relationship between you and a reporter is professional, not personal. You cannot expect a reporter to refrain from publishing facts about your organization that could lead to a damaged reputation. The nature of a reporter's job is to report the good and the bad. Managing a public relations problem entails effective media relations and understanding their perspective. Public relations' crises often entail controversy, and controversy and conflict sell newspapers and increase viewership. It is a matter of knowing this and then responding effectively and efficiently to the media and their questions that dictate the results of a potentially damaging story. Remember that accepting blame and responsibility are two separate things. Even a product that is tampered with is still the responsibility of the manufacturer. It is their duty to ensure its safety even if the problem is not their fault. However, this is different than accepting blame. The blame or fault is on the person who tampered with the product, not the manufacturer. It is, however, the manufacturer's responsibility to make the product safe again and maintain its reputation and brand, just as Johnson & Johnson did when it introduced safety seals to its Tylenol bottles in the early 1980s.

7. **Inability to Emphasize the Important.** Just because something is important to you and your organization does not mean that the media will care as much. Media outlets, in general, know that conflict and human drama sell news. Look at any newspaper or watch any news program, and you will see that the top stories often focus on crime, war, and death. Because of this, positive stories that you develop about your organization will often be left for the back of the newspaper or the end of the nightly news. Your story on the new college department will have a difficult time competing with a story about an armed robbery. You, therefore, need to emphasize and highlight the most newsworthy elements of your story—in other words, answer the question, "Why should they care about this?" If you cannot easily answer this question from

their perspective, it is unlikely that the story has much newsworthy merit and will likely hit the bottom of the recycle bin before it hits the front page.

6. **Lack of Concern.** Even though your organization might be experiencing some difficult times, it does not mean that you can ignore them and hope they will go away. Johnson & Johnson certainly wanted the Tylenol scare crisis to go away on its own, but that would never happen. Your response to a problem will often dictate the resolution of that problem. Ignoring a problem will never make it go away. Therefore, it is the responsibility of the public relations professional to acknowledge the concerns and problems that their organization or its products may cause people—even if the problem is not the organization's fault, it is still its responsibility to address the problem. Imagine what would have happened to Johnson & Johnson's reputation if it had downplayed the seriousness of the Tylenol poisonings. Its response dictated the long-term effects on its reputation. Every organization at some point will experience a problem. The difference between wrecked brands and successful ones comes down to how they were managed by the organization's public relations department when the organization is not doing as well as it might.

5. **Misperceptions of the Media.** Remember that people's perceptions toward issues and information is often as important as the truth behind these issues. What people believe becomes their realities whether they are completely accurate or not. This fundamental is of course one of the greatest challenges facing public relations practitioners. However, the public relations practitioner is a person, and therefore is not immune to the power of perception, or in this case, the misperceptions of the media and what it does. It is true that the media focuses on human drama—death, disease, and conflict. The old expression, "If it bleeds, it leads" is still very true today. The public wants to see conflict and controversy—just think of the last time you drove past an automobile accident and the delay from people slowing down to see what was happening. The media simply provides people what they want. If the public wanted happy, feel-good stories most, they would lead the news, but people seem to prefer conflict, so the media provides its customers with a product they want—the same that any successful organization would do. Knowing this enables public relations practitioners to understand the media's point of view in reporting what it does. If the president, a.k.a. your boss in the position as public relations chief at your community college, was accused of misconduct, it is inevitable that the media will report it. Sometimes, these reports might not be completely accurate, and they might be slanted; however, they will make the news. No public relations professional in the world has the power to stop the media from reporting negative news about his or her organization. Knowing this enables practitioners to develop steps to work

with the media to help ensure that what is reported is as accurate and unbiased in the organization's favor as is possible. Too often, practitioners feel as though the media is out to get them—that is not the case. The media is simply doing its job, and if practitioners do theirs as well, negative media coverage does not have to be devastating to an organization's reputation.

4. **Inability to Control Internal Communication.** The information coming from an organization is proprietary from the start, meaning that it is completely controllable by its source—the public relations department. Because of this, wrong messages, leaked statements, etc., should never occur. Unfortunately, for some organizations, they still do, and result in damage to their professional reputations. Before statements are made to the public, either directly or via the media, they should be scrutinized, edited, proofed, and analyzed for content and connotation (sometimes what you think you said is interpreted very differently). The best means to accomplish this is to have several eyes see the communication before it is disseminated. Too often, time constraints, deadlines, and schedules force statements into the media that later come back to haunt the organization. The time to control communication is before it leaves the organization. Once it is in the public, that control becomes more difficult to possess. Organizations are judged by two things—what they do and what they say they will do. While actions always speak louder than words, do not let the words influence the success of the actions. Actionable steps such as recalls, settlements, and refunds take time to enact. The statements about them always come first because statements take less time to produce and are needed immediately. However, the problem is allowing statements to leave the organization before they are ready. The extra 10 minutes it takes to re-edit a statement is worth the investment of time if you might catch an error that will require additional statements and apologies later. There is nothing worse than making an existing problem more severe than it needs to be because of negligence, ignorance, or arrogance on the part of the public relations practitioner.

3. **Making Statements When There is Uncertainty.** You know that communication is critical to lessening the damage from negative publicity. More importantly, quick communication following the news of a crisis greatly increases the likelihood or brand recovery. Organizations that wait too long, or even worse, make no statement about such an issue, historically feel greater and longer term reputational damage than those organizations that respond quickly. However, as you saw in the last media mistake, acting so quickly that you do not manage the communication's content can cause more harm than waiting to ensure your statement is correct, concise, and clear. Because the tendency on many public relations practitioners' part is to respond right

away, the content of those responses sometimes goes awry. Often spokespersons, when under pressure from reporters to answer questions, fall into a trap of providing responses without knowing the accuracy of their answers. Making promises, accepting blame, and assuring everything is under control are just a few of the problematic statements that can be made when under pressure. Remember that communication from an organization, even at a press conference, is under the control of the organization. Unlike the internally developed communications such as news releases, making a statement on the spot when cameras and microphones are present makes controlling these "spontaneous" statements much more difficult. Remaining calm and collected helps avoid these circumstances. There is nothing wrong with making a statement that states you simply do not know the answers. It is far worse to make a statement when you do not know, and then have to go back and recant your statement—this shows the media that your organization is not in control of its own information, which certainly looks very bad in their reports. It is better to admit that you do not know, state that you will find out the correct answers, and then disseminate them at a later point—to do so prematurely is irresponsible and can make bad situations even worse.

2. **Media Phobia.** Because the nature of media can sometimes make it seem like they are out go expose and destroy reputations—remember they are not; they are simply doing their job—this feeling of persecution on the part of public relations practitioners and their organizations can lead to a complete aversion to and avoidance of the media. The media can and will report on what it wants, how it sees fit. This is an inevitability and a reality from which no organization can hide. Simply pretending that everything is fine without the media and that you do not need them is delusional at best. Remember that the media needs public relations just as much as public relations needs the media. Therefore, there should not be a fear of them. Fear generally comes from an absence of confidence. If you are confident about something, it is unlikely you will fear it. Accordingly, the more public relations practitioners understand and work with the media, the better the relationship, and the dissolution of any fear. Fear often leads to irrational behavior and poor choices, which make the situation even worse—fear breeds more fear. By not involving yourself in this cycle, your public relations decisions and actions will be far better reported on by the media. The best way to avoid the fear cycle is to acknowledge and even appreciate the media for what it offers even though it can be frustrating and damaging at times.

1. **Panic.** All previous nine media mistakes, when left unchecked, will lead to the most destructive force affecting media relations: panic. Destructive media relations come from the difficult circumstances that a company is experiencing. When all is well, media relations is easy. It is when crises develop that negative media coverage

increases. Public relations is about managing these difficult circumstances so that their destructive powers are lessened. This responsibility, however, is impossible to fulfill when panic sets into the organization's leadership, and during crises, public relations practitioners become the most important leaders. The terms "rational, logical, and sensible" should characterize media relations during trying times. "Incoherent, unreasonable, and inaccurate" describe the actions of an organization experiencing panic during a crisis. Preparedness, practice, and professionalism are all hallmarks of proactive media relations. Plans and systems must be in place with the expectation that damaging events and negative media attention will happen at some point. Proactive media relations can simply be summed up, "Hope for the best, but expect the worse." With this expectation, the likelihood of being caught off guard is reduced, as is the fear and panic from it. While any media crisis is going to be difficult to manage, understanding **conflict management** helps make the public relations preparations easier and the organization's responses better.

CONFLICT MANAGEMENT LIFECYCLE

The Conflict Management[59] Lifecycle breaks down any issue or potential problem into four phases: the proactive, strategic, reaction, and recovery. This system enables public relations practitioners to understand the possible media problems that can happen and how to respond best if, and when, they happen. While not isolated just to media, relations, it does offer a means of understanding the importance of preparation in avoiding the 10 most common media mistakes.

1. **The Proactive Phase.** As the name suggests the proactive phase entails preparing for a crisis or problem before it happens. Just as you would study before an exam to help ensure your success on it, the proactive phase includes efforts such as researching, brainstorming, and expecting events and issues that could lead to damaging media exposure. To better understand these elements, think of your position of public relations director for the community college. As with any organization where large groups of people congregate, there are realistic crises that can affect your organization—you hope they never happen, but preparing for them allows you to control them better if they do. In today's society, you know that any college or educational institution must have a plan in place to counter on-campus violence. In addition to developing steps to prevent them, these organizations' public relations professionals must also prepare media relations steps because the nature of the event obviously will lead to widespread media coverage. The Conflict Management Lifecycle can be used to help

prepare all the elements for such an incident, but for our purposes, just the media relations efforts will be discussed. Proactive media relations measures include who should be the spokesperson for your organization, how you will work with authorities, statements to be made to victims and their families, infrastructure needs of the media such as satellite hookups, and support services for your internal audiences. All of these components would encompass the pre-planning, proactive measures your college must take in the expectation that something like a campus shooting could realistically happen.

2. **The Strategic Phase.** The second phase moves the media preparation from the research element to the planning stage, taking what you learned in step one and using it to develop a blueprint to follow when an incident occurs. The first part of this plan is known as the risk communication step. This step forestalls injuries, both physical and emotional, and analyzes the influence of them on your organization. Clearly, the more devastating the crisis, the worse these injuries will be. Accordingly, planning for them allows your organization to sensibly and appropriately respond to them. A campus shooting could result in devastating physical and emotional injuries on the part of the many. With this knowledge, you can then develop plans such as counseling services that can be offered immediately after an incident like this occurs. The second part of this phase is the conflict communication step. This second part anticipates reactions from the court of public opinion. While the court of law offers written rules and guidelines to follow, preparing for the court of public opinion is possible despite its often erratic and sometimes irrational outcomes. Knowing the public's reaction to not only the event, but more importantly your organization's management of the event, enables you to develop messages and strategies that communicate and further your organization's point of view. Your initial responses often influence the future opinions from the public. Developing those messages before they are needed enables you to craft and perfect them as much as possible. Trying to create a message that conveys all of your organization's points when your organization is experiencing such as crisis is difficult and its product will never be as good—remember that the top four mistakes all center on preparedness, especially your communication. At this strategizing point, you can develop the theme and connotation of your message and then adapt it to the actual events. The difficult and lengthy work is done; it is then a matter of customizing its content to match the situation. For example, developing a statement of remorse can be difficult, but done in advance, its power can be maximized because it is written to the best of your ability. The last part of this phase is the crisis management step. If your previous work did not adequately control the situation, this stage prepares for an escalating crisis—in this case with the media. Crises all have lifecycles of their own. Some end quickly while others can drag on for years. Much

of the lifecycle depends on the organization's response, and the response's success is directly related to its preparedness of it. What if your organization is pulled into a national debate over gun control, youth violence, or school safety? These are all possibilities that your college should be prepared for if they occur. By thinking and planning of what your organization should do in these circumstances, you have an added chance of making the right choices when the time comes. The next phase's success or failure directly relates back to all of your proactive and strategic efforts.

3. **Reaction Phase.** This is the time when you ultimately see whether your efforts worked or not, as well as why. Also known as the implementation phase, this part of the process includes putting your strategies and plans that came from your proactive research into practice for the entire world to see. Clearly, the more exhaustive and thorough your work up until this point is, the better the reaction phase. However, because you are dealing with the public and media, which can act unexpectedly, you cannot be assured of your results. But, solid preparation before this phase helps to assure that your reaction efforts are more likely to be success. For example, if you know from your planning stages that working with and allowing investigators to handle questions about the actual criminal incident will likely increase public trust in your organization, then when you implement this strategy, your confidence in your reaction phase improves. Directing questions relating to the crime to law enforcement officials improves your media relations actions, and when you handle enough of these components well, your overall public relations success will increase.

4. **Recovery Phase.** The last component of the Conflict Management Lifecycle includes those efforts and plans to manage your organization's reputation and brand as well as the long-term steps to restore its image. While the early stages of the Reaction Phase include handling the minute-to-minute issues with a crisis, the Recovery Phase entails managing the future actions of your organization relating to the incident. Here, initiating plans such as increased campus security, onsite training of staff, and future steps to work with victims and families all become reality. Remember it is not enough to state that your organization will do everything it can to keeps incidents like this from happening again; it must also follow through with these statements. In doing so, these efforts should also be communicated to the media, which can then pass them on to the public. All crisis present opportunities, and it is during the Recovery Phase that those opportunities usually present themselves. Every competent public relations practitioner sees these prospects even in the direst situations. At the conclusion of any event such as this, lessons should present themselves.

Media relations can be difficult and stressful, but it is how these relationships are managed when problems arise that separate successful from ineffective public relations. The media presents tremendous opportunities along with great challenges. Even today, most people trust the media, and because public relations is focused on improving trust between organizations and their stakeholders, the media presents a great outlet to achieving this critical goal. The media is not out to get anyone, it simply serves an important function in society—the dissemination of information that people find meaningful. Any organization can spend millions on advertising and marketing, but the public is skeptical of these tactics. We expect a television commercial to espouse all of the virtues of a product or company. Because of it, these tactics lack a certain degree of believability and credibility—two necessary components to any successful relationship. A third-party unbiased report from the media will go much further in increasing any organization's image and brand. It is the job of the public relations practitioner to place those stories in the media when times are good, and manage negative media reports when times are hard—failure to do so can result in a failing organization.

IMAGE CREDITS

7 COMMUNITY RELATIONS

Even in today's global economy, the people and places that an organization directly affects can influence organizational success—especially where its image is concerned. Likewise, the people around an organization, who might not have a direct stake in it such as an employee, can also influence what the greater population thinks about the organization. Because of this, public relations must also address and further the relationships between the organization and the people living near it. Traditionally, this has been the case. However, given today's more connected world, neighbors and communities do not always include old definitions such as proximity and physical location. Today, the world is more connected as a global community than ever before. Information can spread instantaneously around the globe in seconds. Now, communities include online; they are social and virtual "neighbors" that organizations need to consider. Their opinions and actions toward an organization can be just as important and influential on the organization as those people who physically live next door. This chapter will examine community relations in general, as well as look at how the term "community" now encompasses much more than streets and towns and how this changing landscape affects public relations practice.

There are several fundamentals to sound community relations—both the physical kind and the technologically connected variety. The overall keys to positive, mutually beneficial community relations rest on knowledge and trust. Without these two essential ingredients, long-term successful community relations efforts will likely sputter and fail. A common problem with community relations is the lack of importance that many organization place on it. As you have seen, there are clear benefits and obvious repercussions to negative employee and media relations; however, sometimes this importance escapes the reaches of the community. Many organizations feel as though community relations just happen because of the nature of the relationship—they are close by, either physically or technologically. Therefore, no extra effort should be made to connect with these individuals on meaningful terms. This, however, is a major mistake, and one that can be easily avoided through sound, sensible, and significant community relations efforts. The first step is understanding what the community thinks about your organization, and from this knowledge, you can then begin to understand how to manage this relationship. As with all stakeholder groups, their perceptions about your organization often create the realities of the relationship—erroneous beliefs lead to negativity, and honest viewpoints lead to positivity. Only by understanding these elements can public relations practitioners expect to develop positive community relations initiatives.

THE BUILDING BLOCKS OF POSITIVE COMMUNITY RELATIONS

Step One: What is their knowledge? When you know what they think about your organization, you can then begin to influence their opinions about it. If what they know is completely false, you know you need to replace these false perceptions with realities. If what they know is inaccurate but has some truth to it, then you know to clarify their thoughts with more information. And, if what they know is correct, then you know to continue your communication plan or even move it to the next step. What you know about their knowledge will dictate what you do and how you proceed with future community relations programs. Moreover, if they know nothing about your organization, then clearly communication is an issue. Imagine, for a moment, that people living near your community college believe that its academic standards and programs will not provide them with anything meaningful—essentially, they look at your college as the high school after high school. How did you find this out?—research of course. Only by looking into your community can you see and hear what they say and think about your organization. Without this knowledge, you may be completely unaware that your college's reputation is weak at best among its most important stakeholder group—remember, it is a community college that you work for and obviously it depends on the community for its students. If they think it does not offer value, they will not attend. Enough of these types of attitudes can lead to devastating effects on attendance, retention, and the future of your organization. Clearly, you can see how communities might play an integral role on organizational image and success. Remember too that word-of-mouth publicity is often the most powerful form of publicity. Too many community members giving negative reviews of your college can spread like wildfire. It is your job as the community college's public relations representative to put that fire out and repair the damage from it. Accordingly, you begin a process of research, planning, implementation, and evaluation to remedy the community's negative opinion of your organization. After finding out that 90 percent of your graduates move on to four-year institutions, and another five percent locate jobs in their field of study within three months of graduation, you have the ammunition to correct this problem. You must change their knowledge of your college and replace the misperceptions with the truth, and the best way to do so is with the hard facts you now possess. You have many communications options available to you—paid advertising, media placements, special events, mailed marketing materials, etc. However, you understand that the best way overcome misperceptions stemming from negative word-of-mouth publicity is to go back to its source—replace the incorrect word-of-mouth publicity with a factual, positive version. If word-of-mouth caused this problem, then perhaps is can help solve it as well. This leads directly into the next step, which looks at where information comes from and the influence these sources can have on community opinion.

Step Two: What are their sources of information? For this step, it is important to note that just because communication is informative does not necessarily mean that it has to be completely accurate. Much of what we know is what we believe to be true—essentially, what we think we know. Because of this, public relations work, and especially community relations efforts, can be quite difficult and often frustrating. If you have ever tried to change people's minds about something that they adamantly thought they knew about, then you are aware of this challenge. Except with community relations, that difficulty could be multiplied by millions. Moreover, word-of-mouth publicity, or word-of-mouth information, can take on legitimacy even if there is no evidence to support it. Opinions can be just as influential as cold, hard facts, and influencing opinion change is never easy. The quickest and most effective means, however, is to look to the source of the opinion and/or the word-of-mouth publicity, which are clearly interconnected. If you can identify the source of this information, then you have chance of influencing the information coming from it. If you can influence this information, then you can stop the inaccuracies in it and replace them with your persuasive message, which includes factual data. From here, you can then shape word-of-mouth publicity in your organization's favor. In the example, misconceptions about your college's usefulness negatively affected the community's view of your organization and its main product—education. When the community sees its community college as meaningless, then that institution's image and brand will certainly suffer. You can avoid this by motivating the community to believe in your organization and what it has to offer. If members in the community influenced the overall community's opinion about your college, then you know where to begin in reversing these negative perceptions. As mentioned before, advertising will go only so far. You need to go to the source—the community itself. Clearly, you have many proponents of your organization already in the community—current and former students who can attest to the quality of your institution's education. By encouraging them to speak directly to the community through friends, family, and organized events such as high school visits, the erroneous, yet equally damaging community opinion can be reversed. Again, the source of the information is trusted—it comes from people the community knows, even if what they know is inaccurate. Therefore, the correct information must also come from the people the community knows. This example helps explain the power and persuasiveness of word-of-mouth publicity, which segues into the next step.

Step Three: What are your organization's personal connections to the community? As you clearly saw in step two, the connection between an organization and its community is critical to its relationship health. If community members' only connection to a neighboring organization is the sign on its building or the traffic congestion it causes, then any attempts at developing strong community ties between an organization and its community will never go far. The more personalized the connections, the more influential and meaningful they are—it is the same as with any relationship. Part of the public relations practitioner's job is to close the gap between his or her organization and the community around it. Getting community members up close and personal with the organization helps them see it as a neighbor, not just a building or an address. Most organizations already have these connections—their employees. The people who work at organizations often are part of the community—the larger the organization, generally the larger the part. Positive employee relations go hand in hand with community relations—it is very difficult to separate the two. When employees are dissatisfied with and distrustful in their relationships with their organization, it eventually will contaminate the community's relationships as well. The simple reason is employees can act as either ambassadors or inside informants about an organization. Even though they may have signed a non-disclosure clause does not mean that employees will never speak of their feelings about their employer. Clearly, when enough employees give their negative views on an organization to the community in which it operates, the organization's reputation will suffer among its neighbors. In many ways, employees are the frontline gatekeepers to the inside information to any organization. Like any form of word-of-mouth publicity, their opinions do not have to rely on fact to be influential. Disgruntled employees' opinions, which might be completely false, can influence community opinions just as much as accurate information from the organization. Why? Because the community sees them as people with inside information who will give the real scoop about the organization, not the company line from the organization's advertisements. Therefore, all successful community relations efforts must include personal, positive connections between the organization and its neighbors. Tactics such as open houses, community days, and civic engagements are all community relations actions that any organization can use to minimize the physical and emotional distance between itself and its community. In your position as community college public relations director, many of these types of community engagement efforts can improve the connection between your organization and your community—specifically the community that has never been on your campus. Simple events like wine and cheese festivals, job fairs, and fall and spring open houses help eliminate the barrier between your organization and the community that it depends so much on. More positive interactions between organizations and their communities will result in better relationships between the two. Isolation and separation will never facilitate positive community relations.

Step Four: How can you include the community in your organization's plan? As mentioned earlier, improved decision-making power results in improved buy-in from those involved in directing an organization's operation. Including the community may seem like an odd choice to improving these operations. After all, what do they know about your organization's functions and goals? However, if you look deeper into the community, you might be able to find people and organizations that can help your organization. Local chambers of commerce, business associations, and local school liaisons are all avenues to be explored when developing community relations programs. Members of these organizations possess some expertise in these areas, and often your organization can benefit from them if you keep an open mind. For instance, clearly local schools would benefit any community college. Students from area high schools are the exact consumers of community college educations. Moreover, most returning and non-traditional students are likely former students at these institutions. If your community relations efforts included working with the local school districts, you not only improve these relationships, but you can also further your organization's mission to educate local college students. The local schools enable you to visit and present assemblies on the costs and expectations of college education, as well as the facts and persuasive messages that can motivate them to attend your school as well. Furthermore, the schools' staff, teachers, and parents of students will not have a greater connection to your organization than they might have otherwise. In return, you invite the schools' experts to offer advice on how to improve the community college's programs to better fit these students—your institution gains new students, and the local community schools gain notoriety, pride, and influence. Of course these efforts need to be realistic and manageable. It would obviously be unwise to offer the local chamber of commerce the authority to affect multi-million-dollar deals, but within every community and with any organization, many partnership opportunities exist. The trick is finding and nurturing them. Too often, these programs begin well, but lose momentum because no one is managing them. These programs can be very beneficial, so, should be accorded the necessary resources to maintain them.

Step Five: **How can you measure your community relations efforts' performance?** Every public relations initiative and effort, no matter how big or small, must be evaluated at some point. No plan or campaign should ever go on and on without it ever being measured for success at all levels. For example, your organization's sponsorship of the local high school football team resulted in great success in bridging the gap between your company and the community. Another initiative, such as partnering with a local organization, did not. You need to know which efforts worked, why they worked, as well as why other initiatives did not work. Without this knowledge, good programs cannot be bettered, and poor ones cannot be improved or eliminated. If sponsoring the local team resulted in great community relations gains, perhaps expanding this effort would result in even greater benefits. If partnering with the local business association did not result in any positive outcomes, then it must be addressed. Perhaps more resources such as investments of time were needed. If those resources are not available, then it might be necessary to eliminate that effort. To illustrate, if your partnerships with the local schools resulted in a five percent increase in 18-year-olds enrolling from your community, then clearly it should be a program that gets more resources and attention. Maybe expanding the program to local eighth-grade students would help too? Or, would expanding the program to outlying areas, which might not be directly in your community, but could offer additional students who can attend your institution improve enrollment? These are all questions that need to be answered. Even the best public relations program can be improved, and over time, will likely need it to maintain its success rate. However, if you do not stop, evaluate, and then learn from your measurements, you would never know how and where to implement changes, and accordingly, might never achieve the successes that are within reach. One of the worst mistakes in public relations is letting a great opportunity slip by without even knowing it. Measurement and evaluation of all programs, such as these community relations efforts, enable you to seize them when they are at their greatest usefulness.

As mentioned previously, today's community relations efforts encompass more than simply the people living near you. The modern world is a global world. This means that the term "community" now extends beyond the physical borders of space and land to the cyber world of new and social media communities. The influence and effect of these non-traditional communities is just as important to today's public relations practice as the conventional communities were in the past. To further illustrate this phenomenon, the five primary steps of community relations will be readdressed using the new, virtual communities as an example. The following will show you how the same principles of community relations management can also apply to the modern online communities.

Step One: What is their knowledge? Just as traditional communities rely mainly on word-of-mouth information from their neighbors and community leaders, a similar phenomenon exists in the virtual communities. Opinion leaders and those with expertise, either authentic or not, gain followers and subscribers who then directly influence the public opinion on important issues. Their power to sway the public's views on issues is very similar to those same types of people in traditional communities. Often the public will look to online "gurus" to help them make sense of the news and find what they believe is the hidden truth behind the traditional media's reports. Much of this information is highly questionable as far as its accuracy, but in the online community, accuracy often takes a back seat to conspiracy. Word-of-mouth publicity and news via blogs, email, and rogue websites, which exist to criticize and damage organizations' reputations, all affect online community relations[60]. They can range from simple aggravations to serious threats that will affect both public relations bottom lines: reputational and financial. The main problem with online community criticisms is the inability to find out who is responsible or even how old and widespread the rumors and mistruths are—this type of content thrives on vagueness as long as the smallest element of truth can be found. For example, pharmaceutical giant Procter & Gamble needed to change their logo because rumors spread that it furthered Satanism; also, stories surfaced online that McDonald's supported the Irish Republican Army (IRA)[61]. Obviously neither of these stories had any truth to them; however, they did gain popularity and many people believed them. Procter & Gamble needed to reinvent its logo, costing it millions in repackaging and rebranding. The main point to remember about the knowledge base from online communities is that they are often anonymous, and because of it, people feel as though they can say anything they want without any fear of reprisals. The biggest problem is that many people believe them. For example, imagine you receive a call from your community college's provost stating that a local reporter called him to answer questions about a Twitter account claiming that your college opposes same-sex marriages. You know the story is completely fabricated, but the fact that the Twitter account's followers began believing and spreading the story now forces your college to make a statement and clear its name despite the fact that it did nothing wrong. Addressing lies has become a part of online community relations in recent years. One of the biggest issues stemming from this problem is the question of how much attention the organization should give these fake stories. Remember that perception is reality to most people—even if they believe a lie, they believe it just as much as if it were true. Therefore, ignoring a seemingly ridiculous story posted on some online community should make sense. However, public opinion management contradicts that idea. Just as you would want to rectify a lie about yourself that is hurting your image, an organization must operate the same. Some acknowledgment of it is necessary before it the fake story gets out of hand and gains momentum. Some stories will go away as quickly as they came; others, however, can get bigger and bigger. The problem is that is it not always easy to know the difference between the two when they start. For your response to the allegations of anti-same sex business practices, you understand that ignoring the issue may help it go away or it might add life to it. Not commenting may lead some people to believe the story because if the organization ignores it, then it must be true. The public might believe that the story is true simply because the organization is clearly afraid to acknowledge it. Commenting on it can further the story, enabling more people to know about it because it gets more coverage. It is a balancing act. Your story deals with a hot-button issue; therefore, it is unlikely to go away on its own. However, you do not want to add too much fuel to the fire, so simply issuing a statement that refutes the allegations, cites your non-discrimination policies, and provides evidence to support your side of the story is probably sufficient in this case. Remember, though, that addressing online communities' allegations can be tricky, and you must find a sensible and appropriate response that addresses the problem but does not help spread it.

Step Two: **What are their sources of information?** As you can imagine, the size of online communities makes the job of locating and understanding the sources of information very difficult, if not impossible. Online communities are inherently anonymous. It is not as if you can easily locate the names and addresses of those who post comments, stories, and allegations on blogs, social media, or rogue websites. The person damaging your organization's reputation may be legitimate and professional, or they may be conspiracy theorists or people who just want to see if their stories will gain popularity—an odd form of the "15 minutes of fame." Moreover, they may be current or former employees who take their anger and frustrations out on their company via the Internet. Regardless of the source or intention, these people and websites can often damage an organization's reputation just as much as the mainstream media. There is a good percentage of the population who believe these faked stories and heavily edited photos, and those people then pass these stories and photos on to to others, and eventually, an online rumor mill begins—essentially, it is a snowball or domino effect. These types of online rumors have several commonalities, such as some aspect of believability; they are difficult to trace; often deal with fear or fear mongering; can spread out of "antiestablishment" viewpoints; and people want to pretend they're in the know or privy to some secret, insider informa-tion. Locating the source of the anti-same-sex rumor would be difficult, and probably fruitless, not to mention taking a great deal of time. Even the most innocuous rumor can cost organizations, if not in financial fallout from damaged reputations, then from lost productivity when the public relations staff must take time to deal with them. Accordingly, you decide that your statement to the media reporter will probably be sufficient in quelling the story before it gains momentum, while at the same time, not lending credibility to the source of the story—whoever or whatever it might be.

Step Three: **What are your organization's personal connections to the community?** Developing personal ties to your physical community is rather straightforward; however, developing a personal connection in rather impersonal media where online communities are established is not so obvious. By now, every organization should have some online presence—a website or email account at the very least. However, as online communities grow and become more fragmented (think about how many more social media sites exist today than just five years ago), organizations' ability to connect with their online communities becomes more complex. There are of course, the most used platforms like Facebook, Twitter, and even Instagram. But every year, new social media sites spring up offering users different features tailored to specific interests and areas. How can organizations stay in touch with all of them? The answer is they cannot. More importantly, they should not. Trying to be all things to all people is an expensive, time-consuming, and difficult endeavor, generally with results that certainly do not warrant these investments. To connect as effectively and efficiently as possible to online communities, organizations need to prioritize and maintain their virtual community members' interests and wants, not the entire online world's. For example, your organization is generally location based— the community college is most interested in its stakeholders within a centralized area. Therefore, it makes sense to offer online content and connections to these people while also offering the world the opportunity to know your organization as well. However, your online community relations focus is still on your most important stakeholder groups— students, parents, educators, local media, and others. Your online presence then enables these people to connect with your organization 24 hours a day, but its focus is still on them. If someone from New Zealand happens to like you on Facebook or follow your Twitter account, then great, but you are not catering and tailoring your messages to him or her. That focus is reserved for your online communities, which still encompass your organization's overall, most important stakeholders. Too often organizations try to connect to everyone on the Internet because the technology enables them. This often results in wasted efforts and content that does not mean much to your critical stakeholder groups, be they customers, employees, neighbors, media, and so on. Even with all of the online community relations tools available, content equates to connection. If your online content is off, then your online community connections will also be off. The fundamental error of one-size-fits-all most often occurs when communicating to online communities. If your key stakeholders (students, potential students, parents, local government, and media) do not care about your online content, then connecting with them via virtual community relations is bound to fail. Moreover, if the platforms you are using do not work for them, then do not use them. Many organizations have Facebook accounts because they think they are supposed to—everyone has one, right? But, if your key stakeholders are not using Facebook, then you should not either.

Step Four: How can you include the community in your organization's plan? Arguably the greatest attribute to online community relations is the direct, and often instantaneous communication that can occur. The best models of communication are those where both parties speak and listen to each other. Online community relations tools, like social media sites, enable this to occur quite efficiently. Second to face-to-face conversations, social media communication is a powerful means of interaction. Therefore, it should also be a great means to include your online communities in your organization, and vice versa. While simple connections like Facebook friends and Twitter followers offer some means of inclusion, other, more meaningful connections are possible. For example, establishing action-oriented initiatives where your online community members can do something is far more meaningful than simply asking them to click "like" or "share" on a social media page. Campaigns, fundraisers, and civic engagements offer meaningful, yet innocuous community connection possibilities. It is important to note the innocuous factor. Often, organizations get themselves into trouble when they offer their online community members free reign to post stories and photos about their relationship with the organization. While initially these ideas seem sound, too often stories about negative experiences, fabricated claims, and outright lies turn these forums into circuses where all the clowns can draw attention to themselves. The outcome is usually overall negativity toward the organization, and it makes the public relations department look silly because they are the ones who asked for it in the first place. While there are many online community relations possibilities for connections, it is important to remember that just about anything goes online, and inviting criticism is always a distinct possibility. Therefore, it is always best to err on the side of caution and not open your organization up to being lampooned in an arena where the entire world can see it.

Step Five: How can you measure your community relations efforts' performance? Today's push to embrace all the opportunities with online community relations also ushers in the practice of finding value and meaning in it. An organization can have a million Facebook friends, but what does that mean for the organization's success? Like any public relations initiative, the outcome should be determined before the process begins. What is it that you want to accomplish through your Twitter account? Is it simply a message board, or will it add to either of the organization's two bottom lines? When social media first exploded into the consciousness of organizational communication, simple impression numbers seemed important, but executives quickly realized that these numbers offered little more than extra vanity for their companies' ego. Online community relations efforts that clearly drive sales or improve reputations are the real valuable numbers when it comes to online community relations measurement[62]. The primary focus to online measurements include reaching your targeted groups, getting them to care about your online presence, allowing them to understand your organization's perspective, encouraging them to like you, and motivating them to do something that benefits your organization. You must focus on content to accomplish these measurement goals. The industry phrase these days is, "Content is King" when it comes to creating Facebook updates, Tweets, blogs, etc.[63] Without meaningful information designed to speak specifically to your target audiences' perspectives, your messages will likely get lost and be ignored in the sea of online content. The communication misnomer "one size fits all" especially applies to online community relations where it often seems that everyone is talking, but no one is listening. Making them listen is the responsibility of the public relations practitioner.

For community relations to really function well, there of course needs to be continuous contact and mutual interdependence. When one side of the relationship has the upper hand, the other side will quickly lose interest in the relationship, or worse, become combative and defense. As you saw with the example of online community relations, many of the problems that affect these relationships stem from fear. Often, this fear comes from erroneous, fake, and misrepresented information posted anonymously where everyone can see it and, unfortunately, many believe it. Managing this type of unwarranted criticism is difficult, yet as you saw, it is possible through sensible and appropriate actions. However, even the traditional community relations between organizations and their physical neighbors can feel the negativity of these fears. Generally, fear and anxiety over organizational plans and actions causes the most damage to community relations efforts. Because of this, it is important to understand how to negotiate understanding and acceptance from the community when difficult organizational decisions must be made. Every relationship will be tested, and how an organization addresses their communities' fears during these tests often will dictate the success of all future community relations actions. There are five principles to dealing with these situations, which will be discussed using an example from the community college public relations perspective to help illustrate their importance and usefulness.

Principles of Community Relations Development

Principle 1: Make Fear More Familiar. Essentially, fear is a lack of confidence. When people are no longer confident in their security in any aspect of their life, then it is possible they will grow to fear that aspect. For instance, when people are no longer confident that their intimate relationships are strong, they may develop an aversion to them—a fear of commitment. When people are no longer confident in their ability to succeed at work, they may develop an avoidance of it—a fear of success. Understanding fear is important if public relations practitioners hope to remove it from or lessen it among their stakeholders. When these stakeholders no longer have confidence in an organization's image, brand, and products, they will also develop an aversion to that organization, resulting in lost reputations, relationships, and the means for the organization to exist: sales. For community members, the risk of fear is much greater because these people are connected to their neighboring organizations by the most important bonds we have—our homes and our families. Accordingly, the damage from community fear is often the greatest to organizations that need community member support and acceptance.

One means to minimize and ideally eliminate these fears is to make them seem familiar. Familiarity with issues and situations reduces fears because when people know and truly understand these issues, then they have confidence in their understanding, which enables them to accept difficult situations. This process helps create reasonable expectations of what can happen in a situation. For example, if someone was given a diagnosis that he had cancer, the likely response is fear, anxiety, and usually, believing the worst outcomes will happen even before he has all the facts. When this same person knows the treatment options, success percentages, and long-term medical probabilities, his expectations become reasonable and less likely to instigate crippling fear. Even if the medical probabilities are negative, at least knowing the realities of the situation lessens the fears that he would likely create in his own mind. Armed with information and facts, people are much less prone to imagine the worst-case scenarios facing them.

Accordingly, because one of the major functions of public relations is communication, it is the practitioner's job to give the facts so community stakeholders are not left to their own devices and imagine their own worst-case scenarios. To illustrate: your community college is doing so well to increase enrollments because of your initiatives, the board of trustees has decided to expand the campus. Initially, this seems great—more opportunities, improved facilities, better reputation, etc. However, as soon as you see the master plan, you notice an impending community relations crisis. The campus expansion plan will require the use of eminent domain procedures to take the property needed for more buildings and parking lots. Your closest community members' homes sit on that property and you know that taking someone's house, no matter the reason, will not sit well with the entire community. You must develop a plan to deal with this impending, yet unavoidable problem. The first step is communicating directly to those who will be most affected: the homeowners. Such dramatic news should never be communicated via secondhand sources like the news media or through impersonal means such as a legal letter. Face-to-face communication on the issue introduces the plan, enables the homeowners to ask questions and clarify issues there and then, and puts a "human face" on the situation. No lawyer's letter can do all of these critical steps.

Addressing issues in an interpersonal manner facilitates understanding of the college's perspective, and enables you to show your empathy with their situation, inform them of the procedure, and overall provide them with reasonable expectations of decision's outcomes. That is not to say that every one of the homeowners will accept the idea. Anger, frustration, and resentment will no doubt color the meeting's atmosphere. However, fear of the unknown will not be one of the problems you or the homeowners will need to face. Being honest, reasonable, and forthright is the best method when communicating news that you know will be difficult for people. In addition, this opportunity provides you the ability to present the college's plan to help these homeowners deal with this difficult situation your organization has put them in.

Principle 2: Illustrate Your Long-Term Commitment. Our organization's plans to assist these homeowners during this trying process illustrates your college's understanding of the severity of the situation. Too often, organizations involved in situations like this appear coldhearted and oblivious to the problems they are inflicting on peoples' lives. Because of this, organizations often are viewed as the powerful bullies pushing people around—something that will never help any organization's image. Communicating and proving your commitment lessens this inevitable criticism. As ever, it is critical back up your organization's commitments with actions. In addition, it is important to publicize these commitments and actions to the world so that when others begin depicting your organization as a power-hungry monster, you have evidence to contradict them—even better, you may preemptively stop some of this criticism. By showing that your college will provide services to help the homeowners sell their houses, find residences elsewhere, and offer real estate services, you illustrate your organization's commitment to those it affected. Moreover, you show the rest of the community, which will likely find your actions reprehensible, that your organization is not just concerned about itself: your college understands its actions and is trying to do the right thing for the people it impacted. By following these steps, you are in a better position to recover the loss of reputation caused by your organization's actions. Remember that you will never be able to convince every one of your community members that your college is right in its actions, but you have put your organization on a path to convincing most community members that your actions are necessary. Every action has a reaction, and these reactions are dictated by public relations efforts early in the process—the better the efforts at the beginning, the more positive the reactions later.

Principle 3: Share Decision-Making Power and be Open to Suggestions. As you have seen, when people feel as though they are part of the decision-making process that affects them (even when the effects are bad), they are more likely to understand them. Clearly, this fundamental of persuasion will help to reduce and minimize the fallout from community fears. While the results of a particular decision might be negative to a group of people, if those people feel empowered to offer their insights, concerns, and ideas to the decision-making process, then they are less likely to criticize it later. Because issues like taking property via eminent domain will undoubtedly result in negative publicity and criticism later, it is important to include those groups, who will likely be the sources of criticism, early on in the process. Just as developing advisory boards and community associations with community members results in positive relations during good times, the same process can alleviate negativity during difficult times as well. Including community leaders in the decision-making process to expand the college can provide additional community support when widespread criticism begins to take hold. If the community feels as though it has a voice and its points of view are being heard and valued by an organization, then they are more apt to feel like their perspective is as important as the organization's. Remember that negative community relations often comes from companies and businesses being seen as all-power monoliths that can do whatever they want in their communities without any fear of reprisals. Positive community relations, however, depends on a feeling of mutual respect and equal coexistence between the two. Therefore, the inclusion of community members in the decision to use eminent domain to expand the campus can result in fewer hurt feelings later and fewer allegations against the college as an uncaring, uncooperative, and unequal partner in the community.

Principle 4: Provide Meaningful Data to Support Your Actions. All organizations propose and develop programs and procedures that will clearly help them succeed. However, the reasons behind these ideas and the proposed benefits of them are often kept inside the organizations' executive offices. This information, however, is very valuable to the public relations practitioner when it comes to handling community criticism caused by these programs and procedures. Information such as this acts as evidence to substantiate and explain your organization's point of view. It helps critics understand the decisions and probable outcomes from them—the best ammunition against fear is fact. Lack of facts leads to rumors, anxiety, and ultimately fear. What people do not know often scares them most—why are so many people afraid of the dark?—because they fear what they cannot see. Facts provide the illumination people need to see reality as it exists. When they see this, the fear of the unknown dissipates; they are then able to sensibly and logically understand that much of what they feared is unfounded and meaningless. For this reason, facts provide public relations practitioners with the greatest weapon against community fears. Being open, honest, and truthful with information is the best means to gain community members' respect, even if gaining their admiration is impossible. For the community college example, factual evidence to support your organization's expansion decision would certainly help your position against the critics who claim the college is bullying the people who live near campus. Clearly, your college's expansion plans were motivated by need. Explaining this need coupled with the benefits of the expansion will help your community relations efforts' persuasive messages. The college attendance rates rose by 25 percent each year for the past three years; current facilities do not offer industry-demanded skills like computer drafting; class sizes grew by 10 percent to accommodate the increased student body. These are all examples of the facts that should be communicated and emphasized in all college communications regarding the expansion efforts. These facts help contradict claims that your college is just expanding for political reasons, to give out more construction contracts, or to substantiate the need for higher tuition. These criticisms lose much of their power when confronted with truths that only facts can provide. Moreover, when the community understands your organization's point of view, they are more prone to accept unpopular decisions, like expanding into the community by eminent domain.

Principle 5: Remove the Source of Fear. All four preceding principles of managing community fears, just as with any stakeholder group, help public relations practitioners accomplish the most important principle: eliminating fear from the public's minds. Of course proactively preventing fear is always the best method to managing it; however, that is not always possible. Issues that you may think are rather benign and innocuous might be very troubling and fearful to others. An issue such as expansion via eminent domain is clearly troubling to those directly affected by it—the people who will lose their homes. However, it is important to remember that anger and fear are infectious and even those people who are not directly affected may become distrustful and angry toward the organization. The feeling that, "If they do these things to them, then they'll do it to me" often creeps into people's minds—usually stemming from irrational thoughts that begin as fears. The not-in-my-backyard mentality that the public can develop usually begins with illogical fears. By not allowing those fears to begin, community relations efforts are much more likely to be successful, even in the face of negativity and criticism. The primary means to accomplish this is being open and proactive with your public relations efforts. Usually, by the time fears set in, trying to reverse them becomes quite challenging. Because most people remember what they hear first, it is critical to be the first with information like the expansion plans. Communicating first to those who will be most affected and then quickly turning to the media to communicate your perspective to the public is the best means to control and stop rumors, speculative reports, and undue criticism, all of which would otherwise lead to the greatest threat to community relations: fear.

Community, whether bound to an organization by proximity or by social and new media, plays an integral role in shaping and affecting an organization's reputation and brand. Because of this, public relations practitioners need to understand, empathize, and empower communities to develop strong, long-lasting relationships. An organization is more than a sign, bricks and mortar, and an address; it is a neighbor, and it must act as a good neighbor to those who physically live with it as well as those who virtually follow it. There is an old saying: "Think globally, act locally"[64]. Every organization must, of course, look at the big picture when it decides on future actions and their repercussions. However, organizational leaders also must remember that their endeavors will ultimately affect those who live and follow the organization most, and therefore, public relations practitioners must act as the liaison between their organization and their communities.

8

consumer relations

In one way or another, every organization depends on consumers for its success. Even though most people think of paying customers when referring to consumers, these integral people may not always be simply buyers of products to be considered consumers. The traditional definition of consumers is, of course, someone who buys a product. However, consumers of ideas, information, and positions are equally important. For example, a candidate running for office needs consumers for him or her to win the office. These are consumers of the candidate's ideas and platforms who then "buy" with their votes, not money. Accordingly, throughout this chapter it is important to keep in mind that consumers are more than people with money in their pockets who buy your organization's products. They are opinion-makers, persuaders, and influencers who affect every organization's ability to succeed. Consumers are voters, donors, and supporters, not just customers. As you can imagine, consumers can be a fickle group who develop and change opinions. Because public relations focuses on affecting opinions in a positive manner, consumer relations is another area of specialization in the public relations practitioner's long list of job requirements.

Because these consumer relations efforts, like all public relations efforts, are dictated by people's perceptions, it is critical to ensure your organization's messages are clear, correct, and convincing. The problem, however, with ensuring your messages adhere to these criteria is they first go through filters. Those filters are the elements of the Two-Step Flow Theory—the media and opinion leaders. As you saw in the chapter on media relations, guaranteeing that your message is printed or aired exactly as you intended it is impossible; that is what advertising is for. However, people trust the news media more than advertising, so it is a "catch-22". Because consumers are highly influenced by the media, the first step to managing consumer relations efforts is often with the media. There are more media channels or "voices" than ever—from ever-expanding cable channel lineups to new social media platforms. The problem, of course, is that with so many voices, so many people are talking and fewer people are listening. Getting them to listen to your organization's messages is therefore more difficult than ever, but it is also more important than ever. "Media noise," or the phenomenon of media overload, often leaves consumers confused and poorly informed about the issues and news most important to them. That is where the public relations practitioner comes in. By researching, planning, communicating, and evaluating consumer relations efforts, the success of these initiatives increases. Consumers expect not only to be listened to, but also to have their requests, and even demands, met by the organizations they are patronizing—by buying their products, donating resources like time, or voting them into office. Part of the problem with today's consumer relations is the focus on individuals' means to voice opinions, whether legitimate or unfounded, to the world. Thousands of new blogs spring up every day. These blogs often deal with consumer-related issues and complaints. Rogue websites set up specifically to denounce organizations, such as www.walmartsucks.org, spread rumors, half-truths, and offer others the means to voice their displeasure with the company. This phenomenon only adds to the problems associated with positive consumer relations. Until the last decade or so, only the traditional, mainstream media had this power, but today, everyone does. Obviously, the mainstream media still holds the most credibility and believability, but even "citizen journalists" can sway and shape public opinion about an organization, usually because of the sensationalism and entertainment value of their "stories"[65]. The notion, "Never let the facts get in the way of a good story" certainly applies to most citizen journalism. But, as always, perception is reality to most people, and perceptions do not rely on truth and accuracy to be believed. Therefore, modern consumer relations must monitor and use traditional as well as new and social media outlets to develop and implement consumer relations initiatives. Consumer-generated media can have an astounding effect on word-of-mouth publicity, and you know that word-of-mouth publicity, both good and bad, directly affects any organization's ability to succeed.

FIGURE 8-1. Aerial View of Walmart in an Underdeveloped Area
http://commons.wikimedia.org/wiki/File:Walmart_em_Bauru_SP.jpg

"**Ombudsman**" is a term that originated in Scandinavia that describes someone who represents the public and protects their rights against policy and legal infringements, usually by those in control. Public relations has taken the idea behind the ombudsman's responsibilities to apply them to consumer relations. Just as the original ombudsman protected the public against government abuses, the public relations consumer ombudsman likewise protects their consumers against abuses from their industry or organization. Therefore, public relations practice plays a large role in shaping how and what people think when they consider the relationship between themselves and companies, businesses, and organizations of all kinds. As mentioned previously, no organization can exist for long without some kind of consumers to support it and its functions.

To further illustrate this point, an organization that has experienced its fair share of consumer-related problems will be analyzed using a **situation analysis**. This type of analysis helps many public relations functions because it outlines the reality of a public relations issue. Situation Analysis can be applied to any initiative or problem experienced by any organization[66]. In this case, Walmart's consumer relations function will serve as the basis of the following situation analysis. Over the years, Walmart's employee relations, consumer initiatives, as well as issues stemming from suburban sprawl to labor practices have put the mega-store in the crosshairs of many protest groups and media critics[67,68]. Even a corporation as large and profitable as Walmart still must try to maintain a positive public image, and using a situation analysis can help understand the problems and solutions associated with these problems.

SITUATION ANALYSIS EXAMPLE

I. Global Ambition—The organization's primary goals and objectives
   A. Reduce negative impressions regarding the opening of new Walmart stores through a positive message campaign while ingratiating the company among targeted communities.
   B. Objective 1: Reduce negative media coverage by 40 percent within the first three months of the campaign.
   C. Objective 2: Increase recognition of Walmart's community-based philanthropic work by 10 percent in targeted locations by September 2015.
   D. Objective 3: Positively affect targeted publics' perception of Walmart by 20 percent six months following the start of the campaign.
II. Real State—History of the organization as it exists today
   E. Management
      i. Current perceptions of Walmart and its management varies greatly among its different stakeholder groups—last year, more than three quarters of American homes made a purchase at Walmart[69]. Those loyal to the company swear it is the best store in the world, while those against the store feel it is an abomination of the American landscape. Several incidents, including the use of non-union labor, undocumented workers, and the perception that Walmart cares only about its financial bottom line have created a growing resentment against the company and its managerial practices.
   F. Target Groups and Other Publics
      i. Again, loyalty among most key publics remains strong, as evidenced by Walmart's commercial success. However, a trend of anti-big-business sentiment has affected the company in recent years. Opinion leaders, vocal activists, and rogue websites continue to spread rumors about the company. In addition, former and disgruntled employees have joined these groups, adding an air of believability to their claims.
   G. Experts
      i. Experts in the field of community relations have stated that Walmart has had mixed results in its relationship with its neighbors and employees most notably, Walmart's anti-union views on labor. Many experts believe that the company is responsible for many economic woes through anti-labor practices. Experts agree that Walmart's low wages and lack of union support for its employees hurt its image with all publics—effectively making the company seem like a monolithic, money-hungry ogre.

H. Literature
    i. The review of the literature substantiates the experts' opinions regarding Walmart's public image. It states that the company receives a "mixed bag" of public perception—some love the store, while others despise it. The literature indicates that the store's low prices cause its public affection, while its labor practices and reliance on foreign goods negatively affects public perception[70].

I. Similar Companies' Responses
    i. Commercial chains like K-Mart and Target come closest to Walmart's scope with their dominance in the market. However, K-Mart's downfall may be attributed to Walmart's success. K-Mart also experienced a lack of public support because of its labor practices. The public outcry resulting from the use of child labor in the manufacture of K-Mart merchandise resulted in company fines, public mistrust, and economic hardships. The company has since dropped the lines of clothing in question and has vowed to be more responsible with its labor force.

J. Issues (1 = least impactful; 7 = most impactful)
    i. Anti-Walmart audiences are capable of spreading negative rumors and attracting unfavorable media coverage (7).
    ii. Several key publics view Walmart as a monolithic, uncaring corporate giant concerned only with profits (6).
    iii. Politicians may enact legislation preventing new construction in their communities because of their constituents' complaints against the company (6).
    iv. Walmart faces possible boycotts by supporters of those who do not want new stores built in their communities (4).

III. Positioning—The ideal state where the organization should exist
    K. Because of the plan, Walmart will become popular, respected, and most importantly, patronized among current anti-Walmart publics, furthering the retailer's dominance in the market.
    L. Ideal versus Real State

REAL ISSUES	IDEAL ISSUES
Negative media coverage resulting in a backlash if anti-Walmart sentiment rises among key audiences and shows a drop in profits.	Use of the media to illustrate Walmart's concern for its communities and employees, increasing brand loyalty, thereby solidifying the company's dominance in the market.
The impression that Walmart does not care about its communities or employees.	Branding Walmart as a compassionate company that cares about its communities, employees, and their families.
The loss of revenue because of anti-Walmart campaigns and boycotts.	The increase of Walmart's market share due to the company's increase in public support. New public support will arise from Walmart's efforts to rebrand itself as a responsible employer and community member.

IV. Audiences

M. Audience rating system (1 = most important, 7 = least important)

AUDIENCE	DO THEY KNOW WHAT I WANT THEM TO KNOW?	ARE THEY FREE TO DO WHAT I WANT THEM TO DO?
1. Community members	Based on formative surveys, most do not know	Yes
2. Media	No	Yes
3. Consumers	No	Yes
4. Employees	Yes	Yes
5. Protest Groups/Opinion Influencers	Yes	Most are probably free, but are not willing
6. Power Leaders (Community leaders, politicians, and others)	No	Yes

N. Behavioral Analysis

i. Community members (external)—Currently, Walmart does not publicize its community relations efforts—grants, donations, etc.—enough to sway community member sentiment to support the construction of new stores. Many community members feel that a new Walmart would be an asset to their towns, but are not vocal in their support. In contrast, anti-Walmart community members are quite vocal in their distaste for Walmart stores. Supporters must be motivated to express their support of new stores, whereas non-supporters should be motivated to seek better, less biased information regarding the construction of new stores. Access to community members must be a priority early on; it is necessary to include them in the planning of new stores (Walmart had access to these audiences to do so simply by reaching out to them during the planning stages). Costs incurred in contacting these audiences may be negligible in terms of their importance. Costs include town meetings, advertising in these communities, and writing letters to editors.

ii. Media (external)—Walmart must be proactive in its efforts to influence media coverage. Media-centered tactics should include information to stem the tide of anti-Walmart publicity from protest groups. Walmart should give timely, newsworthy information to influence the attitudes of the media, namely the attitudes of editors. Motivation on the part of the media includes a tendency to support the most controversial aspects of the issue—namely, the publishing and airing of protestors, while giving less time to Walmart's status quo position. Access to the media must be made early using media contacts to support Walmart's public relations efforts. Costs incurred in media relations include media release writing, special events, and the time of Walmart management to appear on news-magazine programs.

iii. General Public (external) — Information given to the public will come primarily by the media. This information will augment the positive-image campaigns made by Walmart's advertising departments and negate the rumor mill generated by anti-Walmart publics. The attitudes of the public include support for Walmart as well as understanding of its true managerial practices, not just misperceptions if the company proactively explains and describes its position early on. The public is as accessible as the media permits. Therefore, it is imperative to provide the media with relevant information on a timely basis.

iv. Employees (internal) — Keeping employees informed of Walmart's main objectives and ideals must be a priority of the campaign since they are often the first source of information sought by both the media and the public. Employees' attitudes include disgruntlement and apathy toward Walmart's objectives. Accordingly, their motivation is weak as far as becoming a spokesperson for the company. Of all the audience, access to employees is easiest. Through company newsletters, paycheck inserts, and company literature, Walmart should be able to communicate effectively with its employees. The costs of contacting employees are represented in the preceding means to communicate with them.

v. Protest/Opinion Influencers (external) — Information provided to protest groups usually comes from the media but is processed selectively by these groups. Access to protest groups is limited because of their existing prejudices against Walmart; however, gaining access to the leaders of protest groups may help in swaying their opinions. Therefore, their motivation lies in supplementing their anti-Walmart stance and supplanting pro-Walmart messages. Costs of influencing protest groups include time spent with protest leaders and literature to dispel rumors.

vi. Power Leaders (external) — Politicians' and community leaders' information comes from their respective constituents and supporters. Therefore, the groups that power leaders work for shape their attitudes — if constituents do not like Walmart, the power leaders will not, either. Accordingly, power leaders are motivated by the wants of their constituents. Access to power leaders should be relatively easy inasmuch as they seek public attention and therefore must be aware of the issues surrounding Walmart complaints. Costs of reaching power leaders echo the costs of gaining access to the public and protest groups.

V. Messages
    O. Message Table

AUDIENCE	MESSAGE	CHANNEL
Community Members	Walmart cares and contributes to the communities in which it operates	News releases Advertorials Advocacy advertising Town meetings
Media	Walmart is committed to its employees, their families, and the community	News releases Letters to editors Video news releases Special events New conferences
Consumers	Walmart is not a greedy, monolithic company (dispel rumors)	In-store literature (copy of Walmart's mission and/or vision statement on its receipts Silent publicity
Protest Groups/ Opinion Influencers	Walmart is open to criticism but will not stand by and ignore unsubstantiated rumors and fear-mongering	Communication through protest group leaders and opinion leaders Position papers
Power Leaders	Walmart's concerns and ambitions are the same as your constituents'	Face-to-face meetings

1. Unique Persuasion Proposition
    i. Walmart must impart to all its publics, especially the community-based publics, that is cares about its communities, has a proven record of accomplishment and community involvement, and is willing to work with concerned residents to resolve disputes and ease tensions.
2. Force-Field Analysis

FORCES IN FAVOR OF PLAN SUCCEEDING		FORCES AGAINST PLAN SUCCEEDING
Walmart's global name recognition and consumer following		Anti-Walmart factions attract negative media attention and spread rumors
Economic success of Walmart provides the means to accomplish campaign goals	Global Ambition: Reduce negative impressions regarding the opening of new Walmart stores through a positive message campaign while ingratiating the company among targeted communities.	Possibility of boycotts resulting from negative media exposure
Access to satisfied employees and community members to provide testimonials further substantiating Walmart's position		Disgruntled employee and community groups that could add believability and anti-Walmart claims.

VI. Channel/Media Selection
   A. The primary channel to communicate Walmart's messages and achieve the campaign's objectives is through the media, both print and broadcast. The use of news releases, ensuring that reporters have access to company spokespersons, as well as scheduling appearances by company leadership on news programs should aid the success of the campaign.
   B. Face-to-face conversations and town meetings must be used to complete the infiltration of Walmart's message in all publics' psyches.
   C. The employment of special events will provide another means to communicate the company's views to all its audiences.

VII. Competition (Real State)
   D. Because Walmart holds such as commanding lead over similar retailers in the United States as well as abroad, competition should not be an influencing factor unless the campaign is not enacted early. Competition may become a factor if anti-Walmart sentiments influence consumers.

VIII. Budget
Write and distribute news releases..$5,000 (staff time)
Special event..$250,000
Town meeting...$3,000 (management time)
Advertorials..$15,000
Letters to editors/ Op-Ed pieces..................$1,000 (staff and management time)
Video News Releases...$10,000
New conferences (*tentative*)..........................$4,000 (staff and management time)

Total (with news conference): $288,000

Total (without news conference): $284,000

IX. Competition (Ideal State)
   E. Competition should not be a great issue, in either the real or the ideal state.
         With Walmart's commanding lead in the marketplace, competition may not be an issue. However, if the anti-Walmart sentiment is allowed to grow, competition may become a factor with boycotts. Ideally, Walmart's quick, decisive campaign will build consumer loyalty and increase the company's profitability.
X. Final Issues
   F. Final Issue Lost
      i. Propagation of rumors based on anti-Walmart sentiment spread by protest groups.

ii. Negative impressions on key audiences that Walmart is a greedy, uncompassionate organization that cares little about its communities or its employees.

iii. Walmart faces a potential drop in business if protest groups infiltrate the public, leading to boycotts.

iv. If issue #2 (Several key publics view Walmart as a monolithic, uncaring corporate giant concerned only with profits) comes to fruition, power leaders may feel compelled to enact legislation limiting Walmart's expansion into their communities.

XI. Plan

  G. Goal:

    i. Reduce the number of negative impressions regarding the opening of new new Walmart stores with targeted communities.

  H. Objective 1.0:

    i. Positively affect perception of the Walmart in targeted communities by 20 percent within six months of the start of the campaign.

  I. Strategy 1.1:

    i. Increase the amount of positive newsworthy information sent to targeted news organizations. [Analysis: the case literature shows that stories appearing in local news organizations affect community members' attitudes most.]

  J. Tactic 1.1.1:

    i. Assign Walmart staff the task of reporting newsworthy, positive events and/or people of interest to Walmart's public relations department. Walmart's public relations department will compile the most newsworthy stories and use them for news releases to distribute to area print news sources. [Analysis: Research shows that locality affects public opinion most.]

  K. Tactic 1.1.2:

    i. Write Op/Ed pieces to the editors of targeted newspapers. [Analysis: The situation analysis indicates that opinion pieces sent by Walmart management influence public perception since it shows they took the time to address residents' concerns.]

  L. Evaluative Tactic 1.1.1.1

    i. Conduct intercept interviews and telephone opinion surveys prior to the plan's implementation. The public relations department will use data to compare results from similar surveys six months after the plan's implementation to gauge changes in public opinion.

  M. Strategy 1.2

    i. Build personalized relationships with targeted communities. [Analysis: Personal, targeted communication can influence audience perception most. Therefore, personalized communication with targeted communities should work, assuming targeted residents are willing to hear the college out on its position and learn about the benefits that the new expansion will bring to their community.]

N. Tactic 1.2.1

   i. Hold Community Day special events within targeted communities. Walmart will invite consumers, suppliers, and the news media to each event, which will also augment new programs and offerings. [Analysis: Special events in public relations campaigns are powerful channels for gaining public attention.]

O. Tactic 1.2.2

   i. Hold a town meeting that includes presentations on the benefits of Walmart's development in targeted areas as well as a Q&A session with Walmart leaders and community residents. [Analysis: Personal, two-way symmetric communication builds trust between organizations and stakeholders, thereby helping organizations meet their objectives.]

P. Evaluative Tactic 1.2.2.1

   i. Mailed surveys to all homeowners within the targeted communities, asking them to rate (a) their understanding of the issues and (b) their attitudes toward Walmart's positions following the events.

The preceding situation analysis and sample plan provide a glimpse of the process involved in researching, planning, and implementing a public relations solution to remedy an image problem. Remember, these types of image issues, if left unchecked, will affect consumer relations and their trust and patronage of any organization. Actively engaging in and supporting consumer relations efforts is the direct responsibility of the public relations practitioner. To accomplish this goal, several fundamental functions of consumer relations are necessary. The following describes these functions.

Function Number One: Developing Processes to Evaluate Consumer Services. The old saying, "The customer is always right" still rings true with consumer relations today. More so than ever, consumers expect their wishes and efforts to support an organization through purchasing, donations, or even votes to be recognized and appreciated. It used to be that merchandise exchanges always required a receipt; today that is rarely the case. This is because customers voiced their displeasure with the practice, and as a united front, were able to change the retail industry's guidelines in this practice. This is just one illustration of the power of consumers. Because of their strength, organizations must constantly monitor their impressions and perceptions of the organization, its products, and its service. Simple comment cards are an example of this process. If companies do not know what their customers are thinking and what they want, then the leaders of these organizations are making decisions without anything to base them on. Furthermore, making such decisions without reasoning will often lead to not only bad decisions, but costly ones as well. Spending large sums of money and time to cater to customers' wants that they really do not want wastes valuable resources. Knowing what you are doing and why you are doing it is the hallmark of all professional public relations. When dealing with such valuable and influential stakeholders like consumers, it is critical to know what their perceptions are regarding the image and brand of any organization.

Function Number Two: Creating Initiatives to Satisfy Consumer Wants. Knowing what consumers desire is the first step; developing programs to meet their wants is the natural second step. By surveying and researching consumer beliefs and conducting market research, organizations can then satisfy their customers because the organization's decision makers know exactly what to do. Creating programs like these, however, is not always easy and not always immediate. Consumers, like most stakeholders, can be fickle. What they want today may change tomorrow. This fact illustrates the timeliness issue of research. Data must be collected constantly to meet consumers' ever-changing demands. Technology, social issues, and product trends change constantly. With good, current data, however, public relations practitioners are able to develop initiatives to meet these evolving needs. A perfect example of when an organization needlessly spent millions of dollars to meet the needs of consumers, or what the organization thought they wanted, was the introduction of New Coke. Coca-Cola thought that its customers wanted a new flavor of their favorite soft drink. What they got was a dissatisfying and off-putting soda that made them angry. They felt betrayed by the brand they had supported and patronized their entire lives. Clearly, the company's research was not done well and was not adequate to warrant implementing such a risky consumer-centered initiative. Knowing what customers want, then giving it them is the key to positive consumer relations.

Function Number Three: Create Training Programs to Ensure Consumer Satisfaction. Even the best research and the most well-thought-out initiatives will not go far if the people implementing them do not know how to do them. Field training of front-line employees is critical to any consumer relations effort's success. Often, initiatives aimed at improving consumer relations are made by executives and organizational leaders who never meet any of their company's customers. Because of this, a disconnect between the organization and its employees can exist. The employee working at a cash register is the organization's primary spokesperson for its customers. If these employees do not treat the customer correctly, courteously, and capably, then even the best customer relations program will likely fail. Training, educating, and inspiring these employees to not only know how to fulfill these programs' objectives, but also to want to do so is critical. Employees are often the most important stakeholder and should be treated as the most valued resource that any organization can possess. Therefore, they must know how and why their service to the organization is so important. That responsibility falls to the people in charge of maintaining positive organizational image—the public relations practitioner.

Function Number Four: Develop Ways to Measure Consumer Relations Success. Like all public relations initiatives, consumer relations efforts must be measured and monitored to ensure their success, both currently and in the future. If you do not know the pitfalls and problems with something, then it is unlikely that those issues will ever be corrected. However, knowing what consumers think and what they want regarding your customer service efforts enables you to improve, correct, or even eliminate them when and if necessary. Even products fall into this category. Often, organizations will meet consumer demands by offering new products of services. In the early 1980s, a small pizza shop near Eastern Michigan University realized that its business could improve if its products went to the customer, rather than the customer coming to it. Pizza delivery was invented. That company went on to become the second largest pizza chain in the United States: Domino's Pizza[71]. That is not to say that the company has always created great customer-centered products or services. The company introduced a 10-inch dessert pizza made out of Oreo Cookies—needless to say, that product did not last long. Creating consumer relations programs is not always easy and will never be 100 percent successful. However, organizations that do not monitor consumer beliefs, develop programs to meet customer wants, train its employees to implement programs, and measure their success will never achieve their consumer relations goals. The primary goal is to make the customer happy enough to patronize the organization today and in the future. Positive word-of-mouth publicity from consumers is prized by any organization; the best way to gain it is from sound consumer relations initiatives, and the best method of attaining that is completing the four consumer relations functions.

FIGURE 8-2. Ronald McDonald balloon at the Macy's Thanksgiving Day Parade
http://commons.wikimedia.org/wiki/File:Ronald_McDonald_balloon_(2).jpg

Because consumers change, their tastes, habits, and opinions also fluctuate over time. Therefore, it is important for organizations to keep tabs on their perceptions and then meet consumers' changing needs. The largest, most dominant restaurant chain in the world realized this phenomenon in the late 1980s as its customers began to rethink their relationship with their beloved Big Mac. That company was of course McDonald's. By the mid-1980s, Americans became more informed on the health effects of fast food. The media began reporting stories about the damage that high-fat, high-calorie meals were doing to their hearts and their waist lines. Health officials and leading social influencers also jumped on the bandwagon and began blasting fast food as a social pariah. The downfall of western civilization was blamed on the burger and fries, and no other organization felt the heat more than McDonald's. What was the staple of the American dinner table was quickly becoming a punch line for late-night talk show comedians. Something needed to be done to meet the changing perplexities of the fast food consumer. Research, planning, implementation, and evaluation of the entire McDonald's organization and its image were required to get a handle on the issue[72]. The following analysis illustrates this process in one of the most utilized and valuable analyses available to strategic thinkers: the **SWOT analysis**. SWOT stands for Strengths, Weaknesses, Opportunities, and Threats. This type of analysis provides a simple, yet effective way to see the problems or issues facing an organization as well as the possible solutions to them. This method is especially useful when attempting to decipher and understand complex issues and phenomena affecting an organization's ability to succeed. SWOT analyses are not the domain of public relations—they are used in many business and organizational capacities[73]. However, they do offer public relations practitioners an especially valuable tool to grasp issues with many sub-issues that affect their organization's image and brand. This was especially the case for McDonald's in the late 1980s. How does a company that depends on fast food sales survive if the public now thinks it is dangerous to their health? By looking at the issue from outside as well as within the organization, the company was able to make sense of this problem and then offer solutions to ensure future success. The first step is measuring the internal strengths of the company.

Strengths

Because McDonald's is the world's largest restaurant chain with franchises in 119 countries, it has a great arsenal of strengths to rely on when dealing with a changing consumer market. The most obvious of these assets is its size. With the greatness of McDonald's empire come two very valuable strengths: money and power. Every McDonald's sign touts the "Billions Sold" and accordingly, the company has great wealth to develop new products, market them, and change them over time. Small organizations may not have the assets to implement such endeavors on such a large scale; however, every organization does have assets to create new products or services and adapt them to new circumstances. McDonald's wealth allows it to create new products that match customers' wants on a grand scale. Thousands of restaurant franchises also need to offer these products, so having the finances to implement them in so many locations is something that few companies can afford. McDonald's is one of them. With money comes power, or at least influence. McDonald's has been a top-of-mind brand for decades. When people think of fast food,

McDonald's is usually the first brand they think of because the product and the image of the company have been branded into the public's consciousness. From a young age, consumers are introduced to McDonald's through its Happy Meals and playgrounds. Ronald McDonald is as recognizable to most American children as the president. With so much influence, McDonald's has the means to bank on their greatest strength of brand dominance. People get married in McDonald's restaurants; people get

FIGURE 8-3. One of the First McDonald's franchises
http://commons.wikimedia.org/wiki/File:McDonalds.jpg

tattoos of the Golden Arches; people collect McDonald's memorabilia. The company's logo, name, and products are ingrained in society. With so much influence, the company can develop and market products and services that its competitors might not be able to accomplish. Moreover, McDonald's has such a large and fervent fan base, that there will always be thousands of customers who will patronize the restaurant chain regardless of what it does. When it comes to organizational strengths, it is hard to match the assets that McDonald's possesses. Armed with these strengths, the company is able to capitalize on its brand power, implement new products, and market them to billions of customers all over the world. Not many organizations can say the same.

Weaknesses

Even the wealthiest and most influential organization is not without its problems. Every company, person, or product, if given enough publicity, will eventually obtain some detractors. McDonald's is no different. Given its product, the most obvious weakness is what made it such a powerhouse in the fast food industry: its food. Beginning in the late 1970s and especially throughout the 1980s and '90s, facts and knowledge about the damaging health effects of high-fat, high-sodium diets were becoming more universally known. McDonald's hallmark products—burgers, fries, and shakes—certainly did not fit the new healthy lifestyles that were becoming commonplace. Again, McDonald's became the brunt of jokes about obesity and allegations that its products were not everything they were advertised. Urban legends about hamburger meat being made of everything from kangaroo to raccoons made their way through popular culture. Lawsuits ranging from the serious—a multimillion-dollar settlement for a woman who received third-degree burns from a cup of McDonald's coffee to frivolous allegations concerning fried rats and human body parts found in meals—all took a toll on the fast food giant's image. In addition, social commentators derided the company for marketing its "poison" to children through flashy tactics like Ronald McDonald, playgrounds, and Happy Meals. It seemed that all of the assets that made McDonald's so successful were now being used to damage it. In addition, it is possible that some strengths and assets can become weaknesses. While the wealth of McDonald's certainly enables it to overcome major issues that a lesser company probably could not, the size of the operation also hinders its ability to respond and act quickly on fast-changing social trends. Imagine trying to develop, market, and then train thousands of employees on how to serve a new low-fat french fry. A smaller company could initiate these types of quick reactive measures to meet changing consumer demands. A restaurant chain the size of McDonald's needs more time, investment, and resources to enact such a product. Investing millions in research and development, trials, and then marketing new products for a company the size of McDonald's is quite difficult. To illustrate, McDonald's decided to market a product to meet the demands of adult consumers who wanted a more sophisticated burger—after all, even McDonald's needs to keep its Happy Meal consumers coming back after they grow up. McDonald's idea was the Arch Deluxe, which touted a quarter pound of beef, potato flour bun, circular bacon and lettuce, onions, and tomato, along with a secret sauce concoction of mustard and Thousand Island dressing. McDonald's investment in the Arch Deluxe topped out at over $300 million. The product was a flop[74]. Poor advertising, mixed messages, and a target demographic that simply did not want the Arch Deluxe forced the company to abandon the product. A smaller company can take risks and gamble on new products without the massive investment of time and money. McDonald's cannot—it needs to go all in when it comes to addressing changing, whether real or perceived, consumer-buying habits. Even McDonald's efforts to provide more of its product to its customers eventually damaged the company's reputation. "Super Size It" was the offering of more fries and soda with its meals. While successful for some time, eventually the public's concern for their health forced the fast food giant to discontinue the practice. Even the biggest industry leaders are not immune to the sometimes fickle, but always important, consumer trends.

Opportunities

The great advantage of public relations over most other strategic communication fields is that even in the worst of times there are still opportunities to find. McDonald's, even when lambasted and lampooned, can still find ways to reinvigorate and reinforce its dominance in the fast food industry. If the greatest consumer trend that would affect the industry since its inception in the 1950s was the spread of healthy lifestyles, then McDonald's was going to need to change with the times. Before the 1980s it was impossible to fathom that McDonald's would offer anything closely resembling healthy food. Starting with the introduction of salads, then yogurt parfaits, and even oatmeal, McDonald's began adapting its menu to meet the changing fast food market. If McDonald's was going to remain number one in the industry, then its products needed reflect what people now wanted. The problem, however, is that not everyone wants to see healthy items on McDonald's menus, especially if it means that certain products or services, like the Super Size option, go away to make room for smoothies and apple slices. McDonald's core customers still demanded the classic McDonald's menu that they had grown to love. McDonald's realized that it needed to cater to new health-conscious consumers while maintaining positive customer relations with its loyal patrons. Sometimes a delicate tight wire to walk, McDonald's was able to achieve its goal of lessening the negative stereotype of its product while maintaining those same products. There was room for the Big Mac along with the garden salad. In addition, McDonald's social responsibility campaigns and programs became helpful reminders that the company was more than greasy food to a public that was becoming increasingly wary of fast food in general. Charitable programs like the Ronald McDonald House, which provides families of sick children with free lodging while their children undergo treatment, became a public relations plus to show the public that the company was not as evil as some its critics maintained. Out of all problems and setbacks are solutions. It is a matter of how those solutions are implemented and changed over time that determine their success. Beginning in the 1980s, McDonald's solution to the problem of changing diets and healthy lifestyles was to introduce products, which just years before would have seem bizarre and foreign on a McDonald's menu.

Threats

Unlike weaknesses, threats take on a more concrete and clearer nature when it comes to realizing the damaging effects from them. For example, a major weakness for McDonald's was the new demands of its consumers for healthier options. That weakness could take years to manifest itself and the effects would be somewhat ambiguous over that time—perhaps healthier lifestyles are just a fad, for instance? However, threats are generally more obvious. To illustrate, in 2003, a lawsuit against McDonald's alleging it knowingly made people obese make headlines across the country. Even though the lawsuit was eventually thrown out, it left the impression that McDonald's products may be as damaging as cigarettes. After all, lawsuits against tobacco manufacturers alleged the same things as the lawsuit against McDonald's. Legal implications are clearer—the court of law versus the court of public opinion. From these high-profile lawsuits come political threats. Politicians need their constituents to feel as though their interests are the most important. When the anti-McDonald's sentiments really began to gain momentum, politicians were quick to jump on the bandwagon and denounce the fast food chain in an effort to look as though they were fighting the french fry king for the people's benefit. City councils in places like San Francisco even proposed banning McDonald's restaurants from it. Even though most of the allegations made against McDonald's were misleading and contrived, the phenomenon that, "If people hear the same thing enough times, they start to believe it" certainly rang true. For some time, it seemed as though a new allegation and new "scientific data" showed how bad McDonald's food was for its consumers. No evidence against it was more damning than the 2004 documentary *Super Size Me*. The film showed an individual consuming nothing but McDonald's food for one month. An added catch—he would have to eat the then-Super Size version of the meal if a McDonald's employee asked. The results: the documentarian's weight went up, his health deteriorated both physically and psychologically, and overall he made McDonald's food look like poison. The small, independent movie's fallout was dramatic. McDonald's eventually dropped the Super Size option to avoid looking like it was purposely trying to kill its customers with its products. Despite the fact that the film had some serious journalistic issues to it, its effect on consumers was super sized. Arguably, it was the single greatest threat to McDonald's image in the mid-2000s and many of its healthy options came from critics using the movie as "evidence" against the company. As you can see, social and media criticism can be as serious a threat as political or even legal threats. The reason is that these social and media opinion leaders can directly affect the public's knowledge and opinion about major issues, such as the fast food industry's effect on health—especially that of children and the growing social issues of childhood obesity. Here is a clear illustration of the power of the media and opinion leaders in shaping public opinion—the Two-Step Flow Theory.

By using analysis like SWOT, organizations can better understand the consumers' mentalities toward their brand and their product. More importantly though, organizations can realize the opportunities to overcome the weaknesses, and in doing so, avoid as many long-term and reputation-damaging threats as possible. Remember, SWOT analyses are strictly the domain of consumer relations initiatives; they can be useful to understanding any stakeholder group and any public opinion trends affecting your organization—even if it positively affects it. Knowing the state of consumers' opinions about an organization and its products is the first step; the next is implementing this information into public relations programs specifically designed for your customers. In the next section, the keys to positive consumer relations are discussed so you can better understand the complexities of maintaining positive relations with established customers while trying to attract new ones.

THE KEYS TO SUCCESSFUL CONSUMER RELATIONS

1. **Maintaining Established Customers.** One of the great difficulties to successful consumer relations is the balancing act between appealing to existing, loyal customers and attracting new ones. Every organization will need to attract new consumers at some point, but it is the established ones who were so difficult to attract in the first place, and they are the ones who help keep the organization afloat when times are tough. Accordingly, the first priority to long-term organizational success is keeping current customers happy. Established consumers were the first target when branding and image development initiatives began. For example, imagine your organization of the community college and its consumers. While it might seem odd to call college students consumers, the fact is they are the customers served by that institution. Clearly, they come and go as the classes of students graduate. However, even colleges need to establish methods to keep their "existing" consumers content with the organization. Endowments, donations, and word-of-mouth publicity from past students play a huge role in the long-term success and viability of any college. If graduates are dissatisfied with the way their old college is operating, then it is unlikely that they will donate their resources to helping it succeed after they have graduated. The public relations professional at the college must maintain positive contact and interactions with alumni. Even initiatives aimed at improving their old college, like the expansion efforts, might anger some students who want their old school to remain as it was when they attended. These types of issues need to be handled accordingly so that your organization can move forward while not leaving its past consumers behind.

2. **Attracting New Customers.** The longer an organization exists, the greater the need to develop new consumers who can replace the established ones—no one lives forever. More importantly, though, new consumers bring the organization into the contemporary world of its competitors. Companies always compete for those customers who are on the fence—will they support your organization or your competitor's? The determining factor is the services and products that set your organization apart from the rest. This often entails using the latest trends in technology and service, which are often the same. As mentioned earlier, today, consumers expect to have their wants and demands satisfied—the notion that the customer is always right is stronger today than ever before. New technology enables fast, efficient, and convenient customer service that they expect as a right and not a bonus. Moreover, new technology enables them to directly communicate their displeasure about a company through social media and blogs, for instance. New customers are most comfortable with these latest trends, and therefore, they hold a tremendous amount of influence in shaping the future of an organization. It was the new consumers who forced McDonald's to change its tried-and-true menu to one that included healthy options. Accordingly, in your role as

public relations practitioner for the community college, you are responsible for keeping new students not only coming through the doors, but also appealing to the next class every year. Therefore, your duty to attract new consumers is more difficult than that of traditional commercial organizations because you are on such a time crunch. What does the market need graduates to know? What skills are in demand? What technologies must the campus update to remain relevant? These are just a few of the questions that must be asked to determine the best means to attract new student consumers to your campus. You can be sure that your competition is doing the same.

3. **Publicizing Organizational Products and/or Services.** Your organization may have the greatest pre-law department in the nation or the highest rating by a leading national magazine, but the fact is, if no one knows it, it really does not matter. Your organization's consumer relations assets must be communicated and communicated well to appeal to old consumers and attract new ones. Marketing, advertising, and public relations efforts must all incorporate a centralized branding effort that also specifically details the benefits your consumers will gain from your organization's products and services. While this may seem obvious, the difficult part is how to communicate these benefits. Most television commercials last 30 to 45 seconds, which clearly gives little time to describe the products and services in detail. The printed materials even have a limit—not in time, but in attention span. Most people will quickly lose interest in a detailed, complicated-looking pamphlet or marketing material. Therefore, it is important to highlight the "big picture" benefits of your services—such as the specific rates of employment for your college's graduates, the actual costs and affordability of its tuition, or quick looks at the new labs and facilities. These types of communications enable you to quickly, yet memorably, leave impressions in consumers' minds that your college offers the services they want without being too detailed or boring. Remember, the most valuable publicity of word-of-mouth. By keeping alumni, i.e., recent customers, happy, you have a better chance of them attracting new customers based on recommendations.

4. **Dealing with Critics.** Every organization at some point is going to have to manage dissatisfied and discontented customers. The key is to handle them correctly and quickly. As is true with most public relations work, the longer an issue is left to its own devices without any concern from the organization, the more damaging its effects will be on the organization. Similarly, the longer a complainant is left to his or her own devices without any interaction from the organization, the worse the complaint gets. Consumers feel that organizations are obliged to quickly and efficiently handle complaints or criticisms. An organization that waits too long to address complaints runs the risk of intensifying them and making the situation worse. On the other hand, organizations that act too intensely can pull more attention to the complaint than necessary, thereby making the situation worse as well. It is always a balancing act. Weighing the options of response time and response intensity enables public relations practitioners to more appropriately address complaints. For example, in 2013, two

formerly little-known food bloggers began criticizing food mega-company Kraft over the ingredients to one of its flagship products: mac & cheese. The two "expert" bloggers contended that Kraft's use of yellow food coloring caused hyperactivity in children and the food coloring should be banned, despite the fact the FDA found no evidence of these conclusions. The bloggers even went so far as to claim that the food additive leads to cancer, which the FDA did not support. Using specious reasoning and social action organizations as ammunition, the two bloggers went on a coast-to-coast media tour condemning Kraft while, of course, publicizing their blog. Nearly 300,000 signatures made their way to Kraft to change their mac & cheese formula. Kraft addressed the issue with facts supported by the FDA, which enhanced its credibility. Before long, the quick-burning firestorm of criticism died down, and the critics were after another food linked to poor health—probably McDonald's. The point is that Kraft could have acquiesced to the 300,000 critics while forgetting that the product sells to millions every day. The media attention moved on to the next issue, and Kraft remained the favored boxed mac & cheese choice in the industry. Knowing which battles to fight and with how much ammunition is critical to addressing consumer criticisms appropriately and effectively.

5. **Lowering Expenses.** While handling finances may seem out of the purview of consumer relations efforts, sound public relations in this area can help an organization's financial bottom line and improve its reputational bottom line. Eliminating redundancies in handling complaints, customer service, and product marketing all help reduce organizations' expenses. Creating an efficient, consumer-friendly organization clearly helps sell products and services, but is also encourages innovation and creativity when it comes to appealing to customers. For example, in your college's marketing of its services, you might discover that short, to-the-point information packages sent to potential students result in greater attendance than expensive television commercials do. Making your marketing costs more efficient here would clearly help the college save money. Moreover, for-profit companies that rely on sales would likely improve them through better customer service policies. For example, implementing a plan to enable employees working at cash registers the power to issue refunds without their managers' approval could speed up service and reduce customer frustration, simultaneously improving employee morale. While consumer relations may initially seem like a reactive public relations approach where changing consumer habits and complaints are handled after they occur, proactive consumer relations can help reduce operating costs while also improving purchase revenues.

Consumer relations entails a wide variety of responsibilities and functions for public relations practitioners to manage. In the end, three primary duties fall to the public relations department when it comes to consumer relations.

1. **Brand Maintenance.** As you know, brands are hard-won and when they are successful, they are extraordinarily valuable. Brands impart a sense of consistency, quality, and longevity that new products and companies cannot achieve overnight. Because of their value and their inherent connection to consumers, maintaining them as viable and

meaningful entities is critical as times and social tastes change. An old saying, "Change with the times, or the times will change you" rings true with brand maintenance and consumer relations. McDonald's found this out the hard way when it faced mounting criticisms over its products and even its marketing tactics. Loyal customers trust brands and new consumers are open to patronizing a brand; therefore, consumer relations tactics play an important role in the customer-oriented function of any organization.

2. **Customer Service.** Remember that today's customers expect treatment that only a few years ago would have been the exception. If the customer is always right, then they have never been more right than they are today. Efficient and effective customer service is the normal operating procedure of strong consumer-focused organizations. One poor experience can push a customer away from a company, and today, can lead them to publicly and easily criticize the company and gain considerable support.

3. **Addressing Critics.** Whether warranted or not, some people will always find some reason to criticize an organization. When consumers are genuinely wronged, then the organization has a responsibility to right it. Of course, sometimes consumers will criticize a company out of fear or ignorance, or simply to gain attention to themselves. Despite the fact that these types of criticisms are unfounded, they are nonetheless also dangerous. The influence of anonymity in today's society as well as the sound-bite mentality of many media consumers means that organizations must be ready to address these critics quickly, yet carefully. Too much attention from the organization can lead to greater reputational damage than would have occurred had the organization not addressed the issue so forcefully. On the other hand, not paying enough attention can be just as destructive when the critics use the organization's lack of response as fodder to support their positions. Consumer relations is again a balancing act of working with your consumers, but not bowing to their every whim and desire. Of course, this is true of all public relations regardless of the stakeholder group, but consumers' feeling of power at times makes this particular group more problematic than others.

IMAGE CREDITS

9 social media

Arguably, few developments in the modern era of public relations have changed, and affect its practice, more than social media does. The immediacy and pervasiveness of this new type of communication influences the research, development, implementation, and evaluation of all contemporary public relations initiatives. The new platform affords practitioners opportunities never possible before, but just as beneficial as this media is, it also presents a new array of changes to the field. Social media's truest power is to communicate to nearly anyone, anywhere, at any time. New smartphone and wireless technologies, which just ten years ago seemed magical and amazing, are now so much in the mainstream that the public takes them for granted. Apple introduced the first iPhone in 2005, and since then the market has exploded and content for these devices has evolved from simply pale versions of Internet content to platforms designed specifically for these devices. The smartphone and social media boon has created 20-something-year-old billionaires, connected the world, and created a blessing of opportunities and a monster of problems for organizations. This chapter will explore the phenomenon of mobile and social media content and its effects on public relations as well as the means to use this great tool while avoiding the pitfalls that come with it.

First some numbers. The Pew Research Center[75] found:

- 92 percent of Americans use several platforms to find out information every day, meaning that the public is more connected and possibly more informed than ever before.
- 47 percent of American adults use social media sites daily, which is an increase of 10 percent since 2008.
- 46 percent of Americans use at least six media channels to find out news every day through their connected devices, meaning that the 24-hour news cycle is quickly becoming the 24-minute news cycle.

Every minute, approximately 11,000 tweets, which can spike to well over 20,000 during major events, are sent out. About 1.3 billion people now use Facebook, which is nearly four times the population of the United States. These are just a few statistics that really illustrate how widespread and how quickly social media exploded worldwide. Keep in mind that Twitter and Facebook were founded less than 10 years ago. The increasing expansion and popularity of other social media outlets like Instagram and Pinterest in recent years shows that social media is not a trend likely to end anytime soon. Accordingly, social media's pervasiveness requires that any contemporary public relations practitioner understand the uses and problems that this exciting and fast-developing media presents.

To understand the nature of social media more, it is helpful to compare and contrast this relatively new media with the foundation of all media—traditional print and broadcast. The following table breaks down the differences between these two media types and provides the positives and negatives associated with each regarding their usefulness to public relations practice.

TRADITIONAL MEDIA	SOCIAL MEDIA
Centralized Power. The primary power of traditional media is its ability to control itself and its content. Traditional media channels like television and print provide content to that is ultimately determined by media gatekeepers like editors and producers. For this reason, it is integral to understand media relations principles to access these channels. The only means to access these channels without the consent and blessing of these gatekeepers is to buy space, which is advertising. Traditional media are also less feedback-friendly than social media. Most people generally do not have the power to comment enough to influence content on traditional media.	**Share Power.** Social media is egalitarian in its approach to disseminating information. Anyone can sign on to Facebook or make a Twitter account. Everyone is able to post comments, thoughts, opinions, and ideas—whether good or bad—without much interference from anyone controlling the content. Social media are the media of the people where they can access others' content, comment on it, and continuously create and update their own. No one really controls access to and content on it. Accordingly, social media feedback is continuous and constant with "retweets," "hashtags," and "likes" comprising the ongoing dialogue.

Little Accessibility. Because gatekeepers control traditional media, access to it can be difficult. Following the protocols set up by them is the best means to access it other than to pay for space and time. Therefore, traditional media accessibility is composed of the haves and have-nots. Influential people or those who know how to access it can, but most people do not possess these characteristics, and therefore, have little chance of opening the gate to it.

Public Accessibility. The great promise of social media is its universality and open-door policy where all are welcomed and everyone has a voice. Although an altruistic idea, the practicality of this promise is sometimes lost. Nearly 95 out of 100 people use mobile subscription services, illustrating the pervasiveness of smartphone technology. Because social media content entails much of smartphone use, its widespread accessibility cannot be denied.

One-Way Communication. Because of relative lack of engagement between traditional media channels and their consumers, the dialogue between the two is often one-sided. That, "The media tells us what to think about" illustrates the average person does not have much of a voice when it comes to communicating with large media conglomerations that comprise much of the traditional media industry. The influence if the traditional media lies mainly in its control of its content. Control, by its very nature, equates to little sharing of power, and because information, knowledge, is power, traditional media often speak to the people and rarely listen to them.

Two-Way Communication. The ability to say what you want when you want clearly indicates that social media content is predominantly conversational in nature. Twitter, for instance, best illustrates this characteristic of social media. Any follower of any person can state their opinions and thoughts about others' comments and statements. There is no centralized power that controls the content like networks or newspapers do with traditional media. Of course one of the problems with this is that everyone is often speaking and no one is necessarily listening. Discussions turn to arguments and arguments turn to name calling and threats.

Credibility. The nature of controlled and professional communication from traditional media channels means its content is generally more trustworthy and credible than social media. The public expects that a newspaper article was researched, written, and edited by professionals before its publication. This level of trust and respect for the traditional media means that its content is superior when it comes to influencing people through fact and reasoning.

Questionable. The open access, anything-goes style of social media may make it a great tool for the masses to communicate with, but that does not translate to believability or credibility in its content. Often social media possesses an air of anonymity where anyone can pretend to know something or be informed on a topic, but there are no checks in place to assure that this is true. Social media content, while engaging and interesting, often lacks the weight of credibility that traditional media possesses.

Time Restricted. Even though today's traditional media operates on a 24-hour news cycle through expanded platforms and cable stations, it is still for the most part constrained by time. The factors that enable it to be more credible than social media (the researching, writing, and editing) take time to do professionally. Moreover, most traditional media channels are still beholden to set schedules like newspaper and magazine publication deadlines and television news station air times.

No Deadlines. Social media moves fast and without any time restrictions. Content is posted, shared, and replaced thousands of times a day with no regard to any schedule. The fact that most social media content does not depend on research and editing, it can be "broadcast" immediately with little regard for the content's accuracy or readability.

Both traditional and social media clearly have their pluses and minuses when it comes to the usefulness and influence of them. What social media may lack in credibility, it makes up for it in immediacy. The rapid worldwide spread of smartphone technology enables constant and immediate communication through social media platforms. While most traditional media outlets have picked up on social media and nearly all maintain a social media presence, they are still restricted to the time-honored principles of professional journalism, which takes time to complete. User-generated content from unknown and unsubstantiated sources is posted immediately and because it appears first, it is often believed. Remember that most people will believe what they hear first, and because of this phenomenon, anonymous social media content can be very influential in shaping the outcome of public opinion—this is the idea of the influence of anonymity. Clearly, this power can potentially cause great damage and embarrassment to organizations dependent on public trust and their reputations. Even if the content is not true, it can quickly spread, and as it does, it gains momentum and more and more people begin believing it and they in turn spread the information. This snowball or domino effect can leave organizations in a position to address stories and news that may be highly out of context or completely fabricated from imagination. Therefore, all organizations need to maintain a presence and a keep an eye on what it is being said about them throughout the social media universe. To illustrate this important danger of social media, the following scenario will concern your public relations efforts at the community college and the implications of contrived social media stories.

Following your hard work to increase and retain well-qualified students, you discover that your college's online ratings are less than ideal. According to different websites that allow its users to rate companies, businesses, and even colleges, your school is underrated. You notice different postings that state the college is poorly equipped, its faculty underqualified, and student relations nonexistent. You, of course, know this is untrue; after all, the college just spent $500,000 on a new engineering facility. However, you also know that the truth is not always as influential on public opinion as perception is. If potential students, donors, and faculty research the college before they attend, give money, or want to work for it, which they of course will, you know that getting good students, big endowments, and the best teachers will be very difficult. You know that your college is facing a crisis of online inaccuracies and unwarranted criticism. However, that does not really matter right now because what people believe from the websites is what matters. You must address this situation as best you can while not giving the matter too much attention. After all, you do not want to add fuel to the fire by announcing to the world that these critiques even exist. Most people will probably never see them, so addressing them too forcefully can backfire. Then again, ignoring the situation and hoping that it goes away is not a very sound approach either. Again, public relations is a balancing act—knowing how much attention and when to address situations is key. There are five essential issues to overcome: the speed of the spread of rumors, the seeing-is-believing mentality, the ease of faking credibility, the likelihood of finding supporting stories, and the notion that criticism does not let facts get in the way of a good rumor.

NEW MEDIA ISSUES

Issue Number One: The Speed of Spreading Rumors. The instantaneous effect and ease of communicating online make the spread of rumors very fast. Formerly, it took much longer for criticism to spread—either via the media or word of mouth. Today, these types of statements can move like wildfire, and like wildfires, the faster they are contained, the less the damage. Often, people will pick up stories, half-truths, and outright lies because they are salacious and emotive by nature, and people like controversy—just look at the nightly news for evidence of that. Generally, most people will remember negativity over positive stories because they contain more drama. Additionally, they are easy to add content to corroborate them. One claim about some "student's" negative experience with a professor might be supported by an additional "student's" statement about the same subject. In doing so, they both corroborate each other and lend an air of believability. Perhaps the student did have a negative experience, but the facts behind the criticism are missing. Maybe the student was upset they he could not turn in a paper late, and therefore, is angry at the professor and now the entire college. With nowhere else to turn, he decides the post a criticism of the entire school online, out of spite. The problem is that the other people reading and believing the online post do not know the backstory to the claim. This is why online rumors are so dangerous to organizations' reputations. The real question is how to respond. The main determinant to that question is the quantity and quality of the posting. If there are only a few (fewer than five) criticisms, then it is unlikely that they can influence too many people to think less of your organization. Also, if the post contains multiple grammatical and spelling errors, then the credibility of the post decreases, and is also less likely to be taken at face value. With these considerations in mind, you can then plan your response. For example, if 100 posts throughout different websites all contain the same critique that the student facilities are poor, then of course, there might be some merit to them. Just as the other readers to these statements do not know the full story, neither do you. You need to distinguish the possible from the irrational when it comes to dealing with anonymous online critiques. If many people are criticizing your organization over the same issue, then it is important to look into it and address it accordingly. If only a few, random criticisms are posted, and then it is important to acknowledge them, but not draw too much attention to them either. Addressing them on a case-by-case basis is the best way to manage online rumors—there is no one-size-fits-all response.

Issue Number Two: The Seeing-is-Believing Mentality. As with most things related to public relations, perception is everything because to most people perception is reality. If enough people say something then it is likely that even more people will believe it. Even today, a good portion of the population believes that if it is printed, then it must be true. That, of course, is not the case. Anyone can post anything on websites that solicit user responses, and the posts do not need any supporting facts before they are allowed to be posted—that is the main criticism to social media. If enough people read enough negative comments about your college's student relations programs, then it snowballs and more people comment and more people believe those comments, and so on and so on. Quick, rational responses are key. It is always good to stop these types of rumors while they are still manageable by refuting and subduing them early.

Issue Number Three: The Ease of Faking Credibility. Because online posts are generally anonymous, anyone can claim any expertise or experience regarding a subject they choose. Unlike traditional media, social media requires no substantiation or fact checking to ensure that a statement is true before it goes public. A student claiming he had a negative experience at your college may have never even stepped foot on campus. The fact is that online credibility is easy for anyone to fake. Because of this, it is critical to give each criticism a skeptical appraisal before jumping into response mode. Fact checking and research on your part will enable you to verify and justify negative online comments about your organization. If multiple posts all claim the same negative experience with student relations, then it might be wise to look into it first. If warranted, then make changes and correct the situation; and let others know about the fix too. However, it is important not to draw attention to the original problem. For example, if many posts state that student parking is problematic, then after it is fixed, publicize the new and improved parking facilities, but do not mention that the parking lots were improved because of the original criticisms.

Issue Number Four: The Likelihood of Finding Supporting Stories. The corroboration factor influences the strength of and damage from negative online posts more than any other. Therefore, it is critical to investigate the sources and spread of online comments. A few here and there might not be as damaging as multiple sites all stating the same thing about your organization. Today, many websites offer users the ability to post comments and critiques of many different organizations across nearly every industry. Therefore, the spread of online rumors and criticisms is likely to increase in the future. One of the main problems with this advance is that it makes monitoring the web for problematic comments very long and difficult for already overworked public relations practitioners. The good news is that many organizations offer services that monitor the Internet for you. Part of the modern public relations practitioner's toolbox is the ability to use this software. Today, this skill is an expectation, whereas just a few years ago, it was an added-bonus skill. Using these diagnostic software systems enables you to quickly and efficiently monitor what is being said about your organization online rather than spending hours each day surfing through the ever-growing number of ratings-oriented websites.

Issue Number Five: Online Comments Do Not Let Facts Get in the Way of a Good Story. Again, the very nature of online content lends itself to fabrication or at least inflation of the facts. Because there are no real checks in place to ensure accuracy, online posts can be completely true, false, or something in between. Also, since most people like controversial and salacious material, criticism lends itself to online misrepresentation much more than positive comments do. Moreover, if someone feels wronged by an organization and they have no avenues to vent their frustrations other than posting angry comments on some website, then the ferocity of that post's content is likely to be inflated when it comes to objective and practical suggestions for improvement. It is important not to take everything posted online about your organization at face value, even though that may be difficult to do, because the critics may post negative comments about something directly relating to your job or project you worked on for a long time. Professionalism and rationality should guide your appraisal of online comments about your organization.

These five issues are at the heart of understanding and evaluating online rumors and criticisms. The following, however, offers suggestions on tactics to control and deal with them. The first is locating the source of the information. Knowing where something came from helps understand its point and purpose much easier in the vast online universe than simply accepting all statements as is. If, for example, a website that offers comments appears questionable because of its poor quality, then it is likely that others will not believe everything that is posted as it is presented. On the other hand, if a website that is subscriber-only and available just to paying members offers comments and suggestions, then its content might be more believable to readers. Again, a big part of online rumor management is researching and understanding the purpose behind them. When you have figured that out to the best of your ability, then it is more easily managed. Part of the management is the speed in which you respond. Always remember the wildfire simile when it comes to managing online rumors and content. The quicker the response, the less damage is likely to occur.

These suggestions come from the latest studies and cases using social media today. It must be noted, however, that because of the relative newness of social media, there really are no set rules and fundamentals. Much of the work so far with social media has been that of feeling out the new media and its capabilities. Formerly, it was enough to have a Facebook page and ask customers and patrons to "like" the organization. However, it was quickly discovered that having many Facebook friends did not necessarily equate to larger consumer bases and increased revenue. The following tips offer ways to engage and create meaningful content that drives people to your social media outlets and ultimately on to better business success. These steps may change over the next few years as new platforms are introduced and advancing technology changes the way people connect.

SOCIAL MEDIA FUNDAMENTALS

Suggestion Number One: Understand the Importance of Dialogue. Much of the social media content today seems to be heavily focused on self-promotion. Status updates, Tweets, and Facebook "likes" all enable users to focus on individuality—what they are doing, where they are doing it, and exclaiming to world that they are doing it. Much of social media's criticism falls on its lack of engagement and self-aggrandizing content that focuses on the individual, not the social element that it is designed to encourage. Organizations are also not immune to this criticism. A great deal of content from companies focuses on the company—its products, sales, promotions, etc.,—and often leaves the consumers' points of view as afterthoughts. Remember that all good communication should be two-way, and social media is no different. Organizations should embrace the ability of social media to remove the communication barriers that often exist between organizations and their stakeholders. Providing a means of dialogue is important; however, it can also be dangerous. Enabling anyone to voice their thoughts about a company, especially when the company encourages it, helps promote dialogue, but also presents other problems. Many organizations have gotten into trouble when they ask the public to upload their "favorite" experience relating to the company. When often happens is a sounding board of criticism and negativity when in fact the company only wanted to open the lines of communication. Like most things public relations, social media engagement is a balancing act between open dialogue and controlled conversations. This example illustrates the problem with true, symmetrical two-way communication and the fact that most organizational communication is asymmetrical in nature. It is important to open opportunities to communicate, but also control the ability to criticize the organization that is opening the lines of communication.

Suggestion Number Two: Use Social Media as a Tool to Learn More About Your Stakeholders. The amount of data and information posted to social media sites can be a valuable asset to organizations seeking to better understand their publics and the organization's place in society. Stronger relationships often come out of improved knowledge between the parties involved in the relationship. The more your organization can find out about current trends, movements, and changing public opinion via social media, the more prepared it can be to manage its reputation. The contemporary public relations practitioner's research toolbox now must include social media as well because of the pervasiveness and popularity of it, especially among younger consumers who can become lifelong supporters of an organization if they are appealed to early in their lives. As mentioned earlier, people today expect to have a voice and be listened to by organizations, and social media presents the opportunity to do so, but only if the organization knows what to say and how to say it. Researching what is being said on social media is one way of knowing this critically important information.

Suggestion Number Three: Provide Personal Connections. With knowledge of your organization's social media presence, you are better equipped to then provide the type of service people expect as a right—personal service. It is important to focus on the content of your messages and less on the popularity of a social media platform. Not every organization needs a Twitter account, especially if no one in the organization can or will monitor and use it appropriately. You can drive business to your organizations through social media, but only if the content appeals to your audience. In the past, many organizations simply updated and posted marketing information aimed at selling the audience as if social media were an advertising platform. It was not long before that tactic failed to connect with audiences because it became a one-size-fits-all type of communication. With social media comes the ability to ask questions about and seek advice on products, services, and even marketing efforts, but the content in those questions must appeal to your specific audience as opposed to a generic, all-consuming public. Use social media to understand your stakeholders and then use it to communicate with them, not at them.

Suggestion Number Four: Organize Your Online Community. While the original promise of social media may have begun with an effort to connect everyone, the fact is that people assimilate and connect with other like-minded individuals. This is a law of human nature. Therefore, social media sites also arrange themselves according interests, opinions, leanings, etc. Therefore, organizations that take part in these communities can help organize and set them up for these specific audiences. For example, a company that manufactures camping equipment can certainly start an online community of camping enthusiasts where they can discuss the hobby, present suggestions, and publicize their camping feats. The organization that manages this type of online community can offer suggestions, solicit ideas, and occasionally, mention its products as well. This type of social media presence makes more sense than appealing to everyone because only those who will likely patronize the company will be part of it. The content is tailored to the specific interests of a select group of people who can benefit the organization.

Suggestion Number Five: Offer Your Audience Something Meaningful. Content is king when it comes to social media. However, organizations can also offer something more tangible than just good content. Social media provides a great opportunity for promotions, contests, and giveaways. These tactics can draw new members into your online communities who might not otherwise connect to them. Integrating an online giveaway with a television commercial promotional campaign further applies and improves the cohesive messages that all organizations should strive to achieve in today's overcrowded media world.

With today's ease of communicating in the palm of your hand, an advancing emphasis is on utilizing this great virtual opportunity while connecting in tangible ways. The term "SoLoMo" sums up this idea, which stands for social, local, mobile marketing[76]. Essentially, it enables organizations to communicate in real time to consumers who are near their physical businesses. For example, imagine a restaurant in a shopping mall. Hundreds of people pass by the restaurant every day, and one thing that most of them have in common is smartphone connectivity. Therefore, the restaurant can use this capability to drive people into its business. The restaurant can post a special menu, new items, or promotions via its social media platforms to the people walking in the mall. The restaurant sets up an alert system where potential consumers near the mall can receive updates and information about the restaurant's promotions, thereby encouraging them to eat at the restaurant because they received an update. Formerly, dozens of customers would have been missed every day without this technology. The combination of smartphone technology and social media platforms now enables businesses to communicate directly to customers to market its products and increase sales. Of course, with ever-increasing new technologies, it is unknown what the future marketing like SoLoMo will entail, but it offers a glimpse into the new communication possibilities with connected devices and the programs they run.

Social and new media offer a wide array of opportunities that just a few years ago seemed impossible. Moreover, the future of social media-focused public relations also presents a seemingly limitless universe of information and possibilities. While the technology will change and the consumer habits of social media users will evolve, the fundamentals of sound, positive communication will likely never change. Two-way communication that focuses on a conversational quality with meaningful content will undoubtedly remain the driving force in public relations regardless of new technology. Radio, television, the Internet, and now social media all have the same thing in common. They were all new unknowns to strategic communicators like public relations practitioners. Each offered new opportunities as well as new problems. However, all of them still revolve around the solid fundamentals of public relations—stakeholder-centered communication and action. It is unlikely that whatever the future may bring to the field of public relations, it will be enough to change the practice's principles when it comes to solid stakeholder relations.

FACEBOOK

- *Use the assets that the platform affords you.*

  Each social media platform should be viewed as a tool. You cannot use a hammer to do the work of a screwdriver. Similarly, social media platforms are not all the same. Each must be used to maximize the assets they have. Too often, practitioners mistake each social media avenue as the same as the next, when, in fact, they are all different. You must understand that Facebook is not Twitter, which is not Instagram. Each is unique and can accomplish different objectives if used correctly.

- *Good visuals.*

  Showing people something is very different than explaining it. Social media platforms like Facebook lend themselves to visual media, so maximize this opportunity with unique, useful, and interesting video and images.

- *The "About Me".*

  Facebook was invented for the "me" generation. Nearly everything posted on it is about the user. This rather egocentric platform enables users to let the world see and read about what they are doing. Therefore, practitioners must play to that tune, and they must address and concern themselves with what people want—news and information that is useful to them.

- *Integrate your presence with your other platforms.*

  Integrated marketing communications is all about consolidating your presence across various disciplines. Social media is the same. You must connect your Facebook followers to your Twitter and Instagram followers and vice versa.

- *Don't use too many accounts.*

  Each organization should focus on one account per platform. Basically, each company should have one dedicated Facebook account, one Twitter account, etc. Having too many accounts leads to redundancies and missteps in your posting that might result in lost followers.

- *Avoid posting too much and too often.*

  When people talk all the time, few listen to them. It's the same with social media. Too many posts often leads to lost followers because followers think: "What's the point in checking this post out? It's the same as yesterday's." You should only post when there's actually something to say that is meaningful to your followers.

- *Use the metrics.*

  The final and important step in any public relations model is evaluation. Only by knowing what you're doing and how it's working can you expect to grow and learn. Analyzing your results leads to increased productivity and effectiveness.

- *Take advantage of multimedia possibilities.*

  Use the platform's options to maximize your presence. Video and animation can lead more traffic to your account. Again, content is king, so be sure whatever you post is useful and meaningful to your followers.

- *Post at the right time of day.*

  Timeliness is important when planning your posts. Be sure to post items when they're most useful and meaningful to your followers, depending on the content.

- *Respond quickly and thoroughly.*

  The responsiveness of social media is one of its most important and useful assets. Use that availability to communicate to your followers in a timely and complete manner.

TWITTER

- *Consistent use of identity.*
  Being consistent is one of the most important elements of good social media usage. Integrated marketing is all about speaking with one voice in a singularly consistent manner.

- *Follow me, follow you.*
  The ability to follow other Twitter users and be followed is perhaps Twitter's greatest asset. Following like-minded accounts that relate to your organization is a good way to increase your presence while helping similar organizations.

- *Tailor messages to followers.*
  Your followers are your most important social media asset. Therefore, it is critical to provide content they care about most and that is centered on them, rather than just your organization.

- *Use storytelling to move an audience to you.*
  This chapter has outlined the importance of storytelling. Providing good, meaningful, and useful content is critical to attracting followers and keeping them over the long term.

- *Remember mobility.*
  Providing content based on location is a great way to increase your Twitter presence. Posts relating to sales and specials, for example, that can be used when your followers are near your store or location can lead to greater sales and an increase in followers.

- *Organize followers.*
  Different followers want different things. One size fits all solutions never work well for long when it comes to strategic communication. It is similarly important for Twitter communication too. Differentiating between unique groups of followers enables you to communicate directly and clearly to them.

- *Expand through hashtags.*
  Using hashtags can lead to greater presence and association between your organization and important causes or trending issues, thus expanding your net of followers.

- *Measure.*
  All things public relations lead to evaluation. If you do not measure your Twitter account's effectiveness, then you never really know if what you're posting is furthering your communication objectives.

INSTAGRAM

- *Remember it's a visual platform.*
  The basis of Instagram is the pictorial nature of the platform. Therefore, the posts you make need to be visually engaging and meaningful.

- *Track traffic.*
  Measurement of what you're posting and how it's being used by followers is critical to attracting and keeping your followers.

- *Plan posts in advance.*
  In addition to measurement, it's important to plan and post according to your pre-planned communication initiatives. Posting on the spur of the moment is not likely to accomplish your objectives.

- *Promote others.*
  Like other social media platforms, Instagram lends itself to attracting and maintaining relationships. If you promote them, then it's likely that they will promote you too.

- *Ask for followers' contact information.*
  Gaining information about your followers is important to understanding them and their concerns and wants most. By supplying to their demands, your posts take on a greater importance and attraction.

- *Use sponsored ads.*
  Sponsored advertisements enable you to control your content and further your social media objectives.

- *Make content shareable.*
  The very nature of social media revolves around the ability to share content between users. This interactive relationship is at the heart of what makes good social media work for your ad your organization.

- *Look to influencers.*
  Certain users, like celebrities, have millions of followers. Tapping into that market can increase your social media presence and further your reach.

SNAPCHAT

- *Stage events with influencers.*
  Like the celebrities who attract great numbers of followers, linking influencers to events relating to your organization can lead to a greater presence and increased reach.

- *Share promos.*

   Promotions, like sales and specials, can be communicated to your stakeholders directly and when they're in the area of your stores.

- *Provide inside access.*

   Offering users a glimpse into your organization can increase traffic because people like to feel as though they're on the "inside" or have special access to or knowledge about something that others might not.

- *Promote others.*

   You can benefit from helping others achieve their goals by receiving promotion from them too. Locating like-minded organizations and users can further your reach while associating yourself with certain people and causes.

- *Demo your products and services.*

   Showing the features and applications of your organization's products and services lets you "advertise" and increase interest, acceptance, and sales, of your marketable assets.

- *Connect with public opinion.*

   Trending public causes and issues can help keep your organization up-to-date with the pulse of the world. Your organization can find new followers and attract more attention by associating with key issues and causes relating to your organization.

- *Market events.*

   Invitations and information about upcoming events increases attention and gains traction in generating audiences and attention to your events.

10 CRISIS COMMUNICATION

Arguably few other opportunities enable public relations practitioners to show their value and leadership to their organizations more than a crisis. It is during these stressful and difficult times that the public relations functions become the most important part of the entire organization. The fate of many organizations has rested on its public relations response to crisis and criticism. When done well, organizations not only survive, but can fare better than they did before the crisis. On the other hand, poor or inadequate public relations work during a crisis can not only make a bad situation worse, but can cause more harm than the actual crisis does. Accordingly, all aspiring public relations practitioners must understand and appreciate the importance of crisis communication and management as well as the fundamentals of handling a crisis well. This chapter will analyze the different types of crises and preparing for them, as well as controlling them before their power destroys an organization unlucky enough to find itself facing disaster.

CRISIS STAGES

Three basic stages are inherent to all crises: the pre-crisis stage, the crisis stage, and the post-crisis stage. These three stages are hallmarked by specific actions that are common to nearly all public relations crises. During the pre-crisis stage, the organization prepares and practices its crisis response in an effort to perfect and address any problems as much as possible. Also referred to as the prodromal stage, this stage includes all proactive crisis strategies such as research, plan development, personnel assignments for the crisis, and the creation of messages and deliverables such as press releases[77]. The second stage, the actual crisis stage, includes the minute-by-minute management of the crisis as it unfolds. All of the proactive work that took place during the pre-crisis stage comes to fruition during this time. The last state, the post-crisis stage, includes the organization's assessment of its proactive and reactive crisis response as well as the general move to return to normalcy. These three stages organize each public relations crisis fundamental and principle in this chapter to enable you to see how crisis communication and management operate. Even though these stages seem simplistic, the vast amount of work and strategy that takes place during them is formidable. However, through an organized and educated approach to **crisis management**, organizations can not only recover their image but also even improve when facing a seemingly never-ending list of threats and problems.

Regardless of the nature of the crisis, three fundamental steps should always be followed when handling any difficult situation. The first is to identify the source of the crisis, or better yet, identify the source of the problem that could lead to a crisis. The best type of crisis management is stopping a problem from evolving into a full-blown crisis. Small, seemingly insignificant problems and criticism, if handled poorly, can turn into big problems for organizations. Therefore, the identification step enables public relations practitioners to understand where a problem is coming from and then addressing it early. For example, in your capacity as public relations manager for the community college, you realize that a group of protestors is gaining recognition and strength via its growing online presence and influence, then you can identify means to control it before it turns into something more severe. For example, imagine that the group consists of former employees from the state's community college system who make claims of unfair labor practices, nepotism, and misappropriation of funds against the community college system. Because of the nature of the allegations, you realize that these types of statements can damage the entire college system's reputation, and obviously that of your college in the process. Moreover, because of the seemingly unified front from the group and the fact that they have experience, and in some ways credibility, their claims could garner more attention than just one or two disgruntled employees venting their anger can. By identifying the source of the situation before it blossoms into something larger, such as then the traditional media start reporting on them, you are in better position to proactively address the situation, or at least monitor it and be ready for a response immediately. Identifying the source and the likely progression of a problem certainly helps public relations practitioners handle situations when they are small and controllable. Of course the problem with identifying crisis sources is the notion that you can, which is not always the case. Immediate crises like fires, shootings, and accidents cannot always be monitored before they start—if they could, they would never happen. Therefore, planning is key to dealing with unexpected and immediate crises, which will be discussed later in this chapter.

The second step that all crisis responses should follow is isolating and controlling the crisis while it is still manageable. Always remember the simile that crises are very much like fires—they are much easier to put out and a great deal less damaging when they are small; the larger they are allowed to grow, the more difficult to extinguish and the greater the devastation. Isolating and controlling a crisis from the start is like putting out a fire when it is small. Success or failure with crisis management can often be determined by the organization's response within the first 24 hours of the onset of a crisis. This time is known as the "golden hours" because the response during this time can often make or break an organization when it comes to recovering from a crisis. When isolating a crisis you remove the extra fuel that can ignite and spread your crisis. Using the example from step one, if you can isolate the group's complaints, find rebuttals to them, and be ready to provide this evidence to the mainstream media before the group begins their widespread campaign to criticize your organization, then you have a much better chance of reducing their damage. You take away their power of surprise and the method of playing on the public's sympathy. Your quick, correct, and measured response takes the crisis from their control to yours, and the greatest crisis management fundamental is always maintaining control.

The third step to successful crisis communication is managing the crisis as you would with any public relations effort. The problem that often infects organizations during crises is the panic, fear, and chaos of the situation causes normally level-headed and sensible people to lose their control of the situation and then all attempts at returning to normalcy begin to crumble. Public relations practitioners must understand that maintaining order and control during times of turmoil is the most important tool in successful crisis management. Often, the only part of a crisis that is within the control of an organization is itself and its reactions and recovery steps. Once that is lost, all hope of reducing the damage of the crisis and moving forward become lost. Furthermore, one of the often overlooked keys to long-term crisis recovery will also be missed if the crisis if managed poorly: opportunities. Even in the darkest hours of a crisis, there is always light at the end of the tunnel and opportunities to make the organization better than it was before the crisis. An obvious example of this is Johnson & Johnson's actions during the Tylenol crisis where the company came out of it as a beacon of positive public relations actions and the public respected the company more for its handling of the crisis than it had before the poisonings. There are always opportunities in crises; some are easier to see than others, but they are there. For instance, the growing criticism against your college's leadership even holds opportunities. For one, you now see the power and importance of online reputational management and monitoring. Secondly, you can use your research and knowledge of the situation to make the organization's reputation better by implying in its future marketing platforms that the colleges are well run and responsible—without noting why you've posted these, of course. Rational management of a crisis is key to controlling it as it progresses and then recovering from it when the worst has subsided.

Now that you understand the three fundamental steps to all successful crisis responses, it is important to understand the different types of crises that can affect organizations. While categorizing crises into neat, perfect segments is difficult because many of them will overlap into other areas, understanding the nature of the main types of crises will help you appreciate the researching, planning, implementing, and evaluating steps associated with all public relations work—especially crisis management. To develop sensible plans and responses to crises, it is important for organizations to anticipate the types of crises that are most likely to affect them. For instance, an oil company can sensibly anticipate oil spills, environmental criticisms, increased government regulations, and Middle East tensions as likely crises to be ready for. A community college can anticipate decreased budget allocations, changing industry demands on graduates, and changing federal loan regulations as likely problems that could evolve into crises. Therefore, it is not necessary for all organizations to plan for all types of crises—it is difficult to imagine a community college's image being affected by an oil spill—however, the important step is to plan and anticipate for those crises that could affect your organization. With crisis preparation it is better to hope for the best, but plan for the worst.

TYPES OF CRISES

1. **Loss of Human Life and Injury.** These are obviously the most damaging types of crises because of the very nature of them. Loss of money, jobs, and public trust are recoverable, but clearly loss of human life is not. Worse yet, these types of crises are often more difficult to identify than are other categories of crises. As mentioned earlier, if accidents could be identified before they occur, then they would never happen. However, the key to managing these types of crises is anticipating them, and then dealing with them in the event that they do occur. No one wants loss of human life or limb, but the reality is that it does happen. Responding to these types of crises depends on sincerity, compassion, and appropriateness. Helping family and friends recover from these types of losses becomes the priority of the organization that is responsible, even though it might not be to blame for it. On-campus shootings illustrate

that fact that these types of crises do occur and must be planned for even though you hope you never need the plan. Working with investigators, providing counseling services, and trying to maintain some order are all tasks that need to be completed in the face of very difficult times. At some point, organizations affected by these types of crises need to return to normal, which makes the job of public relations during this time even more difficult. You know that public opinion depends on your organization's response, or at least its perceived response, and returning to business too quickly may be seen as insensitive. However, for the organization to survive, it must return to business at some point. This is an illustration of the problematic nature of crisis recovery. No crisis is more important or can be more damaging than those involving the loss of life. A close second is human trauma and injury. This means that public relations practitioners working for organizations that are likely to be affected by these types of tragedies must be planning and working on responses to them well in advance.

2. **Financial.** People are more sensitive to financial and economic crises since the recession of 2008, which means that public relations practitioners need to understand the impact and importance of these types of crises on today's public. Fear and anxiety are the hallmarks of financial crises. Large-scale layoffs, closures, and poorly performing stocks entail just a few of the specific types of financial crises that can affect organizations. Responding to financial crises can be difficult because these types of problems cannot be easily or quickly fixed. Part of crisis response is devising and offering some means to remedy the problem that caused the crisis or at least offer steps to try to prevent it from happening again. Clearly, with financial crises, that is difficult because if there is not enough money, then there is not enough money. A company cannot simply improve its financial outlook overnight. If it could, then most financial crises would never occur. Although not always well received, the sensible one is that of concessions and sacrifices in the service of the greater good. If 500 employees must be laid off to ensure that the remaining 5,000 employees keep their jobs, then that is what must occur. The problem, of course, is the 500 fired employees. Public relations work is difficult because it is nearly impossible to make everyone happy all the time. This is never truer than during financial crises. For example, if your community college needed to reduce staff numbers to make up for budget shortfalls by releasing five percent of its maintenance staff, then that is a tough decision that must be made for the betterment of the entire organization. The task is to enable that five percent to clearly understand the reason, as well as the entire organization to reduce rumors and allegations—ultimately to stop fears before they begin. Once someone starts hearing about layoffs in their organization, the next step is fear of losing his or her own job. Communication and openness, in this case, can help stop a potential crisis before it begins.

3. **Leadership.** People are in control of organizations, but because they are human, they can make poor decisions that can lead to embarrassment and crises of leadership—or lack thereof. Most people expect their company's leaders to be knowledgeable and qualified, of course, but also to look out for the good of the company. That, however, is not always the case. Embezzlement, insider trading, and personal misconduct like sexual harassment all describe actions likely to lead to crises of leadership. However, these types of problems can also stem from poorly planned statements and momentary lapses of judgment. As an illustration, imagine the president of your community college commenting on the recent decision to lay off five percent of the maintenance staff to ensure long-term financial security of the organization. As head of public relations, you counsel him on what to say and the best way to say it, given the nature of the situation. He, in a moment of poor judgment or sheer stupidity, goes off script and decides to give his opinion on the plight of the employees stating, "Those types of people are always losing jobs, so they'll be fine finding new ones." Immediately, you know your organization, through its leader, is facing big trouble. His statement is of course repeated over and over again in the media with emphasis on the fact that 95 percent of those employees let go are of Hispanic descent. Now, a potential financial crisis has turned into a leadership crisis, affecting the image of the entire college. Outrage and condemnation follow from the Hispanic community, human rights organizations, and even the state's leadership including the governor. What should have been a rather clear-cut interview on the reduction of staff caused by budget decreases has turned into a media circus. Apologies and recants are the next step, but the image and reputation of the college will take some time to recover, all because of one statement from one person—the organization's leader and inherent key spokesperson.

4. **Natural Disaster.** In the last decade the number of severe weather events seems to have increased to dramatic levels. Unprecedented hurricanes, tornadoes, earthquakes, tsunamis, sinkholes, and mudslides seem to be common on the nightly news. Organizations must therefore prepare for the types of natural disaster events that can strike them. Even though the organization is not at fault for the disaster, it is still responsible for managing the crisis, especially for those affected by it. Natural disasters can also include the disaster that can affect every organization regardless of its location: fire. Fires cause tremendous destruction and severe interruptions to business operations when no one is injured, but when people are injured, the devastation is even greater. Managing natural disaster crises is different than managing loss of life and injury crises caused by obvious violence such as shootings. Natural disasters do not carry the extra importance of loss of life or injury combined with crime, except for arson; however, that information is unlikely to be available immediately after the

event like it is with violent crimes. Therefore, managing natural disasters removes one layer of issues relating to criminal conduct. However, because both deal with human trauma, they do have some similarities. Responding to the needs of the injured people and those affected by the fire, such as area residents and family and friends, must be the top priority of any organization facing this type of crisis. Imagine that your community college's director of security calls you at 10 P.M. with news of a fire in one of the new labs. In addition to dealing the actual fire, you now must assess the statements your organization will need to make and the actions it must take all in a matter of hours. You also know that the fire occurred during the last week of the semester when the lab is open longer so students can complete their projects. You have no idea yet what the human toll might be, if there is one. Therefore, with natural disaster crises, the wait for information makes managing it much more tedious and nerve-wracking than with other types of crises. You must be careful not to provide too much information because you cannot confirm what you can say without knowing fire and police officials' determinations. While the destruction to the new lab will affect your organization's ability to operate, the question of human losses makes business as usual quite irrelevant at the time. Nonetheless, at some point your organization must return to some sense of normalcy and resume operations, but for the hours following this type of crisis, it is secondary.

5. **Rumors and Accusations.** These types of crises are often the most frustrating because, for the most part, they are avoidable. Unlike true natural disasters, rumors begin with people, and public relations practitioners must be able to understand this influence so that they do not start rumors. While there is always going to be some part of the population that wants to start rumors or make false allegations for profit or fame, most non-malicious rumors are avoidable or at least manageable. Rumors often originate from fears—fear of the unknown. When employees feel that their jobs are in jeopardy, a natural reaction is to fear the worst-case scenario. When consumers believe that products they consume are poisonous, the natural reaction is to believe that every one of these products is deadly. These are natural reactions. However, these types of rumors are manageable and can be stopped before they turn into a widespread panic and crisis. Communication and candidness of information are a good starting point. Because rumors and allegations begin with some level of truth, even if it is very tenuous, people are likely to believe the fabricated parts even more if they are negatively affected by them. The earlier the rumor or allegation is addressed the better the outcomes will likely be for the long-term health of the organization. Imagine that your community college's reputation was being tarnished by rumors that its campus is unsafe. Stemming from a report of a sexual assault two weeks ago, on-campus murmurs and whispers about it have turned into a panic. As public relations

director, you know that the original incident turned out to be a false report, but that will never stop the fears on its own. You realize that you must inform, educate, and persuade your campus community, as well as the outside world, that your campus is safe. Through factual data presented in a persuasive manner, you can start to stem the tide of the rumors. In addition, you decide that your college will step up security presence and offer defense-training programs to help extinguish the last allegations that your college is unconcerned with safety. Rumors, whether person-to-person or online, can cause serious damage to an organization and its reputation. Just because a rumor or allegation is false, does not mean that it cannot inflict real damage. Perceptions stemming from rumors can easily become realities that the organization must deal with, and it is always easier to manage them before they gain momentum.

In addition to the categories of crises, there are also three different classifications of crisis based on the timing of them and their lasting consequences. The first are immediate crises that can occur without warning such as natural disasters and crimes. Because this type is unexpected, dealing with it successfully means preparing for it thoroughly. The immediacy and chaotic nature of these crises mandates that organizations prepare crisis plans well in advance and that they are practicing and updating them regularly. There is less time to develop messages, implement actions, and evaluate responses during immediate crises than during other types of crises, meaning that public relations practitioners are pushed to make split-second decisions that can have long-lasting effects. The second category is emerging crises that take time to develop and reveal themselves. Because they take time, they can be anticipated and dealt with more strategically than with immediate crises. Public opinion trends and poll numbers can illustrate emerging crises. For example, McDonald's crisis of confidence in its food quality and safety did not happen overnight. The health-conscious trends in American began in the late seventies and steadily grew over the next two decades. McDonald's was able to deal with and overcome these issues because it could strategically plan and test its responses. The major benefit of emerging crises for public relations efforts is time. The third classification of crises is sustained. Sustained crises linger and can last for years. They are often the most difficult type of crisis to overcome quickly because whatever issues are causing them cannot be overcome in a short time. For example, a major automobile manufacturer facing a decades-long decline in sales and increased overseas competition is not something easily overcome. However, by steadily and strategically dealing with the issues affecting the entire crisis, the company is able to manage the situation. The problem, of course, is that not all organizations facing sustained crises have the luxury of the time that it takes to deal with the problems. Moreover, sustained crises can take a toll on the organizational culture and morale of the company, which then creates additional problems and issues to overcome. Understanding which classification of crisis your organization is facing enables you to develop and implement policies and procedures to deal with them. Planning and anticipating crises well in advance of their arrival is the surest insurance against long-term devastation caused by them.

CRISIS PLANNING

The first step in planning for a crisis is anticipating and expecting it. Knowing the possible crises that can affect your organization is the best starting point to developing a sensible and logical crisis strategy and response. Often organizations find themselves in trouble when it comes to crisis response because they failed to anticipate them. It is important to keep vigilant and concentrate on those crises that will most severely affect the organization. For instance, an on-campus shooting is likely to be the worst-case scenario that could affect an educational institution. It is, however, by no means the only type of crisis that could occur. Therefore, it is important to prioritize your crises according to the damage they can cause your organization. Strategizing with outside agencies before a crisis hits is also a sound decision. Because most crises are out of the complete control of the organization facing them, it is important to have the outside entities that will likely be involved in the crisis included in the planning stages. Police, fire, and federal agencies are all examples of the types of outside organizations that should be included in any crisis plan. It is also important to consult with the organization's policies and procedures team and/or the company's legal team in advance of a crisis. Because decisions about which steps to take during and after a crisis depend greatly on existing rules, it is important to understand and follow them during the planning stages because it is unlikely that you will have the time to double-check them during the crisis. Media contacts are also very important to consider when strategizing a crisis plan because they are often the ones who dictate how the organization will appear to the outside world. Because the influence of the media is heightened even more during a crisis because the world's attention is on your organization, it is imperative to know whom to contact and where to contact them when it comes to proactively managing crisis media relations, which is often more difficult during a crisis than during periods of normalcy. The importance of internal publics and employees cannot be underestimated during a crisis. It is important to remember that where the organization goes, so do they. Therefore, they have a tremendous stake in the outcomes of any crisis. Nominating and training official spokespersons is critical to ensuring that your organization's statements and messages are consistent, clear, and correct when they must be delivered. The organization's response to a crisis in its initial statements and reactions to a crisis often dictate how the public will remember the organization's handling of the crisis. Because of this importance, media training and reducing redundancies and outright problems with organizational responses at the start is key to overcoming a crisis sooner than later. During a crisis, any employee can be seen as an official spokesperson for the organization. This can kill an organization's response plan. It is impossible for every employee to know exactly what is going on and what the organization is doing at every moment; they are therefore unqualified to speak on the organization's behalf. Employees must know that when a crisis hits, they are to direct questions, especially from the media, to the proper people—such as the public relations department. Credible spokespersons must be trained to handle hostile media professionals who are just fulfilling their jobs, but might appear vindictive to an organization that is undergoing a crisis. One of the worst mistakes a spokesperson can make is going off the record or stating "no comment" to a journalist's questions. Off-the-record statements can and do find their way onto the record—there is no guarantee that they will not. Furthermore, "no comment" connotes "we're guilty" to many people, and while it might seem like a safeguard against legal actions, it is certainly not going to work in the court of public opinion. Spokespersons must establish themselves as the experts on the subject at hand and create a sense of trust and openness for their statements to mean something. Failure to do so can result in confusion and chaos, and the organization can look incompetent and unprepared, which is the worst thing you want your organization to appear to be during a crisis when trust and reputations are on the line.

PLAN IMPLEMENTATION

Even the best-researched and perfectly sculpted plan offers no guarantee of success when managing a crisis because until a plan is put into effect, it is impossible to know for sure that it will work in the real world. Plans are precautions and preparations against the likely problems that can arise during an actual crisis, but it is impossible to plan for everything unless public relations practitioners can see into the future. To assure as much as possible that a plan is solid, it must be practiced and rehearsed to find where any potential problems or oversights exist. Of course, it is never possible to anticipate a crisis exactly the way it will happen in the real world, but initiating a plan into a practice scenario that is as close to real as possible gives the organization a better understanding of the crisis plan's strengths and weaknesses. Too often organizations will build involved and well-thought-out plans, but when the last word is completed, the plans are put on shelves and collect dust until the day they are needed. By then, the functionality of the plan is still an unknown, and the last place you want to find out a crisis plan's problems is when it is being implemented. It is good to think of plan implementation practice like that of a sports team. It must practice its plays, plan for the opposition's efforts, and strive to manage an upcoming game as if it is happening. The practice will never be 100 percent exactly how the game plays out in the real world, but it is a lot better than not practicing and then trying to wing it when everything is on the line. Once a plan does go into effect in a real crisis, it is imperative to continually monitor and assess its effectiveness. A great deal of redundant work and general headaches can be avoided if the plan is evaluated as the crisis unfolds. For instance, imagine that your community college public relations job just got a lot harder because the college president decided to go off script and say some ridiculous things that your organization now must address. Researching your crisis management efforts as the crisis happens enables you to make better choices about your reactions than simply going just by the book—in this case, the book is the crisis plan. For example, perhaps in your evaluation of the crisis you realize that the media really has not focused much on the statements. With this knowledge, you can determine the best next courses of action. Perhaps your crisis plan for such an incident stated that your college would seek greater opportunities to showcase its diversity training. However, because the media, and in turn, the public have not really spoken up about the incident, you realize that continually addressing the statements through actions such as showcasing your organization's diversity that you might make the problem worse. If the public is not outraged, then it is best to not focus on the statements, because in doing so, you might make more people aware of the statements than would if you remained silent. Researching the media's content and public opinion connected with your potential crisis might enable you to avoid a costly and embarrassing crisis recovery. Too often, evaluation happens at the end of a crisis, but solid crisis management dictated continuous measurement of the crisis as it unfolds.

PLAN EVALUATION

As mentioned previously, evaluation plays an important role in the actual implementation of a crisis plan, and is not something that should occur only as the crisis is winding down. Of course, the ultimate, big-picture evaluation of your plan and the success of your efforts is the lasting image of your organization following a crisis; however, because it can take years to ultimately decide if a plan worked, it is difficult to say when the evaluation stage is over. The fact is, it is never over completely because organizations must constantly monitor and assess their image connected with a crisis incident. Without continuous evaluation, determining the next phase of a crisis plan becomes nearly impossible. As you can see, the crisis planning cycle is cyclical rather than linear—there is no stop or start, it is an ongoing effort that really never ends. Solid crisis planning entails constant research and evaluation of not only the plan and its targeted outcomes, but also the public's perceptions of your organization's image and brand, which is constantly evolving and, hopefully, improving. If you do not know what the public is thinking, then it becomes very difficult to develop any plan, crisis or otherwise, that will likely achieve your goals and objectives.

The very nature of crises makes for confusion and high stress levels that can lead to mistakes. The key to crisis planning is minimizing this stress by being prepared. The following checklist offers some of the most important elements to have in any crisis plan.

1. **An Internal Notification System.** Remember that the internal publics and stakeholders must be knowledgeable and up to date with your organization's position during a crisis. They are the organization and the more informed these audiences are, the better the outside world will think of it. An organization in disarray will appear negligent even if its plan is perfect and followed to a tee. A system must be in place before crises hit that enable employees to know what it going on and, even more importantly, what their roles are in the plan. Even if their role is to remain silent and direct questions elsewhere, they must know it before a crisis occurs.

2. **An External Notification System.** Begin at home is a good rule of thumb when planning crisis communications. Of course, the external stakeholders come in a close second. Generally, the most important external stakeholder is the media because with their communication and influence capabilities, they can shape the opinions and perceptions of the other external publics. Statements, protocols, and media relationships play a large role in the external notification system. Today, an additional communication platform to be aware of is social and new media opportunities. People today look to an organization's online presence during a crisis, and will see direct communication from the organization via these platforms. The good part of this is that the organization can have complete control of what it says—it no longer is filtered entirely through the traditional media. However, a problem that can present itself with these new communication opportunities is the ability to say too much. News travels fast via social media, but it is not always completely accurate. A misstatement or poor word choice can come back to haunt an organization; sometimes less is more.

3. **Protective Measures.** Determining who in an organization will take the reins of a crisis is important know well in advance. Clearly, without this knowledge, it becomes quite difficult to train and practice spokespersons' procedures and statements. This step also includes the hands-on preparation work such as setting up command posts and communication centers that the media especially will rely on. Getting infrastructures in place means fewer issues to deal with when your plate is already very full. Stakeholder liaison assignments also come into play during the protective measures step. Any aspect of a plan where an organization's responsibilities and actions are necessary entails a protective measure: protection of the organization from the outside, as well as from itself.

4. **Evaluation Procedures.** Because constant measurement of monitoring is so crucial to crisis management, the people charged with this process must be prepared before a crisis happens. Furthermore, it is important to decide how evaluations will take place. Will they include public opinion polls, and if so, where will the data come from? What type of information does your organization need to know for it to make the best decisions based on your written plan? As the plan is implemented, it will likely change, and these changes are based on new data and information occurring in real time. Therefore, it is crucial to have these evaluation steps determined in advance of a crisis.

5. **Leadership Briefing.** The organization's spokesperson will usually be the leader of the organization, such as a CEO or president. Therefore, that person will be the public face of the company, and remember that the more you can turn your organization into a "person" during a crisis, the better its chances of surviving a crisis successfully. Therefore, it is necessary to determine when these important public appearances will occur and where they will take place. Will they include videos uploaded to your organization's website? Will they include only certain mainstream media outlets? Will they only be regionalized? Will the media be able to ask questions? These are important decisions to make—just as important as the statements that will make up these briefings.

6. **Spokesperson Preparation.** Because the greatest asset an organization can control during a crisis is its communication, spokesperson preparation and training is critical. This person or persons will be responsible for representing the organization to the world during an organization's direst times. Often consulting and appearing with the news media, spokespersons become the main liaison between the organization and the outside world. However, these important people also offer support and encouragement to the organization's most important asset: its employees. You can think of an organization's spokesperson like the president of the United States. During difficult times, he is responsible for pulling the country together, inspiring hope, and leading the nation to overcome whatever adversity it is facing. An organization's spokesperson performs a similar role, albeit on a lesser scale. Accordingly, these individuals must be trained to speak clearly, concisely, and correctly when they might be facing intense scrutiny by the media and public. There are finite opportunities to communicate statements while also conveying the right tone and emotion that your organization wants to elicit in its stakeholders.

7. **Media Management.** By now you realize the important role that the media plays in shaping public opinion. Because the traditional news media still maintains the

greatest amount of credibility when it comes to information about important events, the mainstream media must also be included in nearly every aspect of any organization's crisis preparations. If news media professionals are not included in the organization's communication plan, then they are left to their own devices. Important stories still need to be broadcast, printed, and aired regardless of whether the organization in question will cooperate. Hiding one's head in the sand will never go far in overcoming adversity. Working with the media rather than against it and continuously keeping them informed of the good and bad during a crisis is the best method of media relations. They have a job to do and will do it either with your help or without it. With your help, they can have accurate, timely, and important information straight from the source that is under the public's scrutiny. Without your help, they need to find "experts" on the subject who might in fact say the wrong thing, negatively influence the public, and hurt your organization's crisis recovery efforts. Accordingly, media relationships are among the most important stakeholder relations of all during a crisis.

8. **Maintaining Business Operations.** Just because an organization is going through a crisis does not mean that it can stop all of its normal operations and focus 100 percent of its efforts just on the crisis. All organizations must include a plan to maintain normal functions as much as possible even during a crisis. For example, imagine if Johnson & Johnson decided to stop production, marketing, and sales of all of its products so it could focus just on the Tylenol crisis. Even with its positive outcomes, the company might still not survive because the day-to-day functions that keep it running would have stopped. Even though trying times makes running a normally operating business difficult, it still must operate even at a lesser capacity. The world does not stop when a crisis hits. Organizations experiencing great crises still must make an effort to continue business for its employees and consumers, and to show the world that it can overcome these difficult times.

9. **Rehearse.** Any plan for the future is only as good as its outcomes in the real world. Until a crisis plan is implemented, it is never completely known how it might play out. Of course you do not want to find its greatest flaws when you most need it to be effective. Therefore, practice and rehearsing crisis plans is fundamental to ensuring that as much as possible, the plan is sound. You can think of a crisis plan rehearsal like a fire drill. The worst time to not know where to evacuate in case of a fire is during a fire. Drills, rehearsals, and practices help solidify the plan in an operational sense—they move the plan from a strategic idea to a functioning action. Moreover, they help solidify people's responsibilities and jobs during a crisis. It is one thing to say that the marketing department will be responsible for monitoring public opinion during a crisis, but another to have the marketing department know where to find

public opinion information and how to communicate it and then use it. Rehearsing a crisis plan is just as important as researching and developing it.

10. **Overall Evaluation.** Remember that constant monitoring and measuring of your crisis plan's effectiveness is critical at all stages of crisis. However, at some point it is necessary to evaluate its overall success, failure, or more likely, some combination of the two. Crisis management is never completely great or terrible. It is generally a mix of these two extremes, but at some point, the plan's worth and usefulness should show itself as generally positive or negative rather than polar opposites of wonderful or horrible. When planning a crisis response, it is useful to draw up a guide that gives an idea as to when the plan's overall merits can be determined. The problem with setting a definitive due date for evaluating a crisis plan is that you never know when it will subside. Crises generally never completely end because when dealing with public opinion, you never know for sure what their reaction might include. The public might forget for a while, but they never completely forget, nor is a crisis ever completely erased from history. Imagine if Tylenol was tampered with again, which did happen. The full story of the original crisis is revisited and rehashed by the media and the public is reminded of it as if it were happening now. Because of this phenomenon, putting an evaluation due date in stone is difficult. Trends, poll numbers, and media foci can offer some guidelines to tell you when an overall evaluation might be appropriate, but these times should be left somewhat flexible.

As you can see, there is a great deal that goes into successful crisis preparation because of the great importance of long-lasting effects that its handling can have on an organization. A positive response might result in greater sales, increased reputation, and even a stronger brand than before the crisis. Conversely, a poor handling of a crisis might mean vilification, embarrassment, and even bankruptcy for an organization. Because much of the responsibilities of researching, planning, implementing, and evaluation of crisis management falls to the public relations department, it really is one of the most important public relations functions. It can make or break an organization. The following five principles of crisis management provide a good overall understanding of crisis preparation and recovery.

PRINCIPLES OF CRISIS MANAGEMENT

Principle Number One: Do Not Avoid a Crisis. At some point even the most responsible and best-run organizations can find themselves involved in a crisis situation. More so today because of the explosion of mobile communication, crises can strike at any time and for nearly any reason—justified or not. Organizations can find themselves in deeper trouble by ignoring the telltale signs of a crisis such as increased media scrutiny, investigations from government agencies, or consumer criticisms. While no organization ever wants to experience a crisis, ducking these issues or pretending that they are not happening will never make them go away. Only by accepting, acknowledging, and in some ways, embracing them, can organizations expect to overcome problems. Additionally, by addressing small problems at their start, organizations might even avoid full-blown crises. If a small problem is allowed to fester and become a major issue, then managing it as a crisis can be much more difficult than if it were addressed when it began.

Principle Number Two: Take Responsibility. Social responsibility is an expectation today from all organizations. The public requires all organizations that operate in society act and function according to social standards. An organization facing a crisis must accept that overcoming its crisis is also its responsibility. Just because someone makes up a story online about your organization does not absolve your organization of the task of managing this falsified story because it may turn into a full-fledged issue that the masses might believe as fact. By not addressing it when you could have eliminated it, you condone it and make the fake story believable—after all, it must be true if the organization in question did not refute it. The responsibility for addressing issues, whether they are valid or not, falls to the organization. However, it is important to note that responsibility and blame are two different things. Every organization is responsible to manage and control its reputation and image. Not every organization is to blame for criticisms to its reputation and image. PepsiCo never put needles into its cans of soda; therefore it was not to blame for its crisis of trust. However, the company was responsible for clarifying the facts, communicating its position, and persuading the public that its products were safe. Therefore, it is an important distinction to make that even though your organization may not be to blame for its crisis, it is responsible to lessen the problem and improve its reputation. No one said that crisis management, or public relations for that matter, was fair.

Principle Number Three: Address All Issues. No crisis is composed of just one issue or problem. They are collections of multiple layers of issues—some of greater importance than others, but a mix nonetheless. As you recall, issues management requires public relations practitioners to identify the most pressing problems, situations, or even assets that an organization possesses to arrive at the best solution to a particular condition. Because crises inherently entail many levels of issues as well as a very diversified collection of problems, they are impossible to manage successfully by concentrating on only one or two issues. The main reason for this is that each issue will be interconnected with others and managing one requires managing them all. Think about the Tylenol poisoning crisis and the many issues surrounding that problem. You might think that the main issue with that crisis was the poisoning of the medicine; however, the act of poisoning and the associated deaths are the main problem, and not issues. The primary issue with that crisis was the loss of trust and faith in Johnson & Johnson products and the brand as a whole. If the main issue was just the poisoned pills, then the FBI's findings that it was an isolated incident coupled with the company's repacking and remanufacturing of the medicine should have logically solved the problem. However, just those two actions were not enough to persuade the public to buy Tylenol again and trust the Johnson & Johnson brand. To accomplish that main issue, the company needed multiple tactics and actions. Solving the problem is only part of the solution to overcoming issues connected with it. This is why crisis management is so difficult and complex.

Principle Number Four: Back Up Promises with Actions. During the early stages of a crisis, the public is more sympathetic to an organization's ability to correct a wrong or make a problem better. Logistics such as time and information might be available right away. However, eventually the public does expect to see some action from an organization that backs up what they said during the first phases of the crisis. Generally, part of every initial crisis response will include a vow to remedy whatever the circumstances were that caused the problem that is at the heart of the crisis. In fact, providing actions based on promises is another issue that the organization must address. Johnson & Johnson promised to protect its customers as best it could, and eventually supported that promise with new packaging. Lip service will pacify the public for only so long; eventually they expect and want action from an organization. The organization that makes statements assuring the public that action will take place and does not back its statements up will undergo great public mistrust that can cause the original crisis to pale in comparison to not keeping one's word.

Principle Number Five: Learn and Improve. Crises are emotionally and physically draining experiences for everyone involved, especially the public relations team. Because so much hard work and action goes into managing crises and maintaining public support, it is important to not let these dramatic experiences go to waste. Every problem offers a solution, every issue can be addressed, and every crisis offers lessons to make the organization better and stronger for the future. Some organizations learn these lessons the hard way, but they offer every student of public relations valuable information through case studies. If a solution to a crisis did not work, then be sure to understand why. Only by learning from mistakes as well as success can organizations expect to avoid and reduce future issues connected with a particular crisis. Theoretically, organizations should be able to avoid crises altogether if everyone in the organizations knows exactly what to do by learning from the past; however, in reality that is simply impossible. Therefore, when mistakes do happen, it is important to not only address them, but also gain something from them by turning problems into opportunities.

The preceding chapter highlights just some of the many facets of crisis communication. Public relations crisis communication and management entails a great deal of knowledge and understanding, but as its core are this chapter's main points. Future public relations practitioners can expect much more training and practice in crisis communication and management to fully appreciate this vast, yet critical area of public relations practice.

11 PUBLIC RELATIONS WRITING

No single skill is more valued and important to the practice of public relations than writing[78]. The very nature of public relations dictates that its focus on communication require practitioners to not only know the fundamentals of public relations writing, but also become very skilled in its use. Writing for public relations is unique and quite different than traditional English composition style. Because of its close association with media and journalism, its style closely mimics these disciplines. Usually, students new to public relations find its writing style somewhat daunting and frustrating because of its uniqueness and difference from traditional writing styles that students learned previously. However, when you understand its principles and practices, you can understand why it is so distinct from most traditional English composition writing styles. The primary description of public relations writing is that it is very strategic, to the point, and subtle yet persuasive. Therefore, mastering public relations writing is not something that people can master overnight. It takes years and much trial and error to perfect it. But at its heart is a style of communication that distinguishes public relations from its strategic communication counterparts of marketing and advertising.

THE UNIQUE STYLE OF PR WRITING

As you recall from the chapter on media relations, public relations practitioners must work with journalists and media professionals to get their messages into the media's outlets. Media professionals expect public relations professionals to write in a particular way, focus on specific topics, and present their materials according to the media outlet's protocols. Public relations practitioners who fail to do this also will likely fail to communicate their organization's points of view to the public via the traditional media, which again holds much more believability than direct communication like social media. Moreover, organizational leaders expect their public relations counterparts to be fluent and masterful in their communications to not only the media, but to all stakeholders. Therefore, the importance of sound public relations writing skills must not be underestimated. Some newer students to public relations may find the following lessons and principles on public relations writing to be antiquated. However, be sure that even though this style of writing has been around for decades, its fundamentals have remained the same regardless of the advent of radio, television, the Internet, and now social media. Regardless of what the future holds for communication media, public relations writing's core values will likely not change in the future. Therefore, the following chapter's content that outlines this critical skill will prepare you for the wide complexities of public relations writing, which at its heart, is the focus of all public relations practices and tactics. Even the best public relations strategists cannot succeed without someone to communicate their great ideas. Great public relations writers are the most valuable commodities in the entire field of public relations.

THE NEWS RELEASE

Undoubtedly the most important and most pervasive element of public relations writing is the **news release**. Sometimes referred to as a press release or media release, the news release is the first and foremost component to the public relation's practitioner's writing toolbox. Every competent public relations practitioner must be proficient in news-release writing. The first step to understanding and developing news releases is to remember the fundamentals to newsworthy stories. No newspaper, magazine, or even television station in the world will publish or air a story without a real, significant angle that will appeal to media outlets, and more importantly, its readers and viewers. In the media relations chapter, you were introduced to the newsworthy elements of a good story. Local significance, magnitude, and the unusualness of a story all make solid angles that can help attract media attention. Remember, you are writing your pieces for your media outlet's audience, not necessarily for your organization's consumers. Ideally, they will be the same, but you must attract them by writing for your media outlet's consumers, who will likely be much broader in terms of backgrounds and interests. Therefore, your stories will be a bit more universal in terms of content than an advertisement, which will be much more specialized and specific. Accordingly, your story's content cannot be too personalized in terms of interests, yet it also must be well crafted enough to maintain readers' and viewers' interests. The first step to accomplish gaining that interest is attracting attention immediately. The best way to do this is to compose an interesting and intriguing opening, known as the **lead**. The lead is the first sentence or two that gets your audience's attention at the start. If you lose your audience's interests at the start, then you have little chance of getting them to find out more about your story. For this reason, the lead is the most important component of any good news release, either for print or a broadcast version, known as a video news release. Most leads are short, concise, and to the point while still being interesting; not an easy task. A good rule of thumb is a lead between 25 and 40 words, which must encompass and explain the story's focus and get readers motivated to find out more. Essentially, a lead is the entire story focused into one sentence. You may think that it is odd that one sentence should tell the whole story. After all, why would readers want to read the entire story if they can get it all in the first sentence? While a good point, this is the style of writing that makes public relations writing and journalism unique and different than traditional composition. The lead hits the high points of the story and allows the rest of it to fill in the blanks with more detail and specifics. In a way, the five W's and H of journalism encompass the lead's content. The who, what, when, where, why, and how of a story provide a good starting point, but in reality, it is difficult to include all of these in element in fewer than 40 words while also making it readable. The main task is to pick and choose which elements should be included in the lead. For most stories, the who, what, and when and/or where should be included in the first sentence. Essentially, who did what, when or where was it done, and what is the big deal with it? This system also helps accomplish another important goal of public relations writing—maintaining active voice. Active voice composition makes your stories much more appealing because it focuses the action on the person or entity that did the action rather than the opposite. Remember that people like hearing about other people; therefore, focusing on the element that did something makes your lead better right away. A good equation to active writing is maintaining a sentence construction that includes: Who ... did what ... to whom ... and when. A good way to spot passive voice construction, which is the opposite of active, is to look for auxiliary verbs such as "has," "were," or "was." For example: One person *was killed* and four others *were injured* Sunday morning when their car, which *was traveling* west on Interstate 80, *hit* a concrete bridge pillar and *was engulfed* in flames. You can see the passive verb construction highlighted in italics, which indicate a poorly composed lead sentence. The same story and sentence can be rewritten to make the sentence active, and therefore, much more interesting and intriguing story. Here is a better version: A car traveling west on Interstate 80 *swerved* across two eastbound lanes, *slammed* into a concrete bridge pillar and *burst* into flames, *killing* one person and *injuring* four others Sunday morning. As you can see, the story remains the same, the elements are the same, and the focus of the sentence remains the same, but the composition of the sentence puts the attention on the entity that did the action, in this case the car. You are constantly trying to entice and elicit interest in your story to make readers want to find out more. Something to remember when it comes to readers is the 3-30-3 rule. It means you have three seconds to attract interest to your story, and if you can accomplish this, then the reader will spend another 30 seconds to find out more, and if this is done, then the reader will expend another three minutes to read the entire story. Obviously, you want to get readers to cover the entire story, and that's why the lead, the first three seconds, is so important. In addition to active writing, you want to appeal to readers' interests according to the story's main element that makes the story newsworthy.

LEAD ELEMENTS

Visualization

The following provides some tips and techniques to make your lead sentences as enticing and engaging as possible, all in an effort to turn three-second readers into three-minute readers. The first is to visualize the story. For example, the following story does a decent job at providing the most important information first, yet lacks the extra element of visualization: The council passed an ordinance that will affect all parents and teenagers living within the city limits. While okay, it does not really grab readers' attention. A better version adds that interest-provoking element: The council ignored the objections of the mayor and numerous parents, voting 6-1 Monday to enact a dusk-to-dawn curfew that keeps children off the streets. While a bit longer, it does a better job at creating intrigue and gets readers to find out more. Another example of a poorly written lead is: University officials moved one step closer to increasing tuition and fees for the upcoming school year, leaving students up in the air. This sentence does explain the main story and does offer some interesting elements, but lacks the most important information. If you were reading this lead, you are likely interested in the story's focus—the tuition increase. A more visualized lead sentence that fills in this blank is: The university's board of governors voted Tuesday to increase tuition and fees 10 percent next year to offset cuts in state funding. This sentence offers the "how much" factor and the "why" element that this type of story must include right away. Later in the story, the content can explain more about the tuition increase as well as provide some quotes from the people involved, but this lead offers the story's focus and gets readers to want to find out more.

Magnitude

Another technique to attract readers' interest in the lead is to focus on the "big deal" factor: essentially, the impact of the story on actual people. Remember that people want to read and find out more about other people; this technique does a good job at accomplishing this important goal. For example: The American Cancer Foundation reported that smoking will take more lives this year than previously expected. This lead does offer a bit of magnitude on the people involved. After all, the fact that the American Cancer Foundation expects fatalities to increase certainly encompasses the immensity of the story, but does not offer the extra element that gives real numbers and meaning. A better version is: The American Cancer Foundation reported today that secondhand cigarette smoke will cause an estimated 47,000 deaths and about 150,000 nonfatal heart attacks to U.S. nonsmokers. That's as much as 50 percent higher than previous estimates. While two sentences, this lead provides a better understanding of the big picture component of the story. Hard numbers like 197,000 combined lives mean much more than simply the term "more lives." This type of magnitude can shock readers into wanting to find out more about the story, and can help encourage them to read the rest of the story.

Localize

A third technique to entice interest in your leads is to focus on the area where the story takes place and where it will be published or aired. Most gatekeepers, like reporters and editors, want their content to focus on a particular area because people care about what happens near them. Proximity is a major element to newsworthiness. By localizing a story in its angle, you have a much better chance of your story being published over all of the hundreds of news releases that arrive at media outlets every day. For example, this sentence provides key information, but does not relate to any particular area, and therefore, does not make people care about the story: The FBI reported Tuesday that the number of violent crimes in the United States rose 8.3 percent during the last year. This sentence include the who, what, when, and even the "big deal" element in the percentage, but does not make readers in a particular area care as much as they could. A better version, which includes a specific area, gets readers to care about the story more because it is about their area: The number of violent crimes committed in Philadelphia rose 5.4 percent, compared to a national average of 8.3 percent, the FBI reported Tuesday.

As you can see, the same information is present, but it now includes a specific area. Clearly, if you were writing a news release for the FBI, you would want to tailor your stories to major metropolitan areas with personalized information for that particular area. If you were a Philadelphia resident, clearly you would be much more likely to read the second version than the first. Obviously, you would need to compose each story for the area that it is being sent to, but that is a small investment in time if it improves the chances of the story being published, which is after all the main objective to news-release writing.

From the lead, you then develop your story in descending order of importance. The end of the story is the least important in terms of what you want readers to remember about your story, which is why the lead is so critical to successful news-release writing. This type of construction is known as **Inverted Pyramid** writing. Imagine an upside-down triangle with the lead at the top and the rest of the story then fills in the rest of the triangle to its point at the bottom, the least important part of your story. This arrangement of a story is the hallmark of journalism in terms of writing solid news releases. A good point to remember when developing a news release story is to focus on a good lead at the start and then include a quote from the most important person in the story in the second paragraph. It should be noted that paragraphs in news releases could be just one or two sentences and not the traditional three to five sentences common to most composition styles. It is all about getting to the point as fast as possible and saying the most in the fewest words. A fundamental rule of public relations writing is "less is more." A second fundamental rule is to focus on your reader and not on yourself or your organization. Granted, you want to publicize and generate interest in your organization, but you do not want to turn your news release into an advertisement. In advertisements, you expect the company and its products to be glorified and that the ads emphasize only the positives. News releases, however, must be subtler than that. Nothing will turn off gatekeepers more than a news release that gushes about how great the organization is because it focuses on the organization and not on their most important audience—their readers and subscribers. Many of the problems that haunt public relations writing stem from varying priorities on the part of the organization and the media. Clearly, there must be some middle ground where both entities can gain what they need from the relationships between public relations practitioners and media professionals. In reality, both the media and public relations field provide each other with critical elements, because without them, neither could operate very well for long. Public relations practitioners cannot be the ones communicating every important piece of information to their stakeholders. It would be far too expensive, time consuming, and impractical, as well as ineffective. The media has the means to communicate public relations' work, but the work must adhere to certain guidelines. Moreover, the media cannot possibly research, write, and broadcast every piece of information important to its most critical stakeholders—their viewers and readers. The media needs public relations stories via news releases to fill their pages and airtime. Both parties need each other, but sometimes this working relationship becomes strained. The table below illustrates the two perspectives involved in media relations and public relations writing.

PR COMMUNICATION PERSPECTIVES

PUBLIC RELATIONS PERSPECTIVE	MEDIA PERSPECTIVE
The first concern for public relations is the image, reputation, and ability for its organization to succeed, often linked to the organization's financial stability.	The main concern for the media is gaining and keeping its audience's attention through subscriptions, circulation numbers, and in turn, high advertising rates so that media outlets can make the most money possible.
The purpose of public relations writing is to communicate the organization's point of view on important issues and improve its image in the process	The purpose of the media is generally to give its patrons (viewers, readers, and others) good content that will keep them coming back to a particular media outlet.
The primary stakeholder for public relations writers is the organization's key stakeholders on a given issue. Sometimes it will be employees, other times, consumers, but overall, it focuses on public opinion and perception.	The focus for the media is its audience and what attracts them to choose one media outlet over its competition. In turn, the higher the number of audience members, the more the outlet can charge for advertising and/or subscriptions.
The means to accomplish this process for public relations writers is to give its stakeholders information that they care about.	The function of building a strong, successful media outlet is to give the audience information they care about.

As you can see, despite the many differences in priorities between public relations writers and the media, the way to achieve success for both is in creating and disseminating useful, interesting, and meaningful information to specific audiences. Therefore, a working and mutually beneficial relationship between media professionals and public relations writers should be possible as long as each understands their role in the process. Like any solid relationship, each entity has a responsibility to adhere to for both sides to succeed. For public relations writers, it is critical to use this understanding to build bridges with the media and avoid the unnecessary pitfalls that can arise between the two groups. To do so, you must understand several elements to ensure that your writings' content aimed at your stakeholders is the same as the information the media's patrons care about; therefore, you must know:

1. **The Media Outlet's Patrons' Demographics and Psychographics.** While new technologies and communication tools like social media make our world a bit smaller, people think and behave differently from region to region. Los Angeles's population is not the same as New York's. Each group is different, and therefore a one-size-fits-all message

will likely not appeal to either group. To form successful, working relationships with media professionals, you must know what their patrons want, how they think, and what motivates them. All communication should be personalized as much as possible, and the media expects that what it receives from public relations writers will be tailored to their specific audiences.

2. **The Media Outlet's Reach.** No public relations writer in the world can expect every piece of writing to appear in his or her desired media outlet. There is only one *New York Times*, for instance, and getting stories into highly respected and widely circulated media outlets is difficult. However, not every story needs to be placed into such coveted news outlets. You must of course tailor your public relations writings' content to each audience, but you also must tailor the news outlet to match it. If you are trying to communicate to a group of farmers because your organization wants them to help you stop legislation that could harm your organization, then appealing to a New York audience via its major news outlets will probably not accomplish your goal. Clearly, you must find where your key audiences are, and then appeal to the media outlets in those locations written in a way that appeals to them. One-size-fits-all communication does not work in the material of your writing, but it does not work in the dissemination of it either.

3. **Determine the Needs of the Media Outlet.** Part of developing a solid partnership with a media outlet is to understand their ways of operating. While most media outlets such as newspapers operate in similar ways, no two are exactly alike. Deadlines, means of communication and sending materials, and the technical requirements of each are unique. Therefore, to ensure that your relationship with media gatekeepers like reporters and editors will be as successful as possible, it is necessary to know each one's procedures. Producing video news releases, for example, might be different for two television stations, depending on the software and applications they will use your materials for in their work.

4. **Know What the Media Outlet Considers News.** Just as each demographic and psychographic is unique to each media outlet, so too is its content. Clearly, for a media outlet to succeed it must appeal to its audience through content that attracts and maintains their interests. Therefore, any public relations writer hoping to appeal to a media outlet must know what it thinks is important. Part of public relations writing is researching each media outlet to gauge its content, style, and format. Reading the newspapers and magazines and watching the television stations in your targeted media outlet will help you develop content that matches what they want in their publications and broadcasts.

5. **Understand that the Media Expects Public Relations Content on Their Terms.** The media are in control of what is published or airs on their outlets; therefore, they expect that any material they receive from public relations practitioners will be perfect in content and style. Understanding the audience helps determine content, but it is the style of writing that must also be correct. Most media outlets use Associated Press Style, and all public relations practitioners worth their weight have an Associated Press Stylebook or AP Stylebook on their desk or an online subscription to it. AP Style is unique, and may even seem odd at first, but the more use it gets, the more ingrained it becomes in your writing style. For example, according to AP Style, numbers from zero to nine are always written out as words, and numbers above 10 use figures. These are the types of rules that public relations writers must adhere to because one mistake in the style of your writing can lead to the entire news release being trashed—not because of the content, but because you did not follow the AP Style rules.

6. **Realize that the Importance of Your Content will Determine its Format.** Most news releases will fall into one of two categories: hard news or soft news. Hard news is characterized by its magnitude and immediacy of importance. Most crisis situations would certainly fall into the hard news category. Timeliness plays an integral role in hard news because its content must be communicated immediately. Generally, media alerts as opposed to news releases are used when hard news information needs to be disseminated. News releases often lack the ability to communicate important information immediately because they are usually received by media professionals in bulk. In other words, a reporter's inbox might be filled with many news releases and his or her ability to get to the most important one right away is impeded. Instead, news releases are better suited to information that is not as time constrained, or soft news. Stories on expansion projects, awards, civic engagement, and organizational change will likely find their way into news releases. These stories are not as dependent on immediacy, but rather, they can wait and be aired or printed later, whereas a hard news story will likely need to be disseminated that day. The delivery system you choose for your public relations writing can be just as important as the content in it.

7. **Remember that Success in Public Relations Writing is Dependent on Research.** Like all things public relations, writing begins with research. Knowing the focus of your content, its style, the media outlet to send it to, directing it to the right person at that outlet, and determining the best means of delivery are all aspects that must be planned well in advance. Research always enables you to be more assured that your end goal will be as successful as possible. Knowing what you are doing, why you are doing it, and how to do it allows you to make informed decisions and take deliberate actions. In addition, hitting the send button on your news release does not mean that

you are done with the writing process. Part of sound and successful public relations writing is evaluating its success. Was it published or aired? Did the content capture what you wanted it to? Will it motivate your stakeholders to do something? These are all aspects that must be addressed. In addition, most organizational leaders expect to see your success in real terms. Composing the perfect news release means nothing if it is not used. Even the media's use of your content means little if it does not lead to some measurable result including improved sales, better image, or more respect for your brand. Public relations writing is just as much as about validation of itself as it is the composition of itself. This is an aspect of public relations writing that separates itself from its close cousin, journalism.

Public relations writing and journalism clearly share many characteristics such as newsworthiness and AP Style. However, there are some important differences between the two. Understanding these aspects will enable aspiring public relations writers to realize their roles for both their organization's and the media's needs.

DIFFERENCES BETWEEN PUBLIC RELATIONS WRITING AND JOURNALISM

PUBLIC RELATIONS WRITING	JOURNALISM
1. More Focused on a Direct Outcome. Public relations writing must be focused on creating a meaningful result such as more revenue or improved reputation. Public relations writing does not exist simply to inform, it must also elicit some outcome from its intended audience.	**1. Follows the Facts of a Story.** Journalism is rooted in facts and reality and does not have a predetermined outcome. The audience's reaction to journalistic stories depends on what happens in the world, not on how it is created in the story. Journalism is supposed to be about facts and letting the story tells itself, so it does not have an agenda or a predetermined outcome—it goes where the story and the facts take it.
2. Centered on the Organization. Because public relations writing is outcome centered, it must be focused on the organization's wellbeing. No public relations writer would compose a story that does not include his or her organization or does not intend to improve its image. Public relations writing is about the organization and why the public should understand it, sympathize with it, forgive it, or support it—usually a combination of these.	**2. No Presumed Focus.** At its heart, news is unknown and unpredictable. Anything can happen at any time, and journalism is centered on the task of reporting on anything newsworthy. Therefore, it is difficult to say that any one media outlet will focus entirely on one story for any other reason than its newsworthiness. As soon as this is gone, the interest weans and another focus takes it place. News is finite and ever changing.

3. Subjective in Nature.

Since public relations writing is focused on an organization and its benefits, it clearly takes on a subjective tone. It is difficult to imagine any situation where an organization's public relations writer could compose a story that criticizes and attacks his or her own organization. The focus of public relations writing is on the good and positive of the organization, and when it is facing criticism, it takes on a rehabilitative tone to help the organization, not make the situation worse.

3. Objective in Nature.

Journalism is about being unbiased and determined only by facts and reality. Therefore, its focus is objective and does not seek to benefit any one organization over another. Theoretically, news media outlets do not have a stake in the success of one organization or the destruction of another. Even though most large organizations are owned by or are part of major news media conglomerates, the standards of professional journalism mandate a separation from their success, and therefore, objectivity in its reporting.

4. Concise and to the Point.

Because public relations writing is in competition with other public relations writing, it must be succinct and clear in its content. Moreover, media professionals expect public relations writing to say a lot in as few words as possible. Public relations writers pride themselves on their ability to say in ten words what others need twenty to do. Brief yet thorough are the objectives to public relations writing.

4. Can Elaborate More.

Journalists obviously work for the media outlets that have the power over their outlets' content. Therefore, because they control what goes into their publications and onto their airways, they can take as much space and time as they choose to say whatever they want. Journalists have much more freedom when it comes to the length and complexity of their writings than public relations writers do for the simple fact that they control their content.

5. Sells Self-Focused Points of View.

Public relations writers are charged with a challenge to compose stories that will appeal to the masses yet still sell their organization's image. While public relations writing must be convincing and persuasive, it cannot be obvious that it is. Subtlety in its focus on the organization is the goal of public relations writings' content.

5. Unbiased and Unswaying.

The ideals of journalism dictate that what it covers and how it reports must be accurate, impartial, and fair. No journalist should be able to be manipulated or swayed to report on any story other than in an accurate and balanced fashion. The public expects what it receives from the news media to be impartial and neutral, which can make getting public relations content into it more difficult.

6. More Focused.

The content in public relations writing will target a specific group or stakeholders because it intends to influence a specific audience. Generally, public relations writers do not set out to persuade the entire world because for one, the world probably does not care, and two, because it would be impractical. Public relations treats each audience differently and the one-size-fits-all style of communication will never work well. Public relations writers must home in on a specific group and communicate differently and directly to them.

6. Broader in Scope.

Even though most news outlets cater to a specific audience in terms of location or interests, these groups can still be composed of millions of people. Media outlets make money by appealing to the largest group of people they can, so despite the fact that they are often regionalized, they still serve vast numbers of people. Moreover, today's focus on 24-hour news stations and online content makes these audiences even larger than they were just a few years ago.

7. Generally Anonymously Written.

Public relations writers exist to enhance their organization's image, not their own. Stories published based on news releases will never have the public relation's writer's name in the byline. Instead, the journalists will use the news release's information and compose a story and that person's name will appear in print. Usually, the only time a person from an organization's public relations writing will appear in the news media as a byline or author is when it includes an important figure. For instance, if a public relations practitioner composed an op-ed for her CEO, the CEO's name would appear as the author.

7. Bylined.

Most new organizations are only as good as their journalists. The more famous and well respected the journalists, the better the image of the news outlet. Therefore, media outlets depend on their best journalists and will always want to publicize them. Journalists' main jobs are to research, focus, and present to their audiences complex stories in an easy-to-understand manner. News writers will use the content given to them by their public relations writing counterparts, but the names that will appear in print as the authors will undoubtedly be the journalists'. That is the nature of the news media–public relations relationship.

8. Content May Be Newsworthy.

The final determinant to public relations writings' newsworthiness rests with the media gatekeepers. Until they approve it for publication or broadcast, its overall value is very low. For this reason, public relations writers must adhere to and comply with the news media's demands in terms of quality, style, and usefulness to their audiences.

8. Content Is Newsworthy.

The act of publication or airing of a story inherently makes it newsworthy. The media control its content, and what it says is important, makes it important to themselves. Because they are the final determinants to the newsworthiness of any story, their content dictates what is noteworthy and important to their audiences. For this reason, public relations writers must research news outlets' content and match it to be included.

9. Includes Exclusive Information.

While it seems that the media controls much of the relationship between journalists and public relations writers, public relations does have one advantage—exclusivity. Organizations and companies can control access to themselves and what they say to the media; therefore, the media needs public relations because it offers content and quality of information. Even the most respected journalist in the world must go through the public relations department if he wants to interview a top CEO or president. Public relations does hold some power in the media relationship.

9. Dependent on Outside Information.

If you look at the content of any newspaper, you will notice that much of it comes from sources other than what its writers offer. In fact, most of the content in the news media can be traced back to some public relations work. Reporters cannot be everywhere and report on everything so they need public relations writing to supplement their work and fill the spaces. Remember, the news media professionals need public relations practitioners. While a great deal of competition from other public relations practitioners exists, distinguishing yourself from them enables you to gain greater access to the media for your organization.

10. Most Content Comes from Few Sources Within the Organization.

In addition to the exclusivity of your content, public relations writing usually starts with a few sources from an organization. Generally, if a new product is being introduced, then the developers and perhaps the company leaders will be included in the story. However, most public relations writing is simple in terms of the number of sources in it because its content cannot be too complex or too long. Simple and to-the-point stories preclude public relations writers from expounding too much on their stories.

10. Includes Many External Sources.

For the most part, news writing tries to encompass many points of view from multiple sources to present as balanced and full a picture of the story as possible. Therefore, the complexity of journalism is much greater than public relations writing. News writing exists to explain the depth of a story to many people; public relations writing exists to introduce a story to the media that they will deem as important. From this introduction, journalists then seek out more information to fill in the gaps left in the public relations story.

11. Content is Reviewed by the Source.
The information included in public relations writing should always be checked and double-checked for accuracy and to ensure that what it stated will be interpreted correctly. Word usage, connotations, titles, and dates are all important elements that should be reviewed by the sources included in the content.

11. Content Is Not Reviewed by Its Sources.
The impartial and unflappable nature of journalism restricts itself from being manipulated by the people included in its content. For this reason, journalists are unlikely to allow their sources to review the stories before they are published. It is the responsibility of the journalism to get the facts right and present it accurately and fairly. Enabling the people in the story to read it first is impractical, but also affects the untouchable nature of the news media that the public expects of it.

Despite the differences between journalists and public relations writers, it is the responsibility of public relations practitioners to maintain positive, professional relationships with the media. This task is accomplished easiest by helping journalists and gatekeepers do their jobs, but not necessarily doing it for them. A mutually beneficial relationship with the media entails a give-and-take mentality. You must give them the stories they want on their terms, and in exchange, they include your organization's points of view in their media outlets. The added credibility and trust that comes from mainstream, traditional media makes these efforts worthwhile.

Even though news releases gain the most attention and notoriety concerning public relations writing, it is by no means the only type. Many different forms of public relations writing help practitioners focus their attentions and strategies in a variety of ways. Each type of public relations writing has its own purpose, and collectively, they enable practitioners to communicate more effectively and efficiently with their key stakeholder groups. The following describe some of the elements.

PR WRITING COMPONENTS

1. **Letter to the Editor.** Sometimes known as an LTE, these compositions enable organizations to take a stand against criticism from the media itself, politicians, or even the public. They address issues, usually complex ones, which affect your organization in some way. Often, they address or redress media "opinions" about these issues. Because of the media's influence on public opinion, addressing the media's negative opinion about your organization allows you to have a voice and stand up for your organization's reputation. Issues such as consumer relations problems, political misdealing, or employee abuses are examples of the types of problems that letters to the editor should be written to address. Remember that your statements must be based on fact—you are trying to clarify incorrect or misunderstood information. If the criticism is warranted and real, then a letter to the editor is of no real use. They are often written backward, starting with your position, and then backing it up with facts as it builds momentum. Newspapers include a special section just for letters from

leading experts and those who have special qualifications to speak on important subjects affecting society. Because of this stipulation, the organization's leader such as the president and/or the CEO would likely pen a company's letter to the editor. Occasionally, the public relations personnel ghostwrite these letters because they generally have a better mastery of letter writing, as well as greater knowledge about how to compose an informative, persuasive statement. Remember, that "opinion makers" are your audience because they affect general public opinion. While anyone can read the letters to the editor, they are often directed at a particular group or someone who has unfairly attacked an organization or made misleading statements about it that hurt the organization's reputation with the general public. It is important to be realistic and sensible about your publication options. Obviously, the more influential the publication, the more difficult it will be to get your letter published. Competition for this valuable space is great, and only those letters from key individuals on important issues that are well crafted will be published.

2. **Press or Case Statement.** In some ways press or case statements are similar to letters to the editor in that they both address an issue or problem affecting an organization. However, unlike a letter to the editor, press statements are made available to multiple media outlets at once. The purpose of a press statement is to enable the media to get information about an issue affecting an organization quickly and easily. When a problem arises, it is often too late to send a media release because the information is already well known—in other words, it is no longer breaking news. During these times organizations can become hectic and frantic in their operations, and the press statement allows the organization to make its position and feelings known to the media in an efficient manner. They often begin with an impact statement, which is a single sentence that states what the organization faces. For example: *Gatorade faces a loss of business and customer confidence because of recent reports of brominated vegetable oil.* The next section includes a description (historical, chronological, logical, cause-effect, etc.) of events or facts contributing to the issue. Include some of the following elements: motivation for behavior, environmental influences, intentional or accidental communication, resources expended/available, channels used/available, key players, or organizations. Then, list and prioritize the internal/external/intervening audiences or the communication situation affecting the situation. Address potential target audiences and desired effects you want to accomplish through your communication plan. Remember, PR deals with the understanding, feelings, and actions of the public. It is also important to list management's objectives for your stakeholder groups because, ultimately, you want to provide management with a means to address a problem. Remember to consider what your audience can and will remember and how much you can realistically persuade them. These types of communications are there to offer

your organization's stance on an issue, not necessarily a solution to a problem. You simply want to clear the air and get your organization's point of view available to the media, and in turn, to the public.

3. **Counseling Papers.** One of the primary responsibilities of public relations is counseling the organization's leadership on the appropriate steps to take when dealing with a problem affecting the organization's reputation. Counseling papers enable public relations writers to succinctly and clearly outline the problem and offer suggestions that organizational leaders should take to remedy the situation. The first section identifies the entities or individuals involved and outlines what the problem and/or the challenge is facing the organization. For example, if you were the public relations counselor for collegepapers.com, a possible problem statement is *Collegepapers.com is criticized for providing an academically unethical service to that allows students to buy term papers online and pass them off as their own.* The second section identifies the specific issues involved in the problem as well as the publics affected. Example: *Colleges across the country are calling for collegepapers.com to be disbanded and legally responsible for those students who used the service and were dismissed from the colleges for cheating.* The third sections outlines how an effective decision can be made to address the problem that also identifies those involved in making these decisions. For example: *The organization's public relations department must devise an informative campaign that identifies collegepapers.com as a research-only website, which offers students resources to help them prepare better term papers; it is not a service that writes them for students.* The fourth section offers a variety of solutions and the pros and cons of each so that organizational leaders know their options when making their decisions. Example: *Collegepapers.com can cease operations; change its image to a research-only company; sell itself to competitors; fight to maintain its current operations.* The final section outlines the preferred solution to the problem in hopes of convincing leadership to make the best choice for the organization. For example: *Collegepapers.com should rebrand itself as an educational resource that helps students succeed in college. By outlining the problem, identifying its underlining issues, offering a variety of options, and then emphasizing the best solution, organizational leaders can make better decisions for the organization and its future.*

4. **Media Alerts.** As the name suggests, these alerts are sent to media professional to inform of some important news concerning your organization. Unlike news releases, they are quite short and succinct in naming the who, what, when, where, why, and how of your information without a well-formed composition or story. They simply signal to the media that your organization is undertaking some noteworthy action or campaign that will be of interest to their readers and viewers. They are followed up

on with more information as it becomes available. Essentially, they act as the first line of communication about some newsworthy action taken by the organization between the public relations department and the newsroom.

5. **Pitch Letter.** These invitations to the media ask journalists to either interview a key member of your organization about some important issue or simply attend an event that you are hosting. Like all media correspondence, pitch letters need to note why your request will be worthwhile to the media outlet—what is the big deal about it? They are often short and include necessary information for the media professional to make an informed decision to cover your organization and the logistical details about how to proceed in covering your story.

6. **Brochures.** Common to many organizations, they outline the background and note-worthy elements about your organization to a targeted audience. Usually including histories, important accomplishments, and overall, the "big deal" about your organiza-tion, these colorful and easy-to-read pamphlets provide the highlights of organiza-tion. In addition, they often emphasize why the person who is reading it should want to support the organization in some way. Therefore, brochures offer facts and figures, but also persuade people to support, or at least remember your organization.

7. **Newsletters.** A staple of employee communication, newsletters offer a mini newspaper- or magazine-style format about your organization to an audience that is somehow connected to it. For example, clubs, affiliations, donors, or professional societies might be interested in a newsletter about your organization if they have a link to it. Content is usually light and of a general interest. Stories might include biographies of people in your organization, recent accomplishments or milestones, and upcoming events. Filled with pictures and visual interest, a common practice is also to include readers in the newsletter in some way. Recipients' recent achievements, such as raising money or donating time for a worthy cause, often lead newsletter readers to want to read more. Remember, people like to read about other people, and if it is about them, they really want to read it and share it.

8. **Fact Sheets.** These one-page, often bulleted lists of important information about your organization offer readers (usually the media) a quick reference guide to your organi-zation. They are valuable tools for media professionals who need information quickly so they can accurately give background information about your organization to their readers. Remember that the average media consumer who might read a newspaper or watch the evening news probably does not know many details about your organiza-tion. Therefore, journalists need to add this information to their stories to make them

complete and more understandable. Fact sheets enable them to do so. Fact sheets, like all public relations information, must be updated regularly to ensure that they are current and accurate.

9. **Media Guides.** Similar to fact sheets, but much more exhaustive in their details, media guides are the quintessential go-to book for journalists who need very detailed and, sometimes, past facts about your organization. Often popular with sports teams, these guides provide sports journalists with statistics, player backgrounds, and team histories so they can write a complete story if it warrants these types of facts. Like fact sheets, media guides exist to make the media professional's job easier. If they are going to include your organization in their media channel, then the least you are expected to do is enable them to do so easily. Media guides generally come out once a year, whereas fact sheets can be updated more regularly. Media guides are almanacs about the organization.

10. **Backgrounders.** Nearly all public relations writing caters to the media, and backgrounders are no different. Like fact sheets and media guides, backgrounders provide valuable information for journalists on issues relating to your organization. However, backgrounders are slightly more focused on one of two main categories. One is about a problem or situation that your organization is involved in. This type of backgrounder would outline the situation according to your organization's point of view and describe how it was or will be solved. In many ways, backgrounders of this nature are similar to media alerts in that they both offer an organization's stance on a problem or issue. However, backgrounders are more detailed and thoroughly composed. Therefore, backgrounders often come after media alerts about problematic situations as follow-up information. The second type of backgrounder is one that focuses on a product or service and describes how it began and where it is today. Imagine a backgrounder on the iPhone. It would begin with its development and inception and follow its evolution to its current model, and perhaps give insights into its next generation. Backgrounders are valuable sources of information for the media and enable public relations practitioners to describe and detail a situation or product to better ensure it receives media coverage.

11. **Public Service Announcement.** Also known as PSAs, these types of communications are often the domain of non-profit organizations or the charitable arm of a for-profit company. Because of their altruistic nature, media outlets will air them for free; however, they must adhere to certain guidelines to qualify. First, they must clearly exist for the public's good. Imagine an anti-drunken-driving organization that offers a PSA around graduation time that warns of the dangers of intoxicated driving. This type of message would be for the good of the public, and therefore qualify. Second, the PSA must not

blatantly publicize or advertise an organization or product for its good—remember it must be for the public's good. A PSA about drunken driving that offers a discount on home breathalyzers would be too commercially driven and would likely not qualify for free airing as a PSA. When done well though, PSAs further an organization's image and advocate its message as long as it helps people without selling them something.

12. **Biographies.** As you can guess, biographies provide details and insights into the backgrounds of important figures within your organization. For example, CEOs, presidents, notable figures, and important developers might all be subjects for public relations biographies. They must be accurate and avoid gushing about how great the person is to ensure that journalists do not turn a skeptical eye toward them. They also must be updated and regularly checked for accuracy and relevancy. Media professionals use them as another tool to help compose complete and accurate stories for the public.

13. **Media Kits.** The combinations of many types of public relations writing offer a comprehensive and very detailed portfolio about an organization. Media kits are generally used to offer media professionals a complete package of different kinds of writings in one place. Items often include past news releases, backgrounders, newsletters, biographies, fact sheets, and even brochures. Essentially, you can think of media kits as an organization's scrapbooks. Often given to media gatekeepers before press conferences or events, they provide another means to understand and even appreciate what an organization offers. Additionally, they are often well crafted and professionally designed to highlight an organization's importance and to convince journalists of its quality.

Public relations writing is all about accuracy, relevancy, and appealing to the media's demands in the way they expect stories to be written and delivered. The best public relations practitioners inevitably are also the best public relations writers. Few skills are more important and valued in the field than knowing not just how to write, but also what to write. Despite the advancing technologies and media that seem like they would move public relations writers away from some of the traditional forms of writing, the inherent qualities and criteria for excellent public relations writing will always remain.

EXAMPLE OF A NEWS RELEASE

The following news release illustrates the main points that all good stories must have: a meaningful subject, public appeal, a focus on people, good quotable material, and correct formatting. You will notice the organization's name at the top followed by the date, contact information, and when the information in the release can be used by the media, which in this case is immediately. The story begins with the dateline, which is the location where the story took place. It is followed by the lead that highlights the main story and adds interest to it—what is the big deal?—It is the fact that the Christmas party is months later. The story then progresses to explain the organization and publicize it while offering a story that the public in the area (southern New Jersey) would be interested in. It also includes many people and quotes from them. Remember, the public likes to read about people, and including them is critical for new release success—publication. At the end you will notice the boilerplate that summarizes and provides a biography on the organization. This information would not be used as it looks in the news release; rather, it exists to help the journalist who receives this news release compose a complete story so that any reader can understand the organization in question. The last component is -30-, which is an old printmaker's mark that indicates that the story has ended. Sometimes it is noted as "XXX" as well.

Emmanuel Cancer Foundation: Woodbury, New Jersey

March 29, 2004   Contact: Annamary Kavanaugh
                                  Southern Regional Director
                                  (xxx) xxx-xxxx
                                  children@emmanualcancer.org

                                  Contact: Joe Harasta
                                  Public Relations Consultant
For Immediate Release   (xxx) xxx-xxxx

Belated Christmas Party Brings Joy to Kids with Cancer

Woodbury Heights—Daffodils and dogwood trees may have been blooming outside, but inside the gym at St. Margaret's Regional School, poinsettias and Christmas trees took center stage as the Emmanuel Cancer Foundation's belated Christmas party brought holiday cheer to kids with cancer on Saturday.

Annamary Kavanaugh, southern regional director for the Emmanuel Cancer Foundation, said she had to cancel the first party, originally scheduled for last December because of a winter storm, but was not about to let a few spring showers dampen the fun this time.

"I saw the rain this morning and thought good heavens, we had to cancel because of the snow in December but and now we have the rain. We were disappointed we had to cancel, but having it in March shows the kids we remember and love them," said Kavanaugh.

All of the children, including 9-year-old Fallon Fleming, have been eagerly awaiting the party since its postponement four months ago. "I was disappointed before, but just being here is the best thing. I'm excited to see my old friends," said Fallon. Fallon's mother, Maggie Fleming, credits the foundation for helping her through her daughter's illness.

"My daughter was diagnosed with cancer six years ago and the organization found a family to sponsor us for Christmas—they had Christmas in a bag. The volunteers are a godsend," said Fleming.

Steve Wooton, a long-time volunteer and this year's Santa from the Independent Order of Odd Fellows' Richwood Lodge, which catered the party, said the best part of helping is the look of happiness in the kids' eyes. "We've been helping for about seven years. It's great we can support an organization like this that helps these kids," said Wooton.

Ray Solecki of the Retired Senior Volunteer Program added, "Seeing the children really touches your heart. You see the kids with no hair from chemo, but they're always cheerful and happy to see you."

Fellow volunteer and father of three Ted Whitney added that he feels for the parents who go through the trauma of finding out their son or daughter has cancer. "My mom had breast cancer so my heart goes out to the kids and their families," said Whitney. Many volunteers echo Whitney's words. Volunteer Peggy Kirsch of Pedricktown added, "I've experienced a sibling with cancer. It's near and dear to my heart because I'm a five-year cancer survivor."

Mother of one of about 20 children at the party, Evenlyn Perez of Vineland said when she found out about her 12-year-old son Robert's cancer her world fell apart, but the foundation's volunteers helped her through it. "My car was stolen at the same time I found about my son's cancer and they helped me with bills and food. They couldn't have come at a better time," said Perez.

Jodi Heller, a 24-year-old volunteer from Winslow High School's Leo Club, a teenage version of the Lions Club, said events like these remind you of why you want to help. Heller said, "A lot of us have been affected by cancer, and you really want to help the kids. These events are great because you can interact with the kids, and see you're making a difference in their lives."

Experiencing the pain of despair of their own son's cancer, Susan and Joseph Vizzoni established the Emmanuel Cancer Foundation in 1980, naming it in memory of their 7-year-old son Emmanuel.

ECF was founded to provide New Jersey families with a comprehensive package of in-home individual and family counseling, emotional support, bereavement counseling, and advocacy. Professional caseworkers are available 24 hours a day. All services are provided free of charge. The foundation is a tax-exempt 501©(3) organization privately funded by individuals, corporations, foundations, and community groups[79]. The South Region Branch, located at 1301 North Broad Street, Woodbury NJ 08096, encompasses seven South Jersey counties including Camden, Gloucester, and Burlington counties.

12 GOVERNMENT RELATIONS

While most public relations work revolves around improving an organization's image for key stakeholders like consumers and the media, the government is often overlooked. While it might not be the most critical public that influences an organization's future like customers or the media, it can and does impact every organization's operations. Government agencies from local, state, and federal levels influence and enact legislation that controls organizations' business operations every day. In addition, government leaders impact public opinion about organizations as well. Remember, leaders like mayors, governors, congresspersons, and the president have tremendous followings and as they believe, so too do their supporters. Therefore, if they disparage and disagree with your organization and its operations, then it is likely that their supporters will feel the same way. Just as the media influences public opinion, so too does the government. For these reasons, it is critical to include the government on the list of key stakeholders that public relations work must manage. In this chapter, you will see the different ways that government public relations operates and how to deal with government leaders and legislation for the betterment of your organization. In addition, efforts to improve government leaders will be discussed so you can see the various forms of government-centered public relations, both from the government's side as well as from private organizations.

THE GOVERNMENT'S PERSPECTIVE

The government itself has its own public relations efforts that operate every day to improve its image. Whether it is the senate, White House, or even individual agencies like the IRS or the department of motor vehicles, they all must maintain their own positive image from their consumers—the taxpaying public. While these agencies might not be as dependent on the success of consumer relations as a private organization is, they still need to maintain a positive image to operate well. Public perception about all levels of government service is often reflected by the public's opinion of leadership. Public perception of leaders is often illustrated in their opinions of the services provided by or under these leaders. For many citizens, a highway construction effort that seems to take too long and forces inconveniences for commuters is the fault of the governor or mayor where the construction is taking place. For this reason, the government must maintain a level of communication and candidness for the agency's good, but even more importantly, for the good of the leaders who must maintain a positive image to be reelected. Even the services of schools and school districts can fall under the domain of public relations because it too must appeal and cater to the people (students and their parents) who patronize the school as well as those who support it (taxpayers). Failure to keep these organizations' images up to the expectations of the public can lead to outcry, protest, and calls for change. Currently, in Philadelphia, the city's public schools are facing deficits of over $100 million. The city's school superintendent, mayor, and even the governor all face the daily protests and constant criticisms of that city's residents. No doubt that during the reelection bids of the governor and mayor their opponents will use this situation to denigrate and destroy the image and reputation of these individuals. Political campaign fodder often comes from indecision and inaction of government public relations practitioners. Worse yet, often the negativity associated with poor public opinion for the government is often out of many agencies' control. Lack of funding and increased regulations often force them to make decisions that will negatively affect public opinion, yet must be made anyway. Therefore, the job of the government public relations practitioner is not an easy one even though the future of their agencies might not be as perilous as that of a private company. After all, it is unlikely that the IRS will go out of business if the public does not like it. However, these agencies still must maintain some level of positive public opinion because its consumers fund these agencies through tax dollars. Therefore, these agencies operate more similarly to private entities than you might think. In many ways, the people who file their taxes with the IRS, take out student loans from federal sources, and pay vehicle registrations to the DMV can be seen as government consumers just as account holders at department stores like Macy's are some of its consumers. In this way the government is responsible for maintaining its image and its services to those who support and who can affect it.

PUBLIC AFFAIRS

Partly because of the public's ignorance on what public relations really is—many believe its part huckster and part hack that exists to bamboozle people into believing anything—government public relations often is not called public relations. Instead, the term "**public affairs**" is used to describe the same responsibilities and tasks that any public relations practitioner would do. In many ways, the term "public affairs" or "public affairs officer" is as much a public relations effort as any. It renames and repackages the term "public relations" in a way that makes the public feel better about it and what it does. The responsibilities of the public affairs officer are quite similar to a private company's; however, because of the unique nature of the government, it operates slightly differently. Because the government and its agencies are non-profit, it is not as reliant on customer satisfaction and providing newer, better, and more modern services to its consumers. The United States Post Office, for example, had operated the same way for many decades. Because of this, and the dwindling revenues it was providing, additional new services like online package tracking, flat-rate shipping, and more "hip" postage stamps that replaced presidents with rock stars all helped its image with the public. These efforts entail the kinds of public relations work that government agencies rely upon. Because of the government's rather poor job of symmetrical communication, it will often initiate new services or enact new laws without much notification. Remember, the government works on the Public Information Model of public relations. That model, of course, does a fair job at communicating information, but a poor job at ensuring that the information is understood and known by the public. For example, many students rely on government student loans to pay for their education while in school. These loans of course must be repaid upon graduation. Unfortunately, the crippling levels of debt that many students must take just to pay for college forces them to make equally crippling payments when they graduate, and at the time they are making lower salaries because of their inexperience. To help with this growing problem, the Obama Administration enacted a law that states student loan debts may be forgiven after a set number of years and under certain circumstances. However, as good as this initiative was, the fact that so many graduates do not know about it makes the program a bit moot in its aim to help alleviate the problem. This scenario illustrates the main problem with government public relations and its communication efforts. Many actions are taken by government agencies to help their consumers, i.e., the public, but not enough communication occurs to ensure that their consumers know about them. Therefore, the job of the public affairs officer or professional is to facilitate and encourage more meaningful communication. Remember, simply making statements is not sound communication. Making statements, ensuring that they are listened to and not just heard, and then getting feedback to make future statements better is true, effective communication. This is the first task of the public affairs officer.

THE PUBLIC AFFAIRS OFFICER'S RESPONSIBILITIES

1. **Improving Communication with the Government.** Because of the many pitfalls that exist with government agencies' communication efforts, the first responsibility of public affairs officers is to remedy problems and facilitate improvements. Most communication from the government is one-way, and the first improvement to this type of communication is to make it more two-way in nature. The easiest and best way to accomplish this is to listen and then act on that information. For example, imagine your town's leaders decided to enact a parking tax in addition to the meters it uses to fund the town. Undoubtedly, this would not be a very popular idea among the town's residents. However, the town is losing money, its state funding was cut, and its commercial areas are dwindling. Therefore, it must find money somewhere, and of all the options, the parking tax presents itself as the best option. In this way, the job of the public affairs officer is quite difficult. This person is not responsible for the tax, but he or she is responsible for communicating it—in many ways it becomes the old problem of "kill the messenger." Most private companies' public relations practitioners are not put into this type of situation. Their organizations would not purposely enact a plan that would anger its patrons and the public—that simply would not make sense. However, the government public relations practitioner, the public affairs officer, is put into this type of situation quite commonly. Therefore, the public affairs officer's job is doubly difficult—improve the government's image among the public, but at the same time, communicate unpopular news like parking taxes. However, to make this difficult job as easy, efficient, and effective as possible, sound and successful communication must be at the heart of all public affairs efforts. Even though unpleasant information must be communicated and enacted upon, it does not mean that it must be presented in a way that furthers the displeasure of the public. The best means to communicate bad news like a new parking tax is to include the reasoning behind its initiation. The parking tax exists only because of falling funding from other sources, which used to sustain the town. Given the difficult economic situation, the tax must be enacted to ensure that public services like road improvements, police and ambulance services,

and snow removal proceed uninterrupted. Without this key information, the public is left in the dark and to their own conclusions, which like traditional public relations, is never a good thing. Explaining the situation is the best means to help reduce the negativity and anger toward a parking tax. If the public understands why it must be in place, then they at least know that it is for a good reason. In addition to explaining the tax, the townspeople's thoughts and opinions on the legislation must be listened to and communicated to the town's leaders. With this feedback, the public affairs can learn more about the situation and then use the data to help improve relations. For instance, imagine that the public felt that the parking tax was an annual road tax that every resident must pay, but in fact, the parking tax is a one-time fee to help alleviate the cash-strapped town. If the public affairs officer had not taken the time to listen to the public's opinion and concerns over the parking tax, he or she would never have known this information. Armed with it, the town's public affairs officer can go back to the public with additional communication that explains that it is not a yearly tax, but simply a single payment this year. Clearly, this information would go a long way in swaying the public to understand and accept the new parking tax, which would have been impossible without good research. Moreover, an additional benefit is the public relations fundamental that people will be more likely to accept bad news if they are included in the decision-making process—even if the process creates the bad news. This phenomenon is true in nearly all cases. As long as the people affected are in on the process early enough and feel as though they have a real voice in the decision, then they are likely to accept negative information even if it affects them. Therefore, the public affairs officer for the town should include the public in the decision-making process by allowing them to voice their opinion as well as their suggestions to make the situation better—perhaps they feel there is another means to help support the town other than through a parking tax. This type of consensus building is what public relations is all about. Few individuals in the field know this better than the public affairs officer.

2. **Encourage the Public's Participation in Government Actions.** Part of the public affairs job is to communicate government agencies' news to the public, but also to create a sense of partnership with the public. The best means to accomplish this task is to develop programs and initiatives that make the public care and want to help the government in its duties. One of the most common examples occurs every November. Ordinary citizens who volunteer to help run the election process make this process happen across the country. The people who take your name, show you to the booth, and even give out the "I voted" stickers are all regular citizens who take time out of their schedule to help this important process go smoothly each year. Public affairs officers must enable people to want to participate and facilitate the logistics so they can help. Figuring out who can do what, securing locations, communicating the open

positions and responsibilities, as well as then securing the volunteers are all part of the public affairs officer's job. Even civic engagements like Fourth of July parades and firehouse dinners are all examples of public affairs at work to help build a sense of camaraderie among the public. Remember, the more they are involved in the good things, the more they will accept the bad. Assuring the public that their assistance is not only wanted but also needed makes them more of a part of the government and not just a group controlled by it. The main task of many public affairs initiatives is to break down the barriers that exist between the government and its citizens.

3. **Assess Government Actions' and Regulations' Effects.** The public affairs officer is required to proactively gauge the possible outcomes from government actions on the public to ensure that they are enacted in a way that least harms the agency's image. No one like to pay taxes, but the public affairs department for the IRS must find ways to make the process as painless as possible for the taxpaying public. New initiatives like online tax filing, simplifying new regulations and laws, as well as finding solutions to tax-paying problems are all means to improve the process and help the IRS's image as much as possible. The parking tax scenario provides a good example of this process at work. Understanding what the public's reaction to government actions will be helps make the process run smoother than simply enacting legislation and hoping that the public does not scream too loudly. Research is at the heart of all sound public relations efforts, and public affairs is no different. Knowing the likely outcomes from government actions help the public affairs officer plan and execute the best efforts to help people know, understand, and ideally, like the legislation in question.

4. **Influence Public Opinion.** Because of politicians' influence on public opinion, part of the responsibility of managing this task comes to the public affairs officer. All elected politicians must handle themselves in a manner that both appeals to their constituents and enables them to be reelected. Part of that task is to counter negativity whether warranted or undeserved. Each election season, you will notice many commercials that boast about the qualifications of a candidate and those that lambast the opponent. Part of this job falls to the manager of the candidate and partly to the public affairs officer. Politicians influence the management of government agencies. Public affairs officers must improve these agencies' reputations. Because of this, politicians' images are in part also managed by public affairs officers even though the role of public affairs might not be controlled by or operate under a specific political party. Regardless of affiliation, the public affairs officer must maintain the best image of his or her agency even in the face of negative public opinion toward a specific politician. To accomplish this goal, public affairs officers need to know how and what people think about their agency and the person in control of it. A great deal of this responsibility is constant research

and monitoring of the public opinion process. For example, the nation's president is often associated with all departments of the government like the IRS even though he might not be directly involved. In this sense, the person charged with maintaining the IRS's image must also deal with the president's public opinion as well. Even if it is unwarranted, the public perception of the nation's leader will affect the public's opinion of all levels of the government. In this way, the public affairs officer must address criticisms to his or her agency as well as the government as a whole. Many of the tactics that for-profit public relations practitioners use are the same as those that government public affairs officers use. Influencing public opinion through communication and media placements of key messages plays a large role in accomplishing this objective. In addition, public affairs officers are responsible for counseling and reporting on public perception of their agency to those in charge of it. In this sense, the two major roles of public relations are accomplished. To develop the best reputation possible, the agency must be run in accordance with its purpose as well as appealing to public opinion. Therefore, the public affairs officer acts as a liaison between the public and the agency's leadership. Monitoring public opinion and making decisions based on it is the best means to maintain and improve government agency reputations.

WORKING WITH THE GOVERNMENT

Because of the immense power and influence that the government possesses over private industries, public relations practitioners must find ways to work with as well as influence government legislation. Part of the job is dealing ethically and responsibly, not only because it is the right way to do business, but also because it helps reduce government actions against an organization. Social responsibility provides many benefits beyond the altruistic benefits it offers organizations. Ethical business practices also reduce or at least curtail increased government regulations and scrutiny. This also applies to entire industries. Large industries such as the petroleum industry provide a good illustration of this phenomenon. With every oil spill or environmental disaster due to negligence of poor business practices, such as BP's actions in the Gulf of Mexico, additional and tougher regulations are brought on the entire industry, not just BP. Ensuring that the organization is operating ethically and socially responsibly comes down to sound public relations. Remember that it is impossible for an organization to gain and maintain a positive reputation with any stakeholder group if it is not operating at its best. All public opinion about an organization begins within the organization through sound managerial counseling. This highly specialized branch of public relations often gets a black eye in the opinions of many people. These government-specialized public relations practitioners are known as lobbyists. Lobbyists act as the intermediary between an organization and government leaders who can make and influence policy. Among many responsibilities, lobbyists are charged with four major tasks.

Task One: Research. Because the government cannot possibly know everything about every organization, the lobbyist must educate and inform those within the government responsible for making important decisions. Therefore, lobbyists must know everything about an organization and be able to intelligently and effectively pass this information on to government leaders. In return, lobbyists, who often work and reside in Washington, D.C., then inform their organization's leadership about what the government is doing that might affect the organization. Research is the fundamental to all successful public relations, and lobbyists must rely on sound research to achieve their main goal of influencing government actions in favor of the organization. For example, imagine your organization, the community college, and what it must receive from government entities to run as smoothly and successfully as possible. Even though a public educational institution may not seem like a candidate for this type of work, the fact that it does rely so heavily on government actions requires some representation. Because organizations like it often do not have the funding available themselves to hire lobbyists—who are highly paid individuals—it can join other like-minded organizations and provide them representation as a combined effort. Organizations such as the National Education Association (NEA), which operates as a unified organization representing the individual interests of educators and education-related efforts, can help the nation's educational system from the perspectives of those who work and rely on them such as teachers and staff. In many ways, these organizations are similar to unions in that they protect the interests of those people who otherwise would not be able to have much of a voice with the legislators who make important decisions over academic policies and of course funding. Even non-professional groups like AARP (American Association of Retired Persons) utilize lobbyists to further its members' causes and protect their interests. At the center of all types of lobbyist efforts is a clear understanding of what the people who hire them want and how government actions can affect them. When the government decides on whether to restrict natural gas drilling in Pennsylvania, for example, the petroleum companies that rely on this drilling will certainly have their lobbyists in the offices of those individuals who will make the decision to increase restrictions or not. The purpose of the lobbyist is to maintain and protect the interests of the companies and organizations they are hire to represent, and the first step to doing so is understanding clearly all of the implications of government actions and how they will affect the organizations that hire them.

Task Two: Translate Government Actions. Because lobbyists are highly trained and very specialized in their branch of public relations work, they must be able to describe and detail government actions and plans for their organizations. Often, government actions are complex and time consuming, and can be very broad. Because of this, lobbyists need to be able to simply and succinctly explain these actions to organizational leaders so that they can understand what the government is doing that might affect the organization's future. New proposals, legislation about to be voted on, and even the feel of the government must be clearly described and explained so that the organization can react in the best way possible. For instance, in the last decade environmental concerns and regulations have affected many government bodies' voting and decision-making processes on issues relating to emissions, green technology, and waste disposal. As you can imagine, those companies that will be directly affected by new regulations must understand what could happen on Capitol Hill before it becomes law. Automotive manufacturers hire many lobbyists to interpret what the government is doing on issues concerning emissions requirements and new fuel mileage restrictions. Clearly these types of laws will impact how companies like Ford, GM, and Chrysler develop, build, and sell their products in the future.

Accordingly, the lobbyists need to know what is happening in the legislative bodies in Washington on issues like these and then be able to report back to these companies so they can determine their next course of action. Interpreting government actions is only part of the job, though. Well before actual legislative action is taken, lobbyists need to be able to gauge what the feeling is in Washington to predict and prepare for what might lay ahead. For instance, for decades, increased demands for stricter environmental laws spread across the houses of Congress. With each natural and humanmade disaster came louder calls for reform. Following the Exxon Valdez spill in 1986, a push for harder regulations against the oil companies became widespread. Even natural disasters like Hurricanes Katrina and Sandy, and international events like the Haitian earthquake and Pacific Tsunami all led to increased public opinion pressuring the government to enact stiffer regulations aimed at stemming the tide of environmental catastrophes and climate change. In addition, increased reporting and focus by the news media on climate change and the environment all lead to possible government actions that can affect organizations.

These trends are at the heart of proactive lobbyism. Therefore, for this example, lobbyists would need to monitor several factors that have been found to influence public opinion over environmental issues. Statements made by democrats in support of climate-change legislation; republicans' anti-climate change stances; unemployment figures; the number of times the subject is addressed in *The New York Times*; as well as the release of films such as *An Inconvenient Truth* all contribute to increased public concern for the environment[80]. Therefore, it is not just a matter of actual natural events that lead to greater government attention on environmentally related legislation, but the media's as well as to how the country is performing economically. In this sense, lobbyists act as the fingers on the pulse of not only Washington, D.C., but also the entire country. Knowing the ins and outs of public opinion development and the steps involved are critical skills that every lobbyist must possess to be able to accurately report to their organizations on the actual events in Washington as well as the overall vibe that might lead to actual events like new legislation.

Task Three: Translate Organizational Actions. The same process that lobbyists go through to interpret government actions and the legislative climate of Washington back to their organization is reversed in the third task. Just as lobbyists need to explain what is happening among key government bodies to the organization's leaders, lobbyists also need to interpret their organization's actions to the government leaders. Government bodies such as Congress cannot be expected to know about the workings of even the largest private company; therefore, the lobbyist acts as the direct line of communication between these organizations and the people charged with making widespread and long-lasting decisions. For example, imagine a lobbyist working for the Ford Motor Company. This person would need to explain to key government officials what Ford is doing, how government regulations will affect its ability to operate, and the company's overall points of view on what is taking place in the country. Often, important government officials may simply be unaware of the company's perspectives, and the lobbyist ensures that a greater and fuller understanding takes place between the two entities. Using the Ford example, imagine that the company is currently working on extending the mileage of its vehicles, but it will not be ready for five years. If Congress is debating on whether to pass new legislation requiring better fuel economy to be implemented in one year, then the lobbyist would need to explain to senators and legislators that an immediate vote would harm the company. Of course, in doing, the negative outcomes that might occur if the legislation goes through too soon would be highlighted as well. In other words, it is not just a matter of selling the position of the company, but also persuading legislators that a certain law can and will harm their constituents. Clearly, the best people to speak to about this are those connected with the company—Michigan's representatives in Congress. Part of explaining perspectives of the organization is a bit of persuasion to affect legislation in the company's favor, which is the next task.

Task Four: Advocate for the Organization. Because the lobbyist's number-one job is to influence the government to enact laws and regulations that favor the organizations they represent, the last and most important task is advocating. At the end of the day, the company that hires lobbyists needs them to represent their best interests so that government regulations will either not negatively affect them or even better will help their organizations succeed. For example, corporate tax laws are an important area that lobbyists would want to influence. Government officials in charge of making decisions about how much companies must pay will receive a lot of attention by many industries' lobbyists. Using the Ford example, you can expect that any new proposed law about tougher emissions standards would be of great importance to any automotive manufacturer. New regulations such as these would force car companies to retool their factories, change designs, and create new development processes—all of which will cost the company hundreds of millions of dollars. Therefore, lobbyists working for the automotive industry would want to persuade government officials to relax their emissions efforts a bit so that car manufacturers are not hit as severely as they might be. Strategies could include reducing the level of the law—in other words, not as stringent in its scope or even delaying it until the companies can afford to rework their manufacturing processes. In this way, the legislation is not abandoned, just tweaked enough so that the congressperson feels satisfied as well as the company. Another method might be to reinforce the negative implications that might arise from unpopular laws like the new emissions requirements. If automotive manufacturers must spend nearly one billion dollars to meet the demands of the government's new laws, then the companies must make adjustments to remain in business. These types of concerns would be at the heart of a lobbyist's persuasive message. These messages would rely on speaking to the concerns of the congresspersons in question. One aspect that all politicians have in common at some point is the desire to be reelected. Therefore, an automotive industry lobbyist would target a senator from Michigan. The main focus of this persuasive message would be the loss of jobs due to layoffs stemming from the increased costs of the new emissions regulations. No congressperson wants high unemployment rates in his or her state. Furthermore, a emphasis might be on the fact that if the proposed law went through as is, thousands of automotive workers will lose their jobs, then what would that look like the next time a Michigan senator went up for reelection? By speaking to the concerns of the government leaders, lobbyists can advocate their organization's position and present a convincing and then persuasive message that gets the law enacted in a way that favors the company. At the end of the day, this is the main job of all lobbyists—influencing government actions to favor the operations of private businesses. Clearly, the larger the company and the bigger the industry, the more sway their lobbyists will have in shaping government actions to the benefit of organizations. For this reason, lobbyists have gained a bit of a black eye among most people who see them as manipulating the people's government for the benefit of big business. While not totally unwarranted in this criticism, lobbyists today must adhere to strict rules of conduct to ensure that their persuasive methods do not cross the line into illegal actions. There are set limits, for example, on how much money lobbyists and their organizations can spend on dinners with politicians. Furthermore, regulatory agencies keep a close eye on any type of misdealing among government officials and lobbyists to ensure that the process is upheld to all legal standards. In addition to lobbyists, other groups attempt to influence public opinion and in turn, government actions as well as elections. These groups often use public relations tactics to persuade people to believe and accept that their positions are preferable over their opponent's stance. Often, these groups are rather subtle in terms of who is paying for them and controlling them, and to what end.

■ POLITICAL ACTION COMMITTEES

The first such group is known as a **Political Action Committee** or PAC for short. PACs began in the 1940s by pro-union groups that sought to endorse and help win elections for pro-union candidates. This effort was to avoid legislation that banned direct contributions to candidates, which is known as the Smith-Connally Act. Essentially, PACs were created to get around laws that prohibited union groups from endorsing, usually monetarily, candidates. Because of their effectiveness, groups other than unions began using PACS to get into office those candidates whose platforms would help these groups, where they could, pass official government legislation in favor of the groups the PACs were representing. While politically motivated, PACs often focus on candidates rather than simply party lines in their support. As long as a candidate's position favors the organizations and people a PAC represents, then that candidate will likely receive the PAC's support. For example, the American Federation of Teachers is a labor-focused PAC that obviously supports legislation and positions that favor teachers and their part of the educational process. PACs are group of like-minded individuals who usually donate resources including money and time to help a political candidate gain office. In many ways, PACs can be thought of similar to unions in that they both are made up of individuals who, as a united front, possess the power to influence agendas in their favor. A more notorious political agenda-setting group, though, often possesses much more influence and subterfuge in their tactics—**front groups**.

Front Groups

The organizations often work to purport supporting one stance or issue, while in reality they often seek to win favor for an organization or position that is not clearly presented. In this way, front groups often manipulate public opinion for one agenda while claiming to support another position, which is often less controversial and more easily digestible by the public. The most famous, or infamous, was the Tobacco Institute, which presented itself as a scientifically centered organization founded and run by respected physicians and scientists to clarify the "real" health effects of smoking. In reality, big tobacco companies tried to persuade the public that smoking was not as bad as other scientific findings suggested, most notably the United States Surgeon General's Office. This was during the public opinion development cycle over tobacco use when more evidence pointed to the dangers of smoking, yet the public was not totally convinced yet, so opinion was malleable, and the tobacco companies knew they could influence the public to keep smoking before the public decided that it is in fact a deadly habit. Clearly, the tobacco industry could not advertise that smoking was not bad for you and all the reports saying otherwise were incorrect, because no one would believe it and the government prohibited it. So, the tobacco companies joined together, formed a bogus organization called the Tobacco Institute under the guise of a respected medical research facility, made up reports about smoking's effects, and tried to sell it to the public as being fact. The tobacco industry was eventually caught, and when the reality of the Tobacco Institute was revealed, it only harmed the industry's reputation and solidified the idea that smoking was bad. Because of these types of underhanded tactics, front groups are often secretive about who they represent and often do not disclose where their funding comes from, which is usually the industry or political candidate they are trying to help. Using manipulative, yet often effective tactics, makes front groups a rather dangerous form of political and social public relations. Groups like the National Wetlands Fund sound like they would be in favor of protecting the environment based on their name, which is exactly why front groups choose names that sound altruistic, but are designed to accomplish a specific agenda, sometimes the complete opposite of what they seem like they would do. For example, the National Wetlands Coalition was formed in part by petroleum and chemical companies to persuade the public that increased and more stringent government regulation on protecting wetlands were too strict and hurt them. Clearly, the government's strict laws on wetland protection hurt oil companies' ability to drill in them and use their resources or institute stiff penalties when their companies disturbed them such as with an oil spill. The informed public should always note who is purchasing and airing commercials that purport to defend one agenda, then conduct research on that group to see what they really are trying to accomplish. Unfortunately, a large portion of the public does not do this, and for this reason, front groups can persuade large sections of the population to support what they think is a good agenda, when in fact it is being funded by organizations that sometimes go completely against the advertised statements. Front groups will often seek some kind of public support of their causes through donations, letters to representatives, or asking them to vote for one candidate over another. Front groups are generally most active during times of public opinion development or change, such as when Americans became more educated about the dangers of smoking or during election season.

527 Groups

While PACs can certainly influence public opinion for candidates, the one effect on political and government agendas they are limited in is the amount of funding they can offer political parties. Under law, candidates for the United States Senate and the House of Representatives cannot receive donations more than $1,000 from individuals and $5,000 from PAC groups. However, few candidates seeking a congressional office would be able to fund their campaigns on these meager levels of revenue. Therefore, candidates began developing **527 groups**, raising unlimited amounts of money as long as it does not directly go to the candidate. This type of funding is known as "soft money," which can entail efforts like getting people to vote; however, it often includes some mention of the candidate. So, in reality, these groups can and do help candidates and political parties even though they are designed to be less direct in giving actual money ($1,000 and $5,000 according to the law), they still enable candidates to use large sums of funding to at least help support their efforts for election. Two types of 527s exist: Politician 527s and Public Citizen 527s. Politician 527s support individual candidates and political parties, while Citizen 527s support social ideas, causes, and interests. Despite which category of 527, they both can influence public opinion.

While these types of political public relations efforts seem manipulative and underhanded in their approaches, they do use many types of public relations practices, albeit rather unethically. Aspiring public relations practitioners can learn even from these groups. One important lesson from political public relations efforts is the **grassroots** efforts that seek public support for agendas and ideas. The ideas and agendas are usually to help support an organization's ability to operate or to help a selected candidate win office. Political and government public relations may seem rather unsavory to some; however, when used ethically, they add valuable tools to the public relations practitioner's toolbox of tactics. Grassroots lobbying and public relations can assist in achieving specific objectives for organizations and still be transparent and for the public's good as much as it is for the organization's benefit.

GRASSROOTS PUBLIC RELATIONS

This form of lobbying enables public relations practitioners to earn the public's trust and motivate them to help achieve a specific objective. The following fundamentals of grassroots lobbying provide a foundation on which to build informative as well as persuasive campaigns. In many ways, grassroots lobbying is similar to traditional lobbying. However, professional lobbyists in state and federal capitals do traditional lobbying, everyday people and non-professional lobbyists conduct grassroots lobbying. The result is still intended to influence legislation in favor of a specific group or cause. In this way, public relations takes on a more simplified method of lobbying, which has become synonymous with the term "grassroots." Generally, it starts small and continues to build until the objective is met. Ordinary public relations practitioners can utilize grassroots lobbying, especially smaller organizations without the means to hire high-priced lobbyists. Additionally, public relations practitioners can solicit the public to help a grassroots lobbying effort. Regardless of whether it is done by everyday citizens or trained public relations practitioners, the first step is to ensure your efforts are specific and clear.

1. **Focus Your Energy.** For any grassroots effort to be successful it must first be targeted to a specific objective or result. Too often grassroots lobbying fails because it starts as being too vague or too ambitious. Remember, you are trying to sway the politicians to accept and like an idea; therefore, you cannot confuse them with too elaborate a message or one that is difficult to remember. Clear, concise, and memorable messages are all hallmarks of good grassroots lobbying. Imagine if your community college public relations job required you to start a grassroots lobbying effort. The first step is to clearly spell out what your objective is in tangible terms. For instance, "increase state funding by 10 percent within two years" is a correct objective for a grassroots lobbying effort. From there, you could build a message and develop supporting evidence to help persuade your audience to believe, accept, and want to help achieve your objective. Additionally, it is important to know who you are going to try to persuade and why. Who is the best person or persons who make decisions on budget allocations for public colleges like yours? Undoubtedly, the governor's office is at the top of that list, but state assemblypersons might also be appropriate because they vote on budget issues. In addition to choosing the right people, it is important to select those who will likely be receptive to your message of increasing the state's allocations to its community colleges.

2. **Pick Your Target Audience for the Best Chance of Success.** For any persuasive message to work, it must be received by those who will likely believe and act on it. Therefore, it does not make sense to try to persuade someone who is completely set in his or her ways and will not budge. You can talk until you are blue in the face to these people, but it will not offer much chance of success. Therefore, you must seek out those people who will hear you out and may act on your persuasive message. For example, even though the governor seems like the perfect audience for your grassroots lobbying effort, if she is completely set against increasing the state's budget for its community colleges, then you should not waste your time in trying to persuade her. Instead, look for other prominent and important individuals to make decisions relating to budget allocation who are also likely to be receptive to your message. Perhaps a specific political party would be more prone to help your cause than another would be. If this is the case, then you are already in a better position to make your grassroots lobbying efforts successful. Finding the right people on the state's assembly, for instance, will enable you to talk to not only the right people, but also those who are probably going to help you. Lobbying is not just about getting one person to believe you, but rather a group of individuals who will help your effort. Rarely does one person make important government decisions. At some point, issues like budget allocations are voted on by a group of individuals. It is important to sway as many people in that group rather than just the person who seems to be in charge like the governor.

3. **Find what Motivates Your Audience.** Effective persuasive messages often include not only what is good for the person trying to persuade, but also the person being persuaded. In this way persuasion is most successful when both parties have something to gain from the persuasive action—sort of an "I'll scratch your back if you scratch mine" mentality. Therefore, when developing grassroots lobbying messages, it is important to think about how it will benefit your audience as well as yourself. Each audience will be different in what they want. Economic interests play a large role for most people. However, influence and prestige can also be effective persuasive ammunition. For example, after you have developed your key message of increasing state funding for community colleges and identified the right people to help you, you now need to think about what you can offer them. What is in it for them? For your state assemblypersons example, something they all want and have in common are constituents, specifically votes to keep them in office. Think about how you can tweak your message to include some aspect that relates to their self-interests. Perhaps phrasing your message to emphasize how beneficial an increase in funds would be to their public and how at election time, it will look good for them to include in their platform that they voted to increase funding for education. In this way, you are likely to get your funding increase because now the people who can help you are getting something out of it in exchange. Lobbying in general is as much about how it benefits the person helping you as it is for the person seeking help.

4. **Be Aware of the Environment You Are Working In.** It is important to understand that what can be accomplished is often dictated by the timing or the environment in which you are working. Economic pressures, political strangleholds on power, and changing public opinion on important issues all can affect your grassroots lobbying efforts. What works today might not work a year from now; therefore, you must always gauge what the political landscape looks like at the time you're making your grassroots pitch. For example, the tobacco industry's lobbying efforts to reduce or thwart increased restrictions on tobacco advertising might have worked in the 1960s when the data about the dangers of smoking first came to light. However, those same efforts would be monumentally more difficult today because of the stigma of being associated with the tobacco industry and smoking in general. Therefore, any successful lobbyist, grassroots or traditional, must know and understand how the social and political environment will affect his or her message. Using the community college scenario, you would need to know what the state's economic condition is if you are going to ask for more money. If the state is strapped for cash, then this might not be the best time to solicit grassroots efforts to increase funding. Furthermore, if the state's government is controlled by republicans, for instance, who may not be receptive to funding increases, then you might want to wait until the democrats have

more people in the state's assembly. All of these factors must be considered when developing your grassroots lobbying efforts.

5. **Organize Your Thoughts into a Cohesive Message.** Now that your objective is clear, your audience is selected, your persuasive element of self-interests is factored in, and the timing is right, it is now the moment to develop your message. Every sound grassroots lobbying effort must include a straightforward, sensible, and logical message that motivates your audience to act in your favor. Remember that you are asking for help, so avoiding making the request too big is a good first step in developing a sound message. Logistics and reality play a big role in accomplishing your lobbying efforts. Asking for too much and making your request undoable will likely result in a failed effort. Think about what can be accomplished in the real world—how much of an increase in state funding is doable. If your request is too great, it will often turn your audience off to you and of course your request for their help. Maybe, in a perfect world, the state assembly would increase community college funding by 50 percent, but that is unlikely. Therefore, you need to make your request realistic—perhaps 10 percent is more likely. Remember that 10 percent of something is better than 50 percent of nothing. Your message must also speak to how your request will help you. How will you spend the money? Why is it needed now? Are there other means of funding available? To this end, you need to sculpt a counterargument in your message. It is important play devil's advocate so that when your audience counters your request with a reason to not help, you are already armed with a reply. Better yet, include a counter statement in your pitch so that your audience does not have a chance to question it. A counter argument to increasing state funding to community colleges could be, "If you need more funds, then increase tuition." That seems like a logical argument against increasing state allocations. Therefore, be sure that you are ready to state why the idea of increasing tuition will not solve the problem. Your statement could be, "Our students and families are strapped as it is. Costs of materials like textbooks make increasing tuition impossible for families to afford now. Community colleges are supposed to be for everyone, and increasing the cost of attending puts a college education out of reach for this state's residents. To ensure they receive the best quality education, we need more funds from the state." In this scenario, you have addressed the problem, proactively countered their argument, and reinforced your message and why your solution is best. Well-crafted lobbying messages are a balancing act between being too forceful and too weak. You need evidence to support your claims, but you also do not want to insult anyone's intelligence.

6. **Offer a Simple Solution.** It is always important to remember that you are asking people to help when you lobby them. For this reason, your request should be doable and easy for them. Making a request that is difficult, time-consuming, or overly expensive places a burden on your audience and makes your grassroots lobbying solicitation unattractive to them. You need to consider how you can make your request easy for them to do; how can you simplify and explain the request in such a way that gets them motivated to help, but also enables to them to assist you easily. The more you request, the more you need to think about how they can help you with as little a burden on them as possible. In the funding scenario, you would need to address the problem with your request—more money for the state's community colleges means less money for something else. Therefore, you need to research how your request can work in the real world and what the effects of it might be, not only for you, but also for everyone involved. Where can the extra money come from? More importantly, how can you use the increased funds to improve the lives of those you're seeking help from? To this end, you know that your increased funding will lead to better educational services to the state's residents. The people you are asking money from need to be re-elected by these same people. Therefore, you have the evidence as to why it will help make your audience's lives better. At the same time, you need to consider how your request can happen and how you can make the decision to increase funding as easy as possible for your audience of assemblypersons. Perhaps illustrating the fact that a better educated population leads to higher wages, better employment, and an overall stronger state economy. In this sense, you are making the argument that spending a little now will pay off later because the state will not have to spend as much on programs like unemployment insurance, assistance programs, and even crime-related expenses. In doing so, you make your request as easy for them to approve because it is for their benefit in the long run as much as it is yours. Always remember to keep your message's request as attractive to and as easy on your audience as possible—they are the ones doing you a favor.

7. **Facilitate Interpersonal Communication.** Because you are asking important people for their help with your organization's agenda, it is critical to speak to these individuals in person. Arranging meetings with them, however, can be difficult given the constraints of their time as well as yours. Nonetheless, because interpersonal communication is so important to the success of your grassroots lobbying endeavors, you must seek to see them in person. The primary reason for this is it enables you to talk to them on a human level, which allows for true two-way communication. As always, this model of communication is best because it allows both parties to find common ground and understanding, which is much more difficult through other communication methods. When you see someone in person, you can understand their points of view from what

they say as well as how they say it. Most communication is done through non-verbal signals, such as crossed arms indicating annoyance or lack of trust or confusion on someone's face. When you see these cues, you then change your delivery and add or omit information to speak personally to each individual you are trying to persuade. Always remember that the best communication is personalized communication, and speaking to someone firsthand enables the highest level of personalization. Moreover, because this facilitates two-way communication, the individual can ask questions, clarify ideas, and present their own take on your message. Letters and email will never allow this type of communication, and therefore, those methods will never deliver the same positive results that face-to-face meetings will provide. For instance, imagine the types of communication available when you want to persuade a group of state assemblypersons to provide more funding for your community college. Form letters that outline your plan and your ideas will impart information on your plan; however, they will not clearly communicate your message as well as through meetings. Setting up times that are convenient to your audience members is also an important element to successful lobbying. Their time is valuable and needs to be respected as much as their intelligence and abilities. Providing times and dates that work with their schedules, not yours, should be a priority for your meetings with them. Never forget that you are seeking their assistance, and the more you can appeal to them, the better your chances of lobbying success.

8. **Always be Transparent and Honest.** In the heat of the moment, it can sometimes seem easy to promise outcomes that you really cannot or entertain prospects that you know are unlikely. Evidence is of course one of the mainstays of successful persuasion. However, using specious reasoning or broadly interpreted data to support your points will eventually catch up with you, and any credibility and trust you gained with your audience can be lost forever when the truth comes out. Lobbying audiences will often try to find holes in your ideas because they may be resistant to your plans and ideas. Often, the political minds that you are dealing with have experience with advanced logic—many of them have gone to law school. Therefore, any vagueness of overstating or manipulating data in your message's favor without true substantiation will likely be caught. Then, the situation is even worse because now the person you are trying to persuade is picking apart your evidence. Think about the types of data that could support your request for more funding for your organization. One might be the increase of graduation and retention rates among students who attend colleges with substantial funding available to them. While it may seem like a good idea to promise increased graduation rates, GPAs, or even retention in your message to the assemblypersons, you cannot really promise anything as far as numbers are concerned. You cannot, for example, state that with increased funding your college will graduate 20

percent more students or have a student body with a 3.5 GPA because you do not know for sure what will happen. Therefore, whatever evidence you use to support your request for more money must be stated as a projection, not a promise. You can certainly include data that point to better students and better funding, but you cannot promise that your college will experience an increase in student performance because you do not know what the outcome of increased funding will be once you receive it. Promising too much and manipulating data to suit your needs will cause more harm than good in your lobbying efforts.

Positive government relations comes down to knowing your audience, understanding your organization's points of view, and communicating them correctly yet persuasively to those who can influence its success. Political relationships can be tricky and tenuous. Who is in charge today might be out tomorrow, and a whole new administration can take its place. Like most public relations stakeholder groups, government agencies and the politicians charged with overseeing them can change quickly in their priorities and agendas. Therefore, a successful relationship with the government and in turn politicians comes down to continuous research on what is happening in your town, state, and the country. However, today, the global implications on public relations are stronger than ever. Every aspiring public relations practitioner must understand the importance of the global effects on their organization and how events in other countries inevitably affect what happens here. Therefore, it is important to look at international relations.

INTERNATIONAL RELATIONS

In 1964, pioneering media scholar Marshall McLuhan stated, "Today, after more than a century of electric technology, we have extended our central nervous system itself in a global embrace, abolishing both space and time as far as our planet is concerned"[81]. He referred to technology as the primary influence in integrating the world into one, connected planet. He coined the term "global village" to describe the phenomenon of globalization in terms of technology-driven communication. This unified type of media would enable people from all across the world to connect, and in doing so, make Earth more like an integrated community than a disjointed collection of countries and ethnicities. Exactly 50 years later, this theory has proven itself, no doubt even beyond McLuhan's expectations. Never before can people from all across the planet communicate and connect with one another as quickly, cheaply, and effectively as they can today. Instantaneous communication via smart device technology coupled with improved sharing capabilities on the Internet, and of course platforms like social media, have turned the world into a smaller community. Distances of geography and even cultures no longer restrict the exchange of thoughts and news as they did in the past. For example, events in the Middle East are now communicated directly from the people experiencing them. Their videos shot on smartphones and uploaded to Facebook allow the entire world to see what is happening as it happens. The notion of the global citizen journalists is a viable and important element to today's global village. Because of this, events from tens of thousands of miles away seem closer and closer. People today expect what happens halfway around the world to be communicated and shared by the people being affected and not just from the big news networks. Clearly, this phenomenon has important implications on today's public relations practice.

All organizations need to address this growth toward a communication-connected world. Clearly, the larger the organization, the greater the implications of this growth will be on it. However, even small organizations now face the task of addressing global communities in their public relations practices. With the reduction of barriers between people and cultures, the world today is more intercultural than ever before. Public relations efforts must be inclusive and cognizant of its communications and its actions. Sensitivities stemming from growing cultural groups require today's practitioners to clearly understand what they communicate to different groups and how they connect with them. For example, the Hispanic population in the United States has grown significantly in the past few decades. Projections point to a Hispanic population that will outpace the African American population in the near future. This large and dynamic group is important in its ability to influence and shape public opinion as a whole. Therefore, today's public relations practitioners must understand cultures such as these better than they have. In addition, if your organization operates in a community with a high population of people with Asian backgrounds, then you must know these cultures as well. One-size-fits-all communication rarely works well, and it certainly does not work when the population you are communicating with understands English as a second language. You must know the cultures, how they interact, and then find how your organization can become a part of their community, not vice versa. Language is only part of the equation. Public relations efforts must understand and incorporate correctly the culturally important events, dates, and celebrations of these groups. A safe plan of action is to include someone from these groups to review and recommend your actions before you implement them, especially if you are unsure of or unfamiliar with them. It is always best to err on the side of caution when using a cultural group or trying to appeal to a cultural group through public relations efforts. The worst mistake you can make is to anger, offend, or aggravate a population that you are trying to appeal to.

Clearly, the need for international public relations is greater today than ever before. However, it is important to remember who your key stakeholder groups are for any given endeavor and how growing populations of different ethnicities are included in them. A fundamental to remember when dealing with international public relations is to "Think

Globally, Act Locally." This means that you are aware and understand the implications of today's more diverse populations at home as well as the importance of the global economy on your organization's ability to succeed. However, at the end of the day, you are most responsible for those people and places that are closest to you. Nonetheless, because of the growth of various populations in the areas closest to your organization, your knowledge of and ability to work with new, diverse populations is greater than ever. Mergers, acquisitions, and international trade all play a major role in the contemporary public relations practitioner's job description. But, ultimately, your communities, whether virtual or real, rely on sound public relations that appeals to them and addresses a changing world in terms of technology, diversified populations, and global business implications.

13

STRATEGIC PLANNING

The ability to use public relations formulas such as research, action, communication, and evaluation (RACE) and the identify, segment, prioritize, and rank analysis (ISPR) are what set truly professional practitioners apart from amateurs. Remembering that the two most important elements of these public relations formulas are the research and evaluation stages enables competent practitioners to deliver meaningful results, as well as learn from their campaigns and initiatives. As you will recall in Chapter Four, the ability to plan with meaningful and helpful data allows practitioners to develop means to accomplish goals with as much assuredness of success as possible. In addition, one must remember that even the most successful public relations plans have elements that either did not work or did not go to plan. Only by evaluating the entire plan can a practitioner hope to avoid these pitfalls going forward and improve upon them in the future. The Public Relations Society of America (PRSA) bestows accreditation (APR) only on those candidates that can clearly illustrate their competency in planning, in addition to many other qualifications. Accordingly, the ability to plan a public relations initiative, implement it, and then evaluate it stands at the forefront of professional strategic communication practice.

This chapter explores the main elements most common to public relations planning. It is important to note, however, that no two plans are exactly the same. A plan's development can change as needs and resources change. There is nothing static about the practices of public relations—it is always in a state of constant flux. Accordingly, plans must be adaptable and able to be changed as needed. Some plans might include hundreds or even thousands of tactics, whereas others might only require a few dozen. The plan must be directly connected to the organization's available resources, its current reputation, and its ultimate goal. Accordingly, there is no one, set way to develop a public relations plan. However, there are common elements that are seen in more plans than not. These are the elements that will be the focus of this chapter. The chapter is outlined according to the steps required to develop a successful plan, from inception of an idea (research) to the development of the measurable tactics (evaluation). In addition, examples of these items are presented to illustrate their finished form; however, because an entire plan can be long and complex, the examples below include only one of several major stakeholders. Full plans would include many additional stakeholders. These examples came from the work of Kutztown students Deja Brown, Miranda Harran, Madison Mittnacht, Kimberly Robertson, and Ralla Roth.

STEP 1: SITUATION ANALYSIS

The initial phase of public relations planning entails understanding the ins and outs of the organization. There is no sense in developing a multimillion-dollar campaign if the organization cannot afford it. Similarly, an organization with a terrible reputation cannot hope to change its image with just a few, simple tactics. Only by understanding the realities of the organization can an effective and meaningful plan be developed. Situation analysis is really the start of the research process—in this case, it is about researching the organization itself. Practitioners who work directly for their organization might know more about it than a practitioner who works at a public relations firm and manages several client accounts. Regardless, it is imperative that the starting point of public relations planning lies in researching the organization.

THE INTERNAL AUDIT

The internal audit is just what it sounds like: It is an audit of the organization's internal workings—both good and bad. Knowledge about the inside operations allows practitioners to know what the organization is capable of achieving, and what it is not.

Questions that need to be answered to accomplish the internal audit include:

1. What is it that the organization actually provides? Is it a service, product, or combination of the two?
2. What are the means to rate the quality of it?
3. Is the quality of it accurate? Do its key customers or users actually like it or not? How do you know?
4. Has their impression of the quality changed? How?
5. Does the organization feel satisfied with this impression?
6. Who are the closest competitors?
7. How does the organization's product compare to others in the industry?
8. How does the organization differentiate itself and its product from others?
9. What improvements or changes are necessary to keep the product profitable?
10. Has the organization stayed current with market trends?
11. Do the organization's leaders support the organization's management of the product in terms of marketing and advertising?
12. What resources are available to improve the reputation of the organization and its product?
13. Do the organization's leaders value public relations?
14. Is the organization willing to accept input and direction for future endeavors?
15. Is there a plan for the organization's future in terms of its product and its reputation?

An executive summary is included at the end of the sections. These provide organizational leaders with the main takeaways from each section and are traditionally written in a direct, third-party voice.

Answers to these preceding questions enable a practitioner to more accurately assess what the organization is capable of achieving and what its limitations are before investing too much time and resources on the actual plan. After researching the answers to the questions, the data are then organized and synthesized to make sense of it. This information is often shared with management and/or account managers in the event that the practitioner is employed with a firm. Additionally, this data enables other members of the planning team to understand the direction of the plan and its likelihood of success, and quite frankly, if it is even worth pursuing further.

Examples of each section presented in this chapter come from Kutztown University students Deja Brown, Miranda Hess, Madison Mittnacht, Kimberly Robertson, and Ralla Roth. The organization that is the basis for the plan components is a real restaurant; however, its name was changed for this purpose of this chapter. The restaurant operates in the university town.

Introduction

The Hot Dog House is a takeout and eat-in style restaurant located on North Constitution Boulevard in Kutztown. Before The Hot Dog House, the building was used for a more traditional-style hot dog restaurant called Potts' U. The owners of The Hot Dog House rented out the building and decided to add their own twist to the traditional toppings used on hot dogs and see if a larger and more creative assortment could produce better business in the community.

Performance Audit

The Hot Dog House offers services such as pickup, dine in, and delivery. They stress a strict time of a 30-minute delivery service whereas other businesses in town do not. Their products consist of a variety of unusual hot dog combinations, hamburgers, mac and cheese, pierogis, homemade chili, breakfast sandwiches, and much more. When you walk in you can easily become overwhelmed by their menu and may even take five to ten minutes to decide what you want. Each hot dog is based off a movie and contains an ingredient relating to that movie. For example, they have a hot dog that is called a "Shrek." The hot dog comes bacon wrapped, is deep fried, and is then topped with avocado and jalapeno. Both these ingredients are green, which goes along with Shrek because he is green as well. They use a quote to describe their products, which is "If it ain't homemade, it ain't here!"

The quality is determined by the presentation of the food and the time put into preparing it. They advertise that they use skinless, no-filler hot dogs from Nathan's, which is a well-known brand. Their food is made fresh and homemade. Their fries are fresh cut and every meal is made to order. Their toppings are hand cut and prepared fresh daily.

The owners are pleased with their high quality of food and day-to-day business operations. They strive to outdo themselves every day and set the bar higher. Their past successes lead them to believe that they can grow the business and make it a permanent establishment in the small town of Kutztown.

Since most food places in Kutztown are privately owned and not commercialized, the competition factor is more prevalent in the community. The competitors of The Hot Dog House are mostly other locally owned restaurants such as Mark's, Mama's, Betty's, Tommy Boy's, Spud's, and Pop's Malt Shop. The advantage The Hot Dog House has is their creativity and sense of hominess. Because their menu offers many different choices that are either homemade or created with a movie in mind (all of their hot dogs are named after iconic, well-known movies and many ingredients relate to the movie or the title, e.g., their breakfast sandwiches are based off of characters from *The Breakfast Club*), it offers a more engaging way to view the menu. Maybe the customer will try a certain hot dog just because they like that movie.

There are not many disadvantages with other competitors when it comes to the service; however, there are some when it comes to the food. The Hot Dog House offers a wide variety of different of foods, but you can't really help what a customer may be in the mood for. If someone is craving pizza, they may visit Mama's instead of The Hot Dog House. If someone is craving pasta, they may dine at Camillo's or Ray's instead. Many people just think of hot dogs when they think of The Hot Dog House because its other items are not as heavily advertised; many people may not even realize they sell other products until they physically step into the restaurant and look at the menu.

The specialty that sets The Hot Dog House apart from other competitors is their sense of making you feel at home when you are in their restaurant or eating their food. As mentioned before, having movie titles as names of the hot dogs is a creative and engaging way of advertising their unique topping combinations. The lounge located in the restaurant has comfortable seating, gaming, and movie streaming. There are also board games and other fun activities to do. They invite customers to hang out in the lounge whenever they are waiting for food, while they're eating, or after they finish. This also creates an opportunity to meet new people who enjoy eating there as well.

The Hot Dog House just celebrated their one-year anniversary this past January. Since opening a year ago, they have increased their menu by adding a new hot dog combination. They also now offer brunch bowls as well as their new "Breakfast Club" breakfast sandwiches.

If the service is to change within the next two years, they may create a waitperson-type of atmosphere in the restaurant instead of having the customer come up, order, pay, and then sit down and have their food be brought out to them. The Hot Dog House creates a dog-of-the-week and burger-of-the-week each week, and every week it is something new. Several months ago, they came up with a creation for a hot dog that consisted of pulled pork and coleslaw on top. This dog was a big hit and became very popular, very quickly. The owners saw that customers loved it so much that they made it part of their everyday menu. An instance like this is likely to happen again in the future.

We believe changes should be made to improve the service, such as still offering a quick service to the customers who decide to dine in but have them come in, seat themselves, and be waited on instead of having to come up to the counter to order.

It gives the worker and the customer more of a one-on-one and may make the customer more comfortable with the business.

The owner/manager enjoys being creative and doing things his own way, but in order to keep customers he also must listen to what they want and make changes according to the majority. Changes that need to be made to save business will definitely be made by the owner.

Structure Audit

The Hot Dog House's purpose/mission is to provide quality food for both the students and residents of Kutztown and its surrounding areas in a comfortable and welcoming environment. The Hot Dog House prides itself on the quality of their food. Most items are homemade to ensure freshness and the great taste of home that so many college students miss while away at school.

Their strategic business plan is to offer a new spin on a conventional street food by offering a variety of unique toppings for their hot dogs, and they take it a step further by giving each of their unique hot dogs a cinematic name. The Hot Dog House also offers original breakfast sandwiches, sides, and burgers.

Communication resources that are currently available are their social media accounts and their website: The Hot Dog House's Instagram and Twitter accounts @ thehotdoghouse, their Facebook account The Hot Dog House Hot Dogs Kutztown, and their website maddogskutzown.com. The owners also post from their personal social media accounts on the Kutztown class pages. Lastly, the owners created a Facebook page call Kutztown Eats and Treats as a way of promoting all restaurants in Kutztown.

Within the next three years these resources are likely to increase. The Hot Dog House has only been in business for one year so as technology grows and they learn from their past and future success and failures, there will be more resources available to them. The Hot Dog House owners serve as the public relations/communications staff, so they have all the power in the organization's decision-making process.

Internal Impediments Audit

Obstacles to success would be the way they use social media. If this company wishes to connect with and attract millennials, they must watch the number of times they post a day. Posting too many times a day could become annoying to this group of people. Another thing that needs to be improved on social media are the descriptions; they will often post a picture of food, but the caption will only talk about their fast delivery. If they wish to gain customers off of a post, it would be useful to also post the name of the item in the description so that if a customer wishes to order it, they can know what it is. These impediments are not deliberate or caused by policy and procedure. These impediments are simply caused by the lack of knowledge in how to effectively run a social media account for product promotion. This can be easily fixed. The way that these impediments can be fixed is to simply have a conversation with the owners who are running the social media pages and give them tips and ideas on how to make the posts more effective.

Executive Summary

Melissa, owner of The Hot Dog House, says that the restaurant strives for excellence. With its quick delivery, sizable portions of food, affordability, and cinematic ambiance, the organization continues to grow rapidly, catering to Kutztown University students and the surrounding community.

The owners of the newly opened restaurant strive to utilize public relations in their everyday operations. The restaurant has sponsored local sports teams in the Kutztown School District and at the neighboring university. They are constantly encouraging groups and clubs that are involved on Kutztown's campus to partake in dine-and-donates with The Hot Dog House. When the dine-and-donates take place, The Hot Dog House ends up donating about 15% to 20% of all business earnings from that day to the group or club's charity.

STEP 2: EXTERNAL AUDIT

Following the research on the internal workings of the organization, it is then important to understand its key stakeholders, ranging from employees to customers to legislative bodies. All of these stakeholders affect the organization and its operations and, accordingly, must be fully understood by the public relations practitioner prior to further planning. The more that is known about these groups of people, the more likely it is for the plan to influence them to act in support of the organization and its operations. Simply put, it is very difficult to promote a product to customers if one knows nothing about them. Understanding the demographics and psychographics of the customers gives the plan a much better chance of success than without this knowledge.

Questions that need to be answered to accomplish the stakeholder analysis include:

1. What is this stakeholder's opinion about the organization?
2. What is this stakeholder's opinion about the product or service provided by the organization?
3. What does this stakeholder want from the organization?
4. What does this stakeholder want from the organization's product or service?
5. What problem(s) has this stakeholder experienced in its relationship with the organization?
6. How can this stakeholder influence the organization?
7. How can the organization affect this stakeholder group?
8. Where does this stakeholder group get is information about the organization?
9. Is this information accurate?
10. What communication method(s) does this stakeholder use most?
11. Who/what influences this stakeholder group most?
12. What can the organization offer this stakeholder group that its competitors cannot?
13. What are the socioeconomic traits of this stakeholder group?
14. What are the geographic similarities of this stakeholder group?
15. What are the consumer trends among this stakeholder group?

The information gained from these questions allow practitioners to know as much about the organization's most important stakeholder groups as possible prior to writing any actual strategies or tactics the affect them. As with any research, the more accurate and usable data that a practitioner has about a group of people, the more likely it is to affect and influence them. Remember, this stakeholder analysis should be done with all important stakeholder groups to glean as much knowledge about them as possible. The following illustration provides only the research conducted on the student stakeholder group. Keep in mind that the remaining major stakeholder groups would also be analyzed.

Students

Students are one of the pronounced stakeholder groups of The Hot Dog House. A large majority of college students dislike cooking on a daily basis, or do not know how, so they turn to local businesses such as The Hot Dog House for their meal needs. The Hot Dog House features fun food for a fair price, fitting into student budgets. It appeals to college students because of its retro-themed atmosphere. Most students in this stakeholder group are aged 18–25 and come from the middle and upper-middle class. Students here at Kutztown University want a restaurant that serves quality food at decent prices. It is important to Kutztown students that local restaurants cater to their own needs such as accepting Bear Bucks, offering delivery, and being open late and early hours, as well as offering specials. Being that The Hot Dog House is the first restaurant in Kutztown to put a new spin on traditional street food, the expectations of the restaurant are high. Students expect the food from The Hot Dog House to be of quality because of the unique ingredients on their hot dogs. The Hot Dog House could appeal even further to the student stakeholders by providing a student discount, rewards for visiting often, and continuing to be active within the campus community.

Overall Stakeholder Characteristics Audit

Students

Students are aware that the restaurant is new. The Hot Dog House offers mainly hot dogs, but other fast food items are available as well. They are located just off Main Street. Students are intrigued by The Hot Dog House because of their original and unique twist on the common hot dog. Students do not want to have overpriced food or low-quality service. Students want good food and good service from a trusted restaurant with a nice atmosphere, and they want to be welcomed and treated respectfully. The Hot Dog House closes at 8:00 p.m. every day, earlier than other restaurants in town, which are usually very busy after 8:00 p.m. They also excessively post on social media.

The students expect good, reasonably priced food from The Hot Dog House along with a clean atmosphere. Students also expect fast delivery from them. Students may vocalize to The Hot Dog House that they should stay open later, and if enough students voiced this, maybe they would listen. Since the students have little to no control over the restaurant besides being part of their sales and income, the students are not able to change much or act upon the issue.

Stakeholder Characteristic Audit Specific to Organization

Students

Kutztown is inhabited primarily by college students. If college students are not dining at The Hot Dog House regularly, the business will suffer. Students are also infamous for spreading rumors, both good and bad. Students who speak positively of the establishment will entice others to stop in for a bite to eat. Being that a vast majority of The Hot Dog House' customers are students, if word spreads around about complaints of the restaurant, other students may be turned off and not want to try it out. They know where it is located and some are familiar with the owners via social media.

The stakeholder group thinks it should be open later because many people do not eat before 8:00 p.m., when it closes, or would like hot dogs as a late-night snack and are unable to get them. It is reasonable for the stakeholder group to want the restaurant to stay open later. The stakeholder group expects a clean, neat atmosphere to eat lunch or dinner. Since opening, they have many loyal customers, including students, and recruit new ones each week. New customers often come in after hearing about The Hot Dog House from a friend or family member, and after having it once, it is more than likely that they stop in again.

It is not a big problem because there are many people who would be willing to run through a trial period to test out if The Hot Dog House would generate more business by staying open later Thursday through Saturday. Since the stakeholder group makes up a good portion of sales, they see themselves as very influential. The organization sees this stakeholder group as less influential because there are other, cheaper places to eat around town, but they do have some influence in the unique and creative food they offer, which you are unable to get anywhere else.

Stakeholder Communication Audit

Students

Students take to Facebook, Twitter, Instagram, Snapchat, and other social media platforms to receive information. They prefer to communicate via text message or video when they are not together in person and pay attention to social media pages of news outlets and television. Students are often so overwhelmed with their studies and other college activities that they are not actively seeking information about The Hot Dog House. However, they often pay attention to it when it comes across their news feeds or if a friend mentions it. The Hot Dog House is such a new establishment that most of the student community has not yet formed a connection with it, making it unlikely to act on information it receives. Student peers and word-of-mouth opinions are considered credible by most students.

Stakeholder Demographic/Psychographics Audit

Students

Stakeholders in this group are aged 18–25 (college freshman through senior graduate students) coming from Kutztown and Kutztown University campus. Most students attending Kutztown University are low income regarding spending money. Kutztown University students generally lean toward spending their money on fair-priced food from local restaurants that deliver. The overall enrollment is 8,309 for Fall 2018.

RACE/ETHNICITY	GR	UG	GRAND TOTAL
TWO OR MORE RACES	0.29%	2.95%	3.24%
AMERICAN INDIAN	0.01%	0.17%	0.18%
ASIAN	0.11%	1.50%	1.61%
BLACK	0.57%	6.88%	7.45%
HISPANIC	0.70%	7.85%	8.54%
NON-RESIDENT ALIEN	0.11%	0.82%	0.93%
PACIFIC ISLANDER	0.01%	0.08%	0.10%
UNKNOWN	0.32%	2.23%	2.55%
WHITE	8.93%	66.47%	75.40%
Grand Total	11.05%	88.95%	100.00%

Enrollment also includes 82 students enrolled representing 43 different countries. Most of the student population is at a point in their lives where their political status is not yet important to their identity. Most students are cautious of their spending habits due to the lack of funds, but when funds are available, students are willing to spend. This group is unique because the students are in college, which limits them to a grab-and-go diet. This is much different from a suburban family community where groups of people cook and eat together at home.

Benefits

Students
The Hot Dog House benefits the student population of Kutztown University by offering a different assortment of food from what is commonly sold in in Kutztown. If someone has a certain craving or wants something different, they can go to The Hot Dog House whereas many of the other places around town offer the same kind of items. That The Hot Dog House offers items you cannot get anywhere else helps because it makes this restaurant stand out from the rest.

STEP 3: DATA ANALYSES

THE IDENTIFY, SEGMENT, PRIORITIZE, RANK ANALYSIS

Once a practitioner gathers the necessary data on the organization and key stakeholders, it is then time to understand the information gained. Analysis of the data is crucial to extracting the meaning and usefulness of it.

The ISPR requires practitioners to apply the data gained from the previous research components. This enables planners to start analyzing and understanding their key stakeholder groups. To do so, practitioners need to break out the most important stakeholder groups and distill them down to the characteristics of what makes them tick. Knowing this allows practitioners to make the most informed, sensible, and effective tactics later in the plan. Selecting who the most important stakeholder groups are comes down to the purpose and goal of the plan. If the plan is to increase sales, for example, then the most crucial stakeholder groups would, of course, include consumers and influencers of consumers. If the plan is to inform and convince the student body that a tuition increase is necessary, then students and parents would be key stakeholder groups.

Process

1. Start with the major stakeholder groups and list them in the Identify column. These groups are determined, once again, by the goal of the plan.
2. Break those groups down using demographics and psychographic analysis in the Segmentation column using data from the external audit.
3. Use all of the descriptions from the Segmentation column and order them according to how much impact/influence they have on the organization's ability to operate and succeed. They are then arranged from most influential (#1) to least (last #) in the Prioritization column.
4. The last column is where practitioners start combining the descriptions from the Prioritization column to more clearly identify the people who are most important to the organization. To do so, the practitioner needs to combine the attributes of these people to develop who they are according to their traits and characteristics. Once that is done, these amalgam people are listed from most important to least.
5. Now practitioners know exactly who they need to focus on later in the planning stages. For example, it's no longer just students, but first-year, female students who live on campus.

ISPR Analysis

IDENTIFY	SEGMENTATION	PRIORITIZATION	RANKING
Students Kutztown Community Local Business/ Employees	Students: • On campus • Off campus • Commuters • Freshman, sopho- more • Junior, senior • Male • Female Residents: • In town residents • 0–5 miles away • 5+ miles away Local Businesses/ Employees: • In town/local businesses • Kutztown-area school district • Factories • Employees lunch • Employees dinner/ after work	1. Off campus 2. In-town residents 3. Junior, senior 4. On campus 5. Freshman, sophomore 6. Residents 0–5 miles away 7. Employees lunch 8. Male students 9. Female students 10. In-town local businesses 11. Commuters 12. Employees dinner/ after work 13. Kutztown-area school district 14. Residents 5+ miles away	1. Movie fanatics 2. Nonhealth- conscious eaters 3. In-town residents looking for a quick bite to eat 4. Food fanatics 5. Community members who would like to try something new 6. Employees dinner/ after work

Executive Summary

The primary market lies with those individuals who acknowledge and connect with The Hot Dog House's unique food offerings and atmosphere. The main audience are those who reside nearby who are looking for a quick, inexpensive bite, and who are looking for something unique and not offered by area competitors.

◼ THE AUDIENCE MATRIX OF INFLUENCE

The audience matrix of influence distills down groups of stakeholders into more and more precise individuals. Specifically, the audience matrix of influence finds which individuals from the ISPR's Ranking column are most likely to be influenced and who must be influenced to realistically achieve the organization's public relations goal. The analysis works similar to a map. The intersecting areas on the vertical and horizontal planes show the practitioner who should be the target of the plan. This process helps avoid extraneous work and wasted resources. For example, there is no use in trying to persuade a staunch conservative to vote for a Democrat. The purpose of the analysis is to develop the most effective yet also the most efficient plan possible.

To complete the audience matrix of influence:

1. Identify those individuals listed in the Ranking column from the ISPR analysis who are most likely to be influenced as far as their perceptions and actions are concerned regarding the organization. Can a practitioner realistically get them to support the organization and what it does?
2. Similarly, identify those individuals in the Ranking column from the ISPR analysis who must be influenced in order to achieve the organization's goals as opposed to those who, in a perfect world, would be nice to influence but even if they are not, it would not make or break the success in achieving the goal. The people who would be nice to influence, but who are not required for success, are the Should Influence group.
3. Now, it is a matter of seeing where the individuals overlap. That is, who are both Must Influence and also Likely to Influence, and who are both Should Influence and also Unlikely to Influence?
4. Next, it is time to place them in their corresponding box, like the latitude and longitude on map.
5. The lower, right-hand box now tells which stakeholders to concentrate the plan's efforts on moving forward. These are people who can be affected and also must be affected to achieve the organization's goal.

Audience Matrix of Influence

	SHOULD INFLUENCE	MUST INFLUENCE
Unlikely to Influence	• Those who live 5 or more miles outside of Kutztown • Vegetarians, vegans • People with food allergens • Senior citizens	• Students who live on campus with meal plans • Students on a strict budget • Students/people on diets
Likely to Influence	• Kutztown students who live on campus • Schools activities/fundraisers • Commuters of the University	• Kutztown University students (juniors and seniors) who are off campus • Local residents • Employees on lunch break • Local businesses in town

Executive Summary

The Hot Dog House has an equal number of consumer groups in both categories. Fortunately, there are quick fixes to attract some of the consumer groups who are most likely to not be influenced by The Hot Dog House. The Hot Dog House currently offers a vegetarian hot dog and has several toppings on the menu that are meat free. If customers are concerned about food allergens, employees could lessen concern by frequently changing gloves and asking the customer about their allergy's when they order. Another way to influence more customers is to expand the delivery distance or implement a delivery minimum for delivery over five miles. Others may be harder to influence because of health concerns and dietary restrictions.

◼ THE GLOBAL AMBITION FORCE-FIELD ANALYSIS

The force-field analysis looks at the positive aspects that can influence whether a plan's overall goal, also known as the global ambition, can succeed as well as the negative influences that might cause it to fail. By understanding these two opposing forces, practitioners can adjust their goal and the means to achieve it. In addition, it gives a clearer idea of whether a plan's goal is even achievable before the organization invests time and money in pursuing it. The global force-field analysis takes into account all of the forces, both in the organization's power to control and outside, to give practitioners an overall picture of the plan before the plan is developed.

The first step in developing the global ambition force-field analysis is to think about and list all the driving forces (the things that will help make the goal happen) and all the restraining forces (those things that can hold back the goal from being achieved). After those items are listed, each of them needs an assigned number to measure their weight in terms of their influence of being very driving or very restraining using a scale of 1–5 (5 having the most effect, both positively and negatively). Adding up the numbers will give practitioners a better idea of what needs the most attention and where to devote the most resources during the planning stages. Finally, these numbers are then explained in an executive summary/analysis outcome at the end.

Force-Field Analysis — Global Ambition

DRIVING FORCES	OVERALL GOAL	RESTRAINING FORCES
• Fast Delivery (5)	• Increasing profit	• Closes early (2)
• Free Delivery (5)	• Franchising	• Location (3)
• Homemade Food (4)	• Expand location	• Overuse of social media (3)
• Fair and Affordable Prices (3)	• Positive publicity to The Hot	• Not well established (2)
• Unique/Themed Food (5)	Dog House	• Fairly new business (2)
• Good Reputation (4)	• Customer satisfaction	• Promote themselves better (2)
• Hospitable Employees (4)		• More street advertisement (1)
• Place to Park (4)		• No healthy options (4)
• Retro-Themed Lounge (4)		• Only delivers up to 5 miles
• Community Friendly (5)		away (3)
• More On-the-Go (5)		• Prices high compared to other
		places in town (3)
		• Focused menu Items (2)
		Total: 27
Total: 48		

Summary

Fortunately, The Hot Dog House has more driving forces than restraining forces. While the restraining forces could be considered annoying, many of them could be changed. For example, the restaurant could choose to stay open for longer hours and create more nutritious meals for the health-conscious clientele who may frequent The Hot Dog House. Many of the restraining forces are much more difficult to change, like location and being an overall new restaurant. However, better advertising and other efforts could help ease these problems. You really can't beat the great attributes or driving forces The Hot Dog House has. It caters to the pickiest of populations—college students—and still manages to have a spin of its own without caving into societal pressure.

◼ THE STAKEHOLDER FORCE-FIELD ANALYSIS

The second phase of the force-field analyses is performed the same way as the global ambition force-field analysis, but this time it focuses on the plan's primary stakeholders. These analyses accomplish the same outcomes as the first, but they are performed several times instead of once like with the global ambition force-field analysis. This time there will be one stakeholder force-field analysis per identified stakeholder group.

To perform this analysis, the specific stakeholders that were identified in the Ranking column of the ISPR analysis are used as the basis for which stakeholder groups will be analyzed. Therefore, each stakeholder listed in in the Ranking column will get its own force-field analysis.

From there, the process is the same as with the global ambition force-field analysis:

1. Determine all of the Driving Forces and Restraining Forces for each stakeholder group in terms of how their relationships can help or hurt the organization's chances of meeting the overall goal (global ambition).
2. Provide a ranking on a scale of 1–5, rating the level of their ability to hurt or help the organization meet its goal.
3. Provide an analysis outcome/executive summary that explains the analysis in terms of what it means for the overall plan.
4. Perform steps 1–3 for each listing in the ISPR's Ranking column.
5. The following student analysis provides an example of how this process is done. The same analysis would be conducted for the remaining stakeholder groups.

Force-Field Analysis — Stakeholder Groups

Audience: Students

DRIVING FORCES	RESTRAINING FORCES
• Fast, free delivery (5)	• Location (3)
• Breakfast/lunch/dinner (4)	• Hours are only from 11:00 a.m. to 8:00 p.m. (5)
• Quality food for good prices (5)	• More street advertisement (1)
• Unique menu items (5)	
Total: 19	Total: 9
5 4 3 2 1	1 2 3 4 5

Analysis Outcome

The Hot Dog House is local restaurant most known for their hotdogs. The Hot Dog House provides good quality food for good prices with fast and free delivery. Although their location and operation hours aren't the best, the unique menu items served throughout the day makes The Hot Dog House a great option if you're in the mood for a quick meal. There are more driving forces than restraining forces for The Hot Dog House in this stakeholder segmentation.

▌ MEDIA ANALYSIS

Once the major stakeholders involved in the plan are known, it is then time to analyze how and where they gain information and communicate themselves. Media analysis requires practitioners to consider the best means and approaches to communicate with those stakeholders identified in the Ranking category of the ISPR analysis. Knowing this, practitioners can then consider the best methods of disseminating information in their future plan, as well as how to listen to what these stakeholders are saying about the organization. This knowledge can be used to augment or alter the plan as needed. For instance, if the plan calls for sending a mass email to employees but it is later found that the employees do not open their work email, then the practitioner knows to change that means of communication to a more effective medium.

To complete the media analysis, practitioners must:

1. List all stakeholders from the Ranking column (from the ISPR analysis) across the top of the Media Analysis table.
2. Using the prompts from the far-left vertical column, analyze and answer the prompts according to the stakeholder group being analyzed that is in question.

3. Provide an executive summary at the conclusion of filling out the table that provides a succinct explanation of what the table's findings mean in terms of how this information can be employed moving forward in writing the plan.

Media Analysis

	KUTZTOWN UNIVERSITY STUDENTS	LOCAL BUSINESSES/ EMPLOYEES	KUTZTOWN RESIDENTIAL COMMUNITY
Identify all the media outlets that this group uses	• Facebook • Twitter • Instagram • KU Radio • KUTV	• Facebook • Local TV • Radio stations • Newspapers	• Facebook • Radio stations • Newspapers
Identify the types of messages each medium communicates	• Delivery and menu options • BYOB • Food specials (Sober Sundays) • Special events • Dine-and-donates	• Menu • Delivery, takeout, and dine-in options	• Daily specials • Special events (car shows) • Delivery, takeout, and dine-in options
Identify the frequency of use of each medium	• 4 or more times a day	• 4 or more times a day	• 4 or more times a day
Identify the reasons the stakeholder group uses this medium	• Entertainment • To socialize • Sharing and viewing pictures • To view food options and specials	• Entertainment • Bonding with employees • Upcoming events	• Entertainment • Reading local newspapers
Identify why your organization can use this medium for this stakeholder group	• Students utilize social media more than any other medium • Students listen to the radio while driving to class and out the community	• They are most likely searching for The Hot Dog House in their feeds if they are a regular • Listen to the radio in the car going to and from places • They pay for the newspaper, so they are more eager to read it	• Kutztown residents scroll through Facebook feed on lunch breaks or while at work • They listen to the radio to and from places • They pay for the newspaper, so they are more eager to read it
Identify the drawbacks of this medium	• Social media updates can become intrusive • Because of above, social media updates can get easily lost	• Social media updates can become repetitive and annoying	• Radio time is limited • Newspapers may get thrown out/not looked at

Kutztown University Students

The Hot Dog House reaches out to students using Facebook, Instagram, and Twitter. This is the easiest way of reaching out to students because most use social media daily. Some students might become interested in a certain food item after seeing it posted on the restaurant's social media page and be more likely to visit. The radio is also often utilized by students while driving to and from class or around town. The restaurant offers breakfast specials for hungover students after a night of partying, and the bring-your-own-beer (BYOB) aspect is appealing to some who might want to enjoy a beer or two with their meal.

SWOT ANALYSIS

Of all of the analyses covered so far, the SWOT analysis (Strengths, Weaknesses, Opportunities, Threats) is probably the most well-known. The Strengths, Weakness, Opportunities, and Threats are analyzed according to the organization—and more importantly, the goal—established for it through the global ambition force-field analysis. At the heart of the SWOT analysis is how the organization can take advantage of its strengths to minimize its weaknesses and how it can use its opportunities to diminish its threats.

Keys to Remember

Strengths and weaknesses are internal to the organization. In other words, they both exist from within the organization. Opportunities and threats are external to the organization. For example, good employees are a strength because they exist within the organization. Competition from other similar organizations is a threat because they exist outside of the organization.

In the end, what is gained from the SWOT analysis is how the organization can use its assets (strengths and opportunities) to outweigh or negate its problems (weaknesses and threats).

SWOT Analysis

	HELPFUL TO ACHIEVING GOAL	HARMFUL TO ACHIEVING GOAL
Internal Origin **Attributes of the Organization**	Strengths: • Consistently good food • Fast delivery • Unique menu	Weaknesses: • Restaurant location • Overuse of social media • Hours of operation
External Origin **Attributes**	Opportunities: • Dine-and-donate opportunities • Additional options • Student discounts	Threats: • Competing restaurants • Stigma of hotdogs

Summary

The SWOT analysis shows that The Hot Dog House has an equal number of strengths and opportunities as they do weaknesses and threats. The quality of The Hot Dog House's food and fast delivery sets them apart from other restaurants in town. The biggest attribute of The Hot Dog House is their dine-and-donate opportunities. The location of the restaurant can't be changed, but the overuse of social media could be fixed by cutting back on posts per day. Since The Hot Dog House's main menu items can be bought at a few other restaurants in Kutztown, it is up to The Hot Dog House to find new ways to beat out the competition. The Hot Dog House could become more competitive by creating new burgers and hot dogs, and possibly by expanding the menu.

THE GOSTE PLAN

Once the research and analysis are completed, it is then time to use all of that information to develop to most sensible, logical, and effective plan possible. Remember that all of the work up to this point was to understand the organization, situation, and stakeholders involved as much as possible. Armed with this knowledge, practitioners can then start to develop the actual plan. The plan can best be thought of as a roadmap to accomplishing the overall goal. The development of that plan takes on a top-down model, from the goal through the evaluative tactics that will measure everything required to achieve that goal.

The basic idea is that the plan goes from the broadest element—the goal—to the most specific—the evaluative tactics. The planning model uses the acronym GOSTE – Goal, Objectives, Strategies, Tactics, and Evaluative Tactics.

Step 1: Developing the Goal

The goal is the overarching aim of the plan. It is written in such a way that it is broad enough to encompass a major situation that the organization is involved in yet precise enough as to be as effective and realistic as possible. The goal can be retrieved from the global ambition force-field analysis. The goal is synonymous with the global ambition; basically, they are one and the same. The crucial point is to develop it so that it can be applicable to a wide range of issues affecting the organization.

Step 2: Writing the Objectives

Under the goal comes the plan's objectives. They are more specific and detailed than the goal. They pick up where the goal's ambiguity leaves off, with greater emphasis on how the goal can be achieved. There are two major elements to the objective: how it can help attain the goal and how it can measure the plan's effectiveness. For instance, if the overall goal is to increase profitability, then the objectives of that goal must address how the plan can actually increase sales, donations, increase sales, donations, and the like to actually increase profitability. The other major consideration to objective writing is concentrating each of them on the major stakeholders involved in the plan. They can be identified by using the same stakeholder groups that were analyzed in the stakeholder force-field analyses.

Each objective will have a measurable component and a timeframe, and be concentrated on an individual stakeholder group. Therefore, each group will have their own objective: one objective for each identified stakeholder used for the stakeholder force-field analyses. Remember the more objectives that are accomplished, the more likely it is to achieve the goal, so they need to be both meaningful and realistic at the same time.

To write each objective,

1. concentrate on one stakeholder group per objective according to the stakeholder force-field analyses,
2. develop how much of a change is required from that stakeholder group to help accomplish the goal, and
3. determine the timeframe for each stakeholder to "change" according to the previous step.

Example objective: Increase on-campus students' knowledge of the new PR Major by 30 percent by September 2018.

Step 3: Developing the Strategies

Once the objectives are developed, next come the strategies. Plans should have at least three strategies for each objective. Strategies can be tricky to write—they are more detailed than objectives but less specific than tactics. They can best be thought of as collections of similar types of tactics (which are the hands-on activities). For example, "Increase social media presence" would be a strategy. A tactic that would fall underneath that strategy would be, "Tweet daily lunch specials." Plans can overlap with strategies among more than one stakeholder group.

Examples of Strategies

STAKEHOLDER GROUP	EXAMPLE STRATEGIES
First-year students	Hold involvement events
Commuter students	Create marketing giveaways
In-town residents	Host holiday-related events
Local businesses	Create partnership opportunities

The following graphic (Figure 13–1) gives you an idea of how the strategies fit into the context of the plan.

OBJECTIVE 1	OBJECTIVE 2	OBJECTIVE 3	OBJECTIVE 4
Strategy 1.1	Strategy 2.1	Strategy 3.1	Strategy 4.1
Strategy 1.2	Strategy 2.2	Strategy 3.2	Strategy 4.2
Strategy 1.3	Strategy 2.3	Strategy 3.3	Strategy 4.3

FIGURE 13-1. Plan Objectives

Step 4: Creating the Tactics

Now that the strategies are created, it is time to think about the actual, day-to-day actions that will enable the strategies to succeed, which in turn help meet the objectives, which then allow the goal to be met. They clearly explain to anyone responsible for carrying them out what to do, how to do it, and when it should be done. Tactics need to be crystal clear. Remember that many people might be involved in accomplishing the tactics, so they need to be written in such a way that anyone can understand their role and responsibilities when it comes to implementing the entire plan. Tactics are arranged underneath their corresponding strategies.

For example:

STRATEGY	SAMPLE TACTIC
Increase social media presence	Post daily specials on Facebook by 10:30 a.m. every day
Hold special event	Host end-of-semester sidewalk sale with band and free samples on Friday, May 3

As you can see, the tactics clearly spell out how the strategies will actually be implemented. There is no requirement as far as the number of tactics are concerned; however, plans must have enough tactics so that no strategy and objective is in danger of not succeeding due to lack of effort on the tactics' part.

Step 5: Measuring the Plan with Evaluative Tactics

The final step in the GOSTE Plan is the evaluative tactics. As with the rest of the plan's development, the evaluative tactics fall under the tactics and enable the plan's developers to actually see what succeeded or not and where. In other words, practitioners can learn from the mistakes or problems with their own plan because the evaluative tactics enable them to do so. The evaluative tactics need to address how the plan can be measured as far as the effectiveness of the tactics that came before it, the strategy connected to it, and then the objective that is concerned. It is important to use the objective as a basis for the evaluative tactic. For example, if an objective is to "increase weekend foot traffic by 10% in three months," then how can that 10% be measured? The answer to that question will direct practitioners to what the evaluative tactics should be addressing.

Types of evaluative tactics include:

1. Counting attendance at events
2. Tallying the number or "likes" or retweets
3. Adding gains in donations
4. Adding the number of times a media outlet reports on the organization

Like all tactics, evaluative tactics must be very specific and detailed so that whomever is carrying them out can do so clearly and as easily as possible.

An example of a properly worded evaluative tactic is as follows:

Count the number of returned raffle tickets given out at the Oktoberfest event.

This tactic is correctly worded because it (a) addresses how the event's success will be measured in terms of attendance and (b) identifies the event in question that is to be measured. Like operational plan tactics, plans should have many and a wide variety of evaluative tactics. It would be difficult to measure the outcome of an entire objective with many strategies and a multitude of tactics with just one or two evaluative tactics.

Summary

The ultimate test for any plan, of course, is its implantation and evaluation. No plan is foolproof, and there will always be aspects of it that could be changed, improved upon, or completely eliminated. Unfortunately, this is never truly known until it is put into action. However, with sound research and analysis, practitioners have a much better likelihood of success. Strategic planning without the investment of research and analytics is like throwing darts at a dartboard while blindfolded. You might get lucky one out of every hundred throws and hit the bullseye. However, research and analytical planning remove the blindfold and enable the precision that will hit the bullseye more often than sheer luck can ever afford. The following is an example of a section of a GOSTE Plan. For illustration purposes, it shows only the student stakeholder group

GOSTE PLAN

Goal: The goal as a public relations team is to increase sales and popularity of The Hot Dog House by capitalizing on the Kutztown University Student Population, Residential Community, and Local Businesses/Employees.

Objective 1: Increase the amount of Kutztown University students who eat at The Hot Dog House by 30% by the end of fall semester 2018.

Strategy 1.1: Student Discounts

Tactic 1.1.1: Use Bear Bucks
Tactic 1.1.2: 10% off with student ID
Tactic 1.1.3: Post student specials
Tactic 1.1.4: Student punch card
Tactic 1.1.5: Free drink with on-campus delivery

Evaluative Tactic 1.1.1.1: Evaluated by how many students are using Bear Bucks monthly
Evaluative Tactic 1.1.1.2: Evaluated by how many students are presenting IDs to receive discount
Evaluative Tactic 1.1.1.3: Determined successful by how many students are ordering student specials
Evaluative Tactic 1.1.1.4: Measured by how many students have a punch card, based on order history
Evaluative Tactic 1.1.1.5: Measured by how many on-campus students are ordering for the free drink with purchase

Strategy 1.2: Expand Hours

Tactic 1.2.1: Weekend open until midnight
Tactic 1.2.2: Weekday open for breakfast
Tactic 1.2.3: Weekdays open until 10:00 p.m.
Tactic 1.2.4: One weekend a month open until 3:00 a.m.
Tactic 1.2.5: The Hot Dog House movie night at DMZ, serving food until movie ends

Evaluative Tactic 1.2.1.1: Evaluated by how many students are coming into The Hot Dog House for late night hours
Evaluative Tactic 1.2.1.2: Evaluated by how many students are ordering The Hot Dog House for breakfast over a month period
Evaluative Tactic 1.2.1.3: Determined successful by how much more profits are made by extending hours versus profits made during regular hours
Evaluative Tactic 1.2.1.4: Ask for feedback from students who come to the late-night events to determine if The Hot Dog House should do this more the one night a month
Evaluative Tactic 1.2.1.5: Measured by how many students are purchasing food at DMZ movie night

Strategy 1.3: Campus Involvement

Tactic 1.3.1: Provide hot dog stand for move in day
Tactic 1.3.2: Sell hot dogs at Bear Fest
Tactic 1.3.3: Dine-and-donates with on-campus organizations
Tactic 1.3.4: Late night sales on Main Street with campus organizations
Tactic 1.3.5: Hot dogs sold at all Kutztown University games are The Hot Dog House hot dogs

Evaluative Tactic 1.3.1.1: Evaluated by how many people purchase food from hot dog stand on move-in day
Evaluative Tactic 1.3.1.2: Measured by profits made at Bear Fest, 25% more than the cost of supplies for event
Evaluative Tactic 1.3.1.3: Measured by how many on-campus organizations want The Hot Dog House to cater their events
Evaluative Tactic 1.3.1.4: Work with religious fellowship and sell $1 hot dogs along with the free water offered by the fellowship
Evaluative Tactic 1.3.1.5: Measured by profit of hot dogs sold during sporting events

THE GANTT CHART

The Gantt chart acts as the visual timeline of the GOSTE plan. It enables everyone involved in planning, executing, and evaluating the plan to see when and where their responsibilities fall in the overall context of the initiative. It is named for its creator, Henry Gantt, who developed this system to show the relationships between tactics and the status of the plan at any given time.

Creating the Gantt Chart

Each tactic and evaluative tactic must be accounted for in the Gantt chart. Some activities have definitive dates, such as events, whereas other activities might be ongoing, such as weekly emails or social media posts. There is no one, set way to develop a Gantt chart. The main aspect to remember when setting one up is to be clear about how it is presented, for both clarity and consistency. Everyone involved in carrying out any tactic or evaluative tactic must be able to see when their activity is to take place within the grand scheme of the entire plan. Remember, some plans can have hundreds of tactics carried out by thousands of individuals, so the Gantt chart must be clear and useful to everyone. The example below is set up so that the dotted line shows when the tactic or evaluative tactic will begin and the arrow shows when the activity commences.

GANTT CHART

May 1	June 1	July 1	Aug 1	Sept 1	Oct 1	Nov 1	Dec 1	Jan 1	Feb 1	Mar 1	Apr 1

Tactic 1.1.1:
Use Bear Bucks
-->

Tactic 1.1.2:
10% off with student ID
-->

Tactic 1.1.3:
Post student specials (every Friday)
-->

Tactic 1.1.4:
Student punch card
-->

Tactic 1.1.5:
Free drink with on campus delivery
-->

Evaluative Tactic 1.1.1.1
Evaluated by how many students are using Bear Bucks monthly
-->

Evaluative Tactic 1.1.1.2
Evaluated by how many students are presenting IDs to receive discount
--->

Evaluative Tactic 1.1.1.3
Determined successful by how many students are ordering student specials
--->

Evaluative Tactic 1.1.1.4
Measured by how many students have a punch card, based on order history
--->

Evaluative Tactic 1.1.1.5
Measured by how many on-campus students are ordering for the free drink with purchase
--->

Tactic 1.2.1:
Weekend open until midnight
--->

Tactic 1.2.2:
Weekday open for breakfast
--->

Tactic 1.2.3:
Weekdays open until 10:00 p.m.
--->

Tactic 1.2.4:
One weekend a month open until 3:00 a.m.
--->

Tactic 1.2.5:
The Hot Dog House movie night at DMZ, serving food until movie ends
--->

Evaluative Tactic 1.2.1.1
Evaluated by how many students are coming into Mad Dog for late-night hours
--->

Evaluative Tactic 1.2.1.2
Evaluated by how many students are ordering The Hot Dog House for breakfast over a month period
--->

Evaluative Tactic 1.2.1.3
Determined successful by how much more profits are made by extending hours versus profits made during regular hours
--->

Evaluative Tactic 1.2.1.4
Ask for feedback from students who come to the late-night events about whether The Hot Dog House do this more than one night a month
--->

Evaluative Tactic 1.2.1.5
Measured by how many students are purchasing food at DMZ movie night
--->

Tactic 1.3.1:
Provide hot dog stand for move-in day
--->

Tactic 1.3.2:
Sell hot dogs at Bear Fest
--->

Tactic 1.3.3:
Dine-and-donates with on-campus organizations (once a month)
--->

Tactic 1.3.4:
Late-night sales on Main Street with campus organizations (every other month)
--->

Tactic 1.3.5:
Hot dogs sold at all Kutztown University games are The Hot Dog House hot dogs
--->

Evaluative Tactic 1.3.1.1
Evaluated by how many people purchase food from The Hot Dog House on move-in day
--->

Evaluative Tactic 1.3.1.2
Measured by profits made at Bear Fest, 25% more than the cost of supplies for event
--->

Evaluative Tactic 1.3.1.3
Measured by how many on-campus organizations want The Hot Dog House to cater their events
--->

Evaluative Tactic 1.3.1.4
Work with religious fellowship and sell $1 hot dogs along with the free water offered by the fellowship
--->

Evaluative Tactic 1.3.1.5
Measured by profit of hot dogs sold during sporting events
--->

The Budget

Like the Gantt chart, the budget accounts for each tactic and evaluative tactic. Some items have clear costs such as materials; others are more abstract because they are based on hourly work such as posting items to Facebook. The budget also addresses items that might not have clear costs, such as promotional efforts (see Tactic 1.1.2 for an example). Those items are negligible on expense; therefore, they receive a Negl. listing, meaning that the monetary cost is not significant. The budget is arranged according to the strategies. Each strategy's tactics and evaluative tactics are calculated to show clients where the costs are accruing most and for what purpose. The sums of all the strategies are added to calculate the total cost of the plan. Note that it is important to estimate costs on realistic pricing from outside contractors and vendors. However, it is also important to remember that budgets should be calculated on a more liberal budget that estimates costs on the high side. This is done in budgets so as to not prematurely run out of funds, and from a client's perspective, it is better to come in under estimate. A public relations practitioner who has a reputation for implementing plans under estimate stands a much greater chance of attracting new clients than one who needs more money halfway through the plan.

BUDGET
Strategy 1.1

Tactic 1.1.1: Use Bear Bucks	$600 (machine)
Tactic 1.1.2: 10% off with student ID	Negl.
Tactic 1.1.3: Post student specials	$5/hr.
Tactic 1.1.4: Student punch card	$5
Tactic 1.1.5: Free drink with on-campus delivery	$30
Evaluative Tactic 1.1.1.1 Evaluated by how many students are using Bear Bucks monthly	Negl.
Evaluative Tactic 1.1.1.2 Evaluated by how many students are presenting IDs to receive discount	$8/hr.
Evaluative Tactic 1.1.1.3 Determined successful by how many students are ordering student specials	$8/hr.
Evaluative Tactic 1.1.1.4 Measured by how many students have a punch card, based on order history	$8/hr.
Evaluative Tactic 1.1.1.5 Measured by how many on-campus students are ordering for the free drink with purchase	$8/hr.
Total:	**TBD Based on Hourly Rate. Est. $955**

Strategy 1.2

Tactic 1.2.1: Weekend open until midnight	$100
Tactic 1.2.2: Weekday open for breakfast	$250
Tactic 1.2.3: Weekdays open until 10:00 p.m.	$100
Tactic 1.2.4: One weekend a month open until 3:00 a.m.	$168
Tactic 1.2.5: The Hot Dog House movie night at DMZ, serving food until movie ends	$750
Evaluative Tactic 1.2.1.1 Evaluated by how many students are coming into Mad Dog for late-night hours	Negl.
Evaluative Tactic 1.2.1.2 Evaluated by how many students are ordering The Hot Dog House for breakfast over a month period	Negl.
Evaluative Tactic 1.2.1.3 Determined successful by how much more profits are made by extending hours versus profits made during regular hours	Negl.

Evaluative Tactic 1.2.1.4 Ask for feedback from students who come to the late-night events about whether The Hot Dog House should do this more than one night a month	$5
Evaluative Tactic 1.2.1.5 Measured by how many students are purchasing food at DMZ movie night	Negl.
Total:	**$1,373**
Strategy 1.3	
Tactic 1.3.1: Provide hotdog stand for move-in day	$350
Tactic 1.3.2: Sell hot dogs at Bear Fest	$75
Tactic 1.3.3: Dine-and-donates with on-campus organizations	Negl.
Tactic 1.3.4: Late-night sales on Main Street with campus organizations	Negl.
Tactic 1.3.5: Hot dogs sold at all Kutztown University games are The Hot Dog House hot dogs.	$100
Evaluative Tactic 1.3.1.1 Evaluated by how many people purchase food from The Hot Dog House on move-in day	$8/hr.
Evaluative Tactic 1.3.1.2 Measured by profits made at Bear Fest, 25% more than the cost of supplies for event	$100
Evaluative Tactic 1.3.1.3 Measured by how many on-campus organizations want The Hot Dog House to cater their events	$250
Evaluative Tactic 1.3.1.4 Work with religious fellowship and sell $1 hot dogs along with the free water offered by the fellowship	$50
Evaluative Tactic 1.3.1.5 Measured by profit of hot dogs sold during sporting events	$50
Total:	**$890**
Grand Total:	**$3.218.00**

Summary

As this chapter illustrates, successful public relations planning entails considerable time, effort, and expertise. Plans that are thrown together haphazardly and without solid research are destined for failure. Only through strategic thinking and planning can public relations practitioners expect success rather than simply hoping for it.

THE FUTURE OF PUBLIC RELATIONS and TOMORROW'S PRACTITIONER

14

Public relations is as popular and important today as it has ever been. Beginning with the modern era of public relations that began in the early 20th century, the practice has evolved and changed over time, yet its fundamentals are constant. Technology, public opinion, and social causes have made today's public relations practitioner a valuable and necessary asset to any organization. However, because the field's major tools of communication and its audiences' access to information is greater today than ever, it is important to look at how the field is progressing and where it will likely head into the future. Additionally, this last chapter will offer ideas, suggestions, and tips that any aspiring public relations practitioner can use to begin his or her career in this dynamic and important profession.

Public relations changes and adapts its principles and fundamentals to meet the challenges and opportunities it is presented with. Throughout the 20th century, technology-driven communications shaped the field more than the previous centuries combined. One could argue that the 20th century was the century of public relations. However, as the second decade of the 21st century moves

FIGURE 14-1. First-generation iPhone
http://commons.wikimedia.org/wiki/File:IPhone_hands_on_trial.jpg

forward, it is possible to project where the field may move given the challenges and changes facing it. Clearly, aspiring public relations practitioners can benefit from these predictions given the fact that they will be responsible for moving the field of public relations forward. Three major areas will likely influence the future of public relations: technology, social changes, and globalization. These three areas were chosen because of the great influence they had in shifting public relations from a practice of deception and propaganda in the early 1900s to one that operates responsibly and as ethically as possible today.

TECHNOLOGY

It is hard to remember the days before cell phones and smart device technology; however, for most of the public, this was less than 10 years ago. Apple's 2005 launch of the iPhone changed the way the public connects and communicates with each other as much as the change that the Internet ushered in during the 1990s. Because of this great shift in communication in so few years (10 years is a drop in the bucket of time), you can feel confident in thinking that instantaneous, convenient, and even cheaper forms of communication will be available as the 21st century continues. Because of this phenomenon of pushing communication forward, at least technologically, tomorrow's practice of public relations will focus more on managing information and communication than simply making statements and sending messages. Even today, most people are bombarded with news, links, advertisements, and messages that make true, meaningful communication difficult. Technology enables the world to be more connected, but at a price. Similar to the notion of everyone talking and no one listening, the state of communication will likely only get more efficient but less effective. Therefore, public relations, and its critical role in communicating an organization's point of view, will be even more difficult despite the advances in technology that enable people to be more connected. How can you manage an organization's image and its communication in a world where dialogues via advancing technology never cease? Managing the online presence of an organization will likely become the number-one job of future public relations practitioners. Safeguarding against erroneous reports, online rumors, and misinterpretations of information will add additional pressures and problems than organizations already face today. With advancing communication technologies come a vast number of problems that can arise from them, which the current state of public relations is beginning to face now. This trend will likely continue in both the ferocity of the problems and the speed at which they arise. The

24-hour news cycle has already become the 24-minute news cycle, and all indications point to a 24-second news cycle in the near future.

SOCIAL CHANGES

With great advances in technology come great changes to society and how it functions. The advent of the airplane forever changed the way the world thinks of its planet. People who had never traveled 20 miles from their homes were now traveling the globe. The radio changed the way people got news and entertainment. Television fostered a new generation of media consumers. The Internet connected the world and enabled anyone with a modem to speak to the world. Today's smart device technologies are currently ushering in a new socially connected world. Whether that is a good thing or not does not affect the fact that it already happening and will continue in the future. Public relations practitioners, socially engaged to begin with, will need to proactively and reactively address today's mobile connected society. The PRSA Leadership Assembly found in 2014 that future practitioners will require greater specialization and an emphasis on embracing these changes. Despite this need, the group's findings point to the fact the essential and fundamental elements of public relations practice will remain the same. With social changes revolving around shifts in communication, the need for more public relations practitioners versed in and able to communicate effectively with new platforms and technologies will be greater than ever. Currently, however, only about 53 percent of practitioners use the main means of online communication—content marketing focus. However, given the increased demands for a substantive return on investment from organizational leadership for social and online media work, the demand for more evidence of its effectiveness will increase. Today's emphasis on SEO (search engine optimization) will likely evolve into larger areas of return on investment of online public relations operations. SEO entails the efforts to make your organization and its online presence rise among the search engine results rankings. How can you get your organization to be the first result when people use search engines to look for businesses like yours? Imagine if you worked as the public relations practitioner charged with managing your organization's SEO. If your company was Home Depot, for instance, what can you do to keep it ranked as the number-one search engine result over its main competitor, Lowe's Home Improvement? The primary responsibilities of the future public relations practitioner will remain the same; however, the means and techniques to accomplish new and evolving demands will change. Essentially, the future asks how you can use new technologies to manage and operate fundamental public relations responsibilities. Vocus' State of Public Relations 2014 study, which polled 325 senior and mid-level public relations practitioners found:

While the role of a public relations professional remains the same—generating and creating goodwill for an organization with its stakeholders through a variety of tactics—how they accomplish their main goal remains an intriguing evolution. As social and digital media continue to be impacted by technology developments, PR practitioners will be challenged to optimize and cut through the noise with the right mix of strategy, creativity, channels, and campaigns[82].

GLOBALIZATION

Clearly, with advancing technologies enabling the world to communicate quickly, easily, and cheaply, the lines between cultures and countries will likely to continue to blur. With this greater emphasis on communication on a global scale, the public relations practitioner of tomorrow must be adept at using the technologies available but also understanding their limitations. Face-to-face communication will likely never be replaced in terms of effectiveness with mediated technologies. The need for interpersonal communication will remain. However, with technology enabling the world to communicate so easily, the availability of face-to-face communication may lessen. For instance, technologies today enable people to use smartphones to talk to one another using video chat capabilities. Given these advances, organizations might be less inclined to budget travel and related expenses to facilitate face-to-face meetings. Therefore, as a chief communicator for an organization, the public relations practitioner will likely need to understand when and how to utilize these media while also utilizing the tenets of true, two-way communication. Globalization on a business scale also adds to this complexity. Multinational conglomerates and business buyouts force public relations practitioners to represent companies and organizations that are composed of many smaller businesses based all over the world. The mix of backgrounds and experiences makes representing one organization more difficult because its main message can be misinterpreted or misconstrued by various stakeholder groups. Essentially, the one consistent message from an organization becomes jumbled among many different companies operating under the umbrella of one large conglomerated organization. The future for tomorrow's public relations practitioner will certainly be more complex and confusing, even though the actual means and technologies associated with the job will improve. It is through these improvements that most of the complexities lie—too many tools and not enough people who know how to use them.

To this end, it is important to recap the major skills that today's public relations practitioner must possess because, as you might suspect, most of them will remain the same in the future. Interestingly, the PRSA Leadership Assembly predicted the major job demands for a practitioner entering the field in 2015. Its predictions were made in 2009, and as you can see, many of the same requirements of the future practitioner are the same as the past. It defined the top 10 areas of knowledge, skills, and abilities. They are:

1. Business literacy
2. Communication models and theories
3. Researching, planning, implementing, and evaluating programs
4. Media relations
5. Ethics and law
6. Management skills and issues
7. Crisis communication management
8. Using information technology efficiently
9. History and current issues in public relations
10. Advanced communication skills

As you can see, these 10 key skills align nearly perfectly with the major elements of this textbook, and they have remained constant in the field for decades as well. Therefore, while technology, public issues, and society as a whole fluctuate over time, the essential public relations skills to manage them remains constant.

INTEGRATED MARKETING COMMUNICATIONS

A shift in strategic communications efforts began about 20 years ago with the introduction of Strategic Marketing Communications. First coined at Northwestern University, the idea behind **Integrated Marketing Communications**, or simply IMC, is the combined efforts of marketing, advertising, and public relations into one, focused effort[83]. The major benefits of IMC are efficiency and effectiveness in achieving these formerly separated areas of communication. In the past, the disciplines of marketing, advertising, and public relations operated on their own. Therefore, each department would utilize their own personnel and resources to achieve what are the same objectives and goals. Each segment strives to improve the brand and notoriety of the organization, and therefore, each area should work with the others. However, redundancies and inefficiency would naturally affect these areas' ability to achieve their goals. Now, through IMC, each department works with and complements the others and, through this combined effort, achieves its goals more easily and effectively. Also, organizations do not need to staff and fund three departments or hire outside firms. Now, one efficient and effective department handles the communications needs of the organization. Therefore, it is also much more cost effective and effective in achieving an organization's strategic communications objectives.

ENTERING THE FIELD

A career in public relations today generally begins in college. In the past, most public relations practitioners came from other fields—usually journalism or a strategic communication background in marketing or advertising. However, today's greater understanding and appreciation of the field among all industries has changed the requirements for aspiring public relations practitioners. The major demands include education in the field coupled with experience using this education. Because of this, the need for job or internship experience has never been greater. Most graduates of public relations programs who have not worked in the field are at a great disadvantage in terms of hiring compared to those who have. Increased competition among job seekers continues to make this demand even greater. Therefore, in addition to solid academic credentials, tomorrow's public relations professionals must possess experience and demonstrable knowledge. This means evidence of knowing the essential requirements of public relations—not just in terms of grades, but also a portfolio.

Most first-time jobseekers' portfolios should include a few essential items. One is a solid, well-crafted new release that demonstrates the writing ability of the applicant as well as his or her understanding of media relations and placement. In addition, some illustration of the public relations planning process is good. For instance, a sample plan that shows the research abilities of the applicant and his or her ability to apply implementation and evaluation strategies shows potential employers the level of the applicant's abilities. In addition, social media skills are an expectation that most employers today have, especially with young applicants. Therefore, being able to demonstrate your knowledge and ability to develop social media content places you in a good position for your potential job. Lastly, many job openings ask for some real-world examples of public relations work. In the past, classroom projects and grade point averages were sometimes enough to persuade an employer to hire one applicant over another. However, given today's highly competitive job market, even entry-level positions will often ask for clear evidence of public relations knowledge and skill with evidence of success. Because of this, the importance and necessity of internships mustn't be underestimated. Internships were once an option; today they are an expectation. To this end, it is important to understand the realistic internship application process. Like all job listing websites, internship postings attract thousands of applicants for a few hundred internships. Therefore, trying to find an internship through these sites will be a long, frustrating, and often fruitless endeavor. Therefore, it is best to be proactive in your search. Rather than looking for postings of existing internships, actively seek out potential employers who might benefit from an intern. Most organizations would love to have an intern, but many employers either do not have the time to look for them or think the process of developing an internship partnership with a college or university will be too complicated. Therefore, students who ask employers if they would like an intern and who can explain the school/employer process will often find more success in securing an internship than the student who relies on internship listing sites. When communicating with potential internship locations, it is important to outline the following:

1. Why you think your qualifications make you the best candidate for them.
2. Why you want to intern at their organization.
3. How the internship process works between your college or university and the organization.
4. Some examples of your public relations knowledge and how it can help them.
5. Your availability and how you can fit their requirements with yours.

Clearly, using the public relations principle of customized communication is especially important in this process. You need to research the organization and the person most likely to oversee a public relations internship. Using this process you can locate organizations near you and those that work in areas that interest you most, such as sports, entertainment, or the arts.

Tomorrow's public relations leaders are only as good as the education and training they receive today. Successful organizations have relied on sound public relations for decades, and future demands on organizational reputations will only increase the importance of this key function. The future of public relations has never looked more demanding. However, because of these demands, the future of public relations has also never been brighter.

IMAGE CREDIT

Fig. 14-1: Copyright © 2007 by Jylppy / Flickr, (CC BY 2.0) at http://commons.wikimedia.org/wiki/File:IPhone_hands_on_trial.jpg.

BIBLIOGRAPHY

1. Tesser, A. (1988). *Toward a self-evaluation maintenance model of social behavior.* In Berkowitz, L. advances in experimental social psychology. New York: Academic Press.
2. Grunig, James E; Hunt, Todd (1984), *Managing public relations* (6th ed.), Orlando, FL: Harcourt Brace Jovanovich.
3. Phillips, David (2006), Towards relationship management: Public relations at the core of organizational development. *Journal of Communication Management, 10*(2).
4. Michel, W., Shoda, Y., & Smith, R. E. (2004). *Introduction to personality: Toward an integration.* New York: John Wiley.
5. Young, Gregory G. (1978). *Your personality and how to live with it.* New York: Atheneum/SMI.
6. Oldham, John M. & Morris, Lois B. (1995). The new personality self-portrait: Why you think, work, love and act the way you do. New York: Bantam.
7. Bennett, P. D. (1995). The American Marketing Association dictionary of terms. New York: McGraw-Hill.
8. Grunig, James E. and Hunt, Todd. (1984). *Managing public relations 6e.* Orlando, FL: Harcourt Brace Jovanovich.
9. Neumeier, M. (2004), *The dictionary of brand.* New York: AIGA Center for Brand Experience.
10. Standard & Poor's (2005). *The Standard & Poor's 500 guide.* McGraw-Hill Professional: New York.
11. New York Times. (1985). Topics: Cars and colas coke jokes. *New York* Times. Retrieved from http://www.nytimes.com/1985/10/23/opinion/topics-cars-and-colas-coke-jokes.html
12. Oliver, Thomas. (1986) *The real Coke, the real story,* London: Penguin.
13. Donsbach, Wolfgang. (2008). *The international encyclopedia of communication.* Malden, MA: Wiley-Blackwell.
14. Cialdini, R. B., Borden, R. J., Thorne, A., Walker, M. R., Freeman, S., & Sloan, L. R. (1976). Basking in reflected glory: Three (football) field studies. *Journal of Personality and Social Psychology*, 34, 366–375.
15. The Coca-Cola Company. (2012). The real story of New Coke. Retrieved from http://www.coca-colacompany.com/history/the-real-story-of-new-coke
16. Bernays, E. (2011). *Crystallizing public opinion (Reprint edition).* New York: IG Publishing.
17. Katz & Lazarsfeld (1955). Personal influence. New York: Free Press.
18. Staubhaar, LaRose, Davenport (2009). *Media now.* Belmont, CA: Wadsworth Cengage Learning.
19. Harasta, J. (2014). Jersey strong, right?: A communications analysis of New Jersey's post-Hurricane Sandy tourism recovery. *Case Studies in Strategic Communication*, 3.

20. Lovett, Mitchell; Peres, Renana; Shachar, Ron. (2012). On brands and word-of-mouth. *Journal of Marketing Research, 50*(4), 427–444.

21. Yankelovich, Daniel; David Meer. (2006). Rediscovering market segmentation. *Harvard Business Review*, 1–11.

22. Rogers, Everett M. (1962). *Diffusion of innovations.* Glencoe, Ontario: Glencoe/McGraw-Hill: Free Press.

23. Strategic Business Insights. (n.d.). About VALS. Retrieved from http://www.strategicbusinessinsights.com/vals/about.shtml

24. Cantril, H. (1965). *The pattern of human concerns.* New Brunswick, NJ: Rutgers University Press.

25. Public Relations Society of America. (2012). What is public relations: PRSA's widely accepted definition. Retrieved from http://www.prsa.org/AboutPRSA/PublicRelationsDefined/#.VAYiG0u4mFI

26. McClam, E., & Weber, H. R. (2010, June 11). BP's failure made worse by PR mistakes. NBC News. Retrieved from http://www.nbcnews.com/id/37647218/ns/business-world_business/t/bps-failures-made-worse-pr-mistakes/#.VAYkOUu4mFI

27. Norman, Wayne; Chris MacDonald (2004). Getting to the bottom of 'Triple bottom line.'" *Business Ethics Quarterly, 14*(2), 243–262.

28. Farris, Paul W., Neil T. Bendle, Phillip E. Pfeifer, & David J. Reibstein (2010). *Marketing metrics: The definitive guide to measuring marketing performance.* Upper Saddle River, New Jersey: Pearson Education, Inc.

29. Farris, P. W., Neil T., Bendle, P. E., Pfeifer, & Reibstein, D. J. (2010). *Marketing metrics: The definitive guide to measuring marketing performance.* Upper Saddle River, New Jersey: Pearson Education, Inc.

30. Bell, R. (n.d.) The Tylenol terrorist. Crime Library. Retrieved from http://www.crimelibrary.com/terrorists_spies/terrorists/tylenol_murders/index.html

31. Stansberry & Smith. (2008). *Public relations practice: Managerial cases and problems, 7th ed.* Upper Saddle River, NJ: Pearson.

32. CNN. (2009, Feb. 5). Law enforcement to review Tylenol murders. CNN. Retrieved from http://www.cnn.com/2009/CRIME/02/04/tylenol.murders/index.html

33. JM Moses (1995), Legal spin control: Ethics and advocacy in the court of public opinion. *Columbia Law Review.*

34. USA Today. (1997, Feb. 5) Racial factor tilts the scales of public opinion. *USA Today.* Retrieved from: http://usatoday30.usatoday.com/news/index/nns212.htm

35. Flock, E. (2011, July 6). Casey Anthony verdict shocks media: attorneys black "talking heads." *Washington Post*, Retrieved from http://www.washingtonpost.com/blogs/blogpost/post/casey-anthony-not-guilty-verdict-shocks-media-attorneys-blast-talking-heads/2011/07/05/gHQAHhIXzH_blog.html

36. Litwin, L. (2003). The public relation's practitioner's playbook: A synergized approach to effective two-way communication. Dubuque: IA: Kendall-Hunt.

37. Marston, J. (1963). *The nature of public relations.* New York: McGraw-Hill.

38. Kunhardt, Philip B., Jr.; Kunhardt, Philip B., III; Kunhardt, Peter W. (1995). *P.T. Barnum: America's Greatest Showman.* New York: Alfred A. Knopf.

39. Harrison, S. & Moloney, K. (2004). Comparing two public relations pioneers: American Ivy Lee and British John Elliot. *Public Relations Review,* 30, 205–215.

40. New York Times. (1995, Mar. 10). Edward Bernays, 'Father of public relations' and leader in opinion making dies at 103. *New York* Times. Retrieved from http://www.nytimes.com/books/98/08/16/specials/bernays-obit.html

41. Sweeney, Michael S. (2001). Secrets of Victory: The Office of Censorship and the American Press and Radio in World War II. Chapel Hill, N.C.: University of North Carolina Press.

42. Bernays, Edward L.; Cutler, H.W. (1955). *The Engineering of Consent.* Norman, OK: University of Oklahoma Press.

43. Bernays, E. (1928). *Propaganda.* Brooklyn, NY: IG Publishing.

44. Grunig, J. E. (1984). *Managing public relations.* Independence, KY: Cengage Learning.

45. Mohr, Betty. (1994). The Pepsi Challenge: Managing a crisis. *Prepared Foods.* Retrieved from http://www.highbeam.com/doc/1G1-15312359.html

46. Stansberry & Smith. (2008). Public relations practice: Managerial cases and problems, 7th ed. Upper Saddle River, NJ: Pearson.

47. Federal Trade Commission. (n.d.). Statutes enforced or administered by the commission. ftc.gov. Retrieved from http://www.ftc.gov/enforcement/statutes

48. United States Supreme Court. (Mar. 9, 1964). *New York Times v. Sullivan,* (376 U.S. 254). Retrieved from http://www.bc.edu/bc_org/avp/cas/comm/free_speech/nytvsullivan.html

49. Maslow, A.H. (1943). A theory of human motivation. *Psychological Review,* 50(4), 370–96.

50. Pierce, W.D., Cameron, J., Banko, K. M., So, S. (2003). Positive effects of rewards and performance standards on intrinsic motivation. *The Psychology Record.* 561–579.

51. Fair III, E.M., Silvestri, L. (1992). Effects of rewards, competition and outcome on intrinsic motivation. *Journal of Instructional Psychology.* 3–9.

52. Dunham, R.B. (1977). Relationships of perceived job design characteristics to job ability requirements and job value. *Journal of Applied Psychology.* 760–763.

53. Cotton, J.L., Vollrath D.A., Froggatt K.L., Lengnick-Hall M.L., & Jennings, K.R. (1988). employee participation: Diverse forms and different outcomes. *Academy of Management Review,* 13, 8–22.

54. Pew Research. (2013). Climate change and financial instability seen as top global threats. Pew Research Center. Retrieved from http://www.pewglobal.org/2013/06/24/climate-change-and-financial-instability-seen-as-top-global-threats/

55. Boykoff, M. & Boykoff, J. (July 2004). Balance as bias: global warming and the US prestige press. *Global Environmental Change Part A, 14*(2), 125–136.

56. Lippman, W. (1922). *Public opinion.* San Diego: CA. Harcourt, Brace, and Co.

57. Shoemaker, Pamela J. & Vos, Tim P. (2009). *Gatekeeping Theory.* New York: Routledge.

58. The Associated Press. The Associated Press Stylebook 2014 (Associated Press Stylebook and Briefing on Media Law). New York: Associated Press.

59. Rahim, M., Antonioni, D., & Psenicka, C. (2001). A structural equations model of leader power, subordinates' styles of handling conflict, and job performance. *International Journal Of Conflict Management, 12*(3), 191.

60. Fearn-Banks. K. (2011). *Crisis communications.* New York: Routledge.

61. Emblemetric. (n.d.). Procter & Gamble's new logo: By the numbers. Eblemetric. Retrieved from http://www.emblemetric.com/2013/05/06/procter-gambles-new-logo-by-the-numbers/

62. Taylor, M. & Kent, M. L. (2010). Anticipatory socialization in the use of social media in public relations: A content analysis of PRSA's Tactics. *Public Relations Review, 36*(3), 207–214.

63. Goumans, F. (2014, Jan. 3). Friday five: Social media tips for 2014. PRSAY. Retrieved from http://prsay. prsa.org/index.php/2014/01/03/friday-five-social-media-tips-for-2014/

64. Barash, David (2002). *Peace and conflict.* Thousand Oaks, CA: Sage Publications.

65. Bowman, S. and Willis, C. (2003). We media: How audiences are shaping the future of news and information. *The Media Center at the American Press Institute.*

66. Steenberg, T., & Avery, J. (2010, Feb. 4). Marketing analysis toolkit: Situation analysis. *Harvard Business Review.* Retrieved from http://hbr.org/product/marketing-analysis-toolkit-situation-analysis/an/510079-PDF-ENG

67. Kabel, M. (2006, July 18). "Wal-Mart, critics slam each other on web." *The Washington Post.*

68. Norman, Al (2004). The Case Against Wal-Mart. *Raphel Marketing,* 7.

69. Zook, M., & Graham, M. (2006). Wal-Mart nation: Mapping the reach of a retail colossus." *In Brunn, S. D. Wal-Mart World: The World's Biggest Corporation in the Global Economy.* New York: Routledge. 15–25.

70. Hodal, K, Kelly, C., Lawrence, F. (2014, June 10). Revealed: Asian slave labour producing prawns for supermarkets in US, UK. *The Guardian.*

71. Nations Restaurant News. (2012, Nov. 12). Top 100 Chains: U.S. Sales *Nations Restaurant News.*

72. International Business Times. (2008, May 22). McDonald's Holds down Dollar Meal, Making Menu Healthier. *International Business Times*

73. Armstrong. M (1996). *Management processes and functions.* London: CIPD.

74. Bhasin, K. (2011, Aug. 30). 12 McDonald's menu items that failed spectacularly. *Business Insider.* Retrieved from http://www.businessinsider.com/failed-mcdonalds-items-2011-8?op=1

75. Pew Research Group. (2013). Social networking use. Pew Research Group. Retrieved from http://www. pewresearch.org/data-trend/media-and-technology/social-networking-use/

76. Techopedia. (n.d.). SoLoMo. Retrieved from http://www.techopedia.com/definition/28492/solomo

77. Coombs, W. Timothy (2012), Parameters for crisis communication in "The Handbook of Crisis Communication" Eds. W. Timothy Coombs & Sherry J. Holladay, West Sussex, UK: Blackwell Publishing Ltd.

78. Basso, J. & Randall, H. (2012). The writer's toolbox: A comprehensive guide for public relations and business communication. Dubuque: IA: Kendhall-Hunt.

79. About the Emmanuel Cancer Foundation. (2017). Retrieved Sept. 06, 2018, from https://www.emmanuelcancer.org/about-us/

80. Revkin, A. C. (2006, May 22). 'An Inconvenient Truth': Al Gore's fight against global warming. *New York Times.* Retrieved from http://www.nytimes.com/2006/05/22/movies/22gore.html?_r=0

81. McLuhan, M., Powers. B. R. (2012). The global village: Transformations in world life and media in the 21st Century. Oxford, UK: Oxford University Press.

82. Vocus. (2014). Vocus releases "The state media 2014 report." Vocus. Retrieved from http://www.vocus.com/about-us/press-release/vocus-releases-the-state-of-the-media-2014-report/

83. Journal of Integrated Marketing Communications. (n.d.). What is IMC? Northwestern University. Retrieved from http://jimc.medill.northwestern.edu/what-is-imc/

GLOSSARY OF
KEY TERMS

527 group—A tax-exempt group set up to influence and affect public opinion regarding elections and political nominations

absolute privilege—The right to report the statements made during official proceedings that would otherwise be deemed as defamatory or with malice

agenda-setting theory—Max McCombs and Donald Shaw's 1968 theory that examines and explains how the media coverage on any given event can influence and affect public opinion and action

appropriation—The act of using someone's image or description without their consent

brand—The connection or feeling associated with a person, organization, or product

case study—The research method that uses past events to help gauge future actions for an organization experiencing a similar situation

communicating—In addition to counseling, the second major function of the practice of public relations

conflict management lifecycle—The process by which an organization can organize and address needs of various groups during a crisis

counseling—In addition to communicating, the second major function of the practice of public relations

court of law—One of the two main courts in which public relations practitioners operate; dictated by established verdicts and precedents, making it much clearer than the court of public opinion

court of public opinion—One of the two main courts in which public relations practitioners operate; built on shifting public opinion, making it more difficult to manage than the court of law

crisis management—The function of public relations that plans and executes actions when an organization is facing a major public image disaster

deception—The act of intentionally misleading someone with misleading actions or statements

defamation—The act of negatively impacting someone's character through untrue statements

early adopters—A group who accept new ideas after deliberation and the influence of innovators

early majority—A large group who believe in new ideas following debate, deliberation, and influence from early adopters

Edward Bernays—The primary developer of using psychology in the practice of public relations for the first time; best known for his work in propaganda during the World War I

fake news—The phenomenon by which information disseminated by media outlets is criticized or invalidated by those who are critical of the information's content

false light—Placing someone in a situation or place that negatively affects their reputation

Federal Bureau of Investigation—U.S. government agency responsible for investigating and prosecuting major federal offenses

Federal Communications Commission—U.S. government agency responsible for regulating media broadcasting and establishing rules for content

Federal Trade Commission—U.S. government agency responsible for protecting consumers and consumer rights

Food and Drug Administration—U.S. government agency responsible for regulating consumable products such as food and drink as well as the pharmaceutical industry

front group—Organization set up by various entities to influence public opinion against or for a proposed action so that the organizations setting up the group are not directly connected to its actions

gatekeepers—Individuals in the media industry such as editors and producers who decide upon the content that is disseminated via their media outlet

grassroots—The efforts by a small group to convince and persuade individuals to favor their position, generally by untrained individuals with small budgets

Hadley Cantril (1906-1966)—Psychologist renowned in the field for his innovate work and theories concerning public opinion

innovation diffusion process—The theory that explains how new information and technology spreads across varying communication platforms to large groups of people

innovators—The group of select individuals who are most likely to accept new ideas quickly because of the ideas' uniqueness and innovativeness

integrated marketing communications (IMC)—The combination of public relations, marketing, and advertising efforts into one cohesive approach

internal audit—The analysis of an organization's operations from the inside out

intrusion—The act of infringing upon someone's solitude

inverted pyramid style—The unique style of journalistic writing that emphasizes the most important information first and presents lesser news later in the piece

issues management—The method of controlling a given situation through the step-by-step analysis and execution of the situation's various components

Ivy Lee—The first practitioner credited with understanding and applying the principles of counseling to public relations; credited with developing the press release

James Burke—CEO of Johnson & Johnson during the Tylenol crisis who is credited with initiating positive public relations responses to save the company

James Grunig—Practitioner most widely known for his efforts to professionalize the practice of public relations and develop its inclusion in college and university programs; the co-developer of the four models of public relations

laggards—A group who are most unlikely to accept new ideas and are the most difficult to persuade because of their longstanding beliefs

late majority—A large group who accept new ideas after they have been tested against alternatives and proven themselves

lead—The first sentence in journalistic writing; includes the necessary information to entice and encourage readers to continue to read the rest of the material

leaders—Those individuals who understand the vision and possibilities inherent in organizations and employees

libel—The written form of defamation

Ludlow Massacre—The April 20, 1914, incident that resulted in deaths and injuries following a mining strike and demonstration; credited with being the first major incident that an organization had to use public relations for to counter negative media exposure and affect public opinion

managers—The day-to-day operators of organizations who lack the ability to foresee opportunities within their organizations

margin of error—The statistical means of expressing the confidence in polling results; the lower the margin of error, the more likely the data are accurate to the population polled

Maslow's hierarchy of needs—Abraham Maslow's 1943 model that expresses the personal growth and stages of developmental psychology needed to achieve individual self-fulfillment

mass sentiment—The final stage of the public opinion formation model where the majority of a group of people share a feeling or disposition toward an event, issue, or topic

media—The collective group of outlets that affect individuals' perceptions about organizations

media kit—An assortment of various public relations and marketing materials used by media professionals as a reference for an organization

news release—The most pervasive form of public relations; used to inform and interest media outlets to report and cover events important to an organization

ombudsman—The individual responsible for representing the interests and concerns of the public within an organization

Pepsi case—The 1993 incident where a consumer purported to find a syringe in a can of Pepsi; the case showed the impact of perception on people's beliefs and actions in spite of the fact that the contamination was done by the consumer and at no fault to the company

personal approach to public relations—The method of practicing public relations based on micromanagement of relationships to macrolevel organizations

political action committees (PACS)—Organizations that collectively fund efforts to affect elections, legislation, or political initiatives

press agentry/publicity model—The first, and most basic, model of public relations; most associated with P. T. Barnum, it is known for its basic emphasis on publicity at any cost

primary research—Data collected by the researcher

privacy—The expectation that certain information about and actions of an individual will not be held to public information or ridicule

private facts—Information about someone deemed not to be necessary or available for public consumption

P. T. Barnum—Legendary showman who operated one of the largest sideshow museums in history; famous for his hucksterism-style of publicity and is most associated with the press agentry/publicity model of public relations

public affairs—The name ascribed to government or noncommercial public relations practice

public information model—The second model of public relations; focuses on supplying the public with news with no regard for the public's understanding of it; mostly associated with government communication

public opinion—The collective sentiment held by a majority of people about an important event or newsworthy topic

public opinion formation model—The development sequence that describes how large groups of people share similar dispositions on important topics and issues

qualified privilege—The right to report statements made during official proceedings as long as they are not deemed as being made with malice

qualitative research—Methodologies that use personal interactions rather than numerical means of data collection

quantitative research—Methodologies that rely on numerical accuracies and statistical realities

RACE—The public relations acronym formula for research, action, communication, and evaluation

return on investment (ROI)—The amount of reward, often financial, that comes from venturing resources into an initiative

RPIE—The public relations acronym formula for research, planning, implementation, and evaluation

secondary research—Data acquired by the researcher that originally came from a previous source

Securities and Exchange Commission—U.S. government agency responsible for regulating the securities industry including the stock market

situation analysis—The research method by which an organization's reputation, media presence, and actions are measured to determine the best course(s) of action

slander—The spoken or broadcasted form of defamation

stakeholders—Groups of people who can impact an organization's ability to operate and who are in turn impacted by the actions of the organization

SWOT analysis—Research and planning methods that looks at the strengths, weaknesses, opportunities, and threats facing an organization in any given circumstance

Times v. Sullivan—The landmark 1964 Supreme Court case that established the precedent of actual malice, which placed additional burdens of proof on public figures seeking to sue the media for defamation; the case resulted in a freer ability of journalists to question and criticize public figures, such as politicians

two-step flow theory—The model that describes the movement of information from its source or event through media and opinion leaders' influence, and their effects on the public's interpretation of news and information

two-way asymmetric model—The third model of public relations; the most widely practiced model, with an emphasis on communication with the public but focused on how it can benefit the organization most

two-way symmetric model—The fourth model of public relations; focuses on creating an equal exchange of information between organizations and the public; an aspirational model but one that is difficult to practice in the real world

Tylenol case—The 1982 poisoning of Chicago-area residents who consumed cyanide-laced Tylenol-branded acetaminophen; the case is famous for its strategic public relations efforts that illustrated the importance of the field to corporate America

uninformed mass sentiment—The earliest stage of the public opinion formation model where a public has not developed a cohesive sentiment about a topic; it is when public relations activities are at their most effective

Index

Printed in the USA
CPSIA information can be obtained
at www.ICGtesting.com
LVHW060718280723
753680LV00008B/29